Tradition and Reform in Education

Tradition and Reform in Education

Stephen Tonsor

Open Court Publishing Company
La Salle, Illinois

Contents

III. Christian Education

To be sure, those who held this view were not altogether wrong. The campuses are quieter. The revolution in Academe has come and gone and the chief casualties seem to be those administrators and professors who are beached on the farther shores of ideological mania. One even hears now and then echoes of the concern of liberal professors in the 50s about campus conformity.

Appearances, however, are deceptive. Though American education is quieter there can be no thought of setting things into the accustomed order which existed on the eve of the time of troubles. That, quite simply, is impossible. Too much has changed. Both our society and our schools have lost that certainty, that innocent unawareness and sureness which is one of the great sources of creativity and vitality. Things will be put back in order but that order will be a new one.

It is quite appropriate that the old order should pass. One wonders why and how it lasted so long. One wonders why the assumptions on which it was based went unchallenged through so many decades. Sometimes the way to destroy an idea or an institution is simply not to challenge it; to heap it with the rewards which come with success, to still the small voices which can be heard at every school board meeting and at every self-congratulatory commencement address. The time of troubles in American education did not follow on a golden age. The past may have been serene; it was not golden. There was waste, personal and institutional. Vision was lacking and values non-existent or corrupted. The desire for excellence was muted and a systematic analysis of ends and methods was neglected. Obviously, the mood on campus and in the schools was more conducive to educational achievement before than after the day of the long knives at Berkeley, San Francisco State, Columbia and Madison. However, the problems out of which the collapse of education was generated had been present for many years.

They were not the recent development of the first half of the 1960s. In 1964 the internal crisis in American education matched the moment of external crisis in the polity and culture. That is why the general and sustained collapse took place so rapidly. Overnight it became clear to everyone that American education was not achieving even those goals which it set for itself, let alone satisfying the expectations which it had created in the society at large.

All of which does not argue that American education and educational ideals were bankrupt. Few efforts in the realm of the spirit have been so intense, so prolonged and in individual instances, so successful, as the American educational effort. The goals and methods of mass education have been remarkably successful and in one sense, certainly, our problems are the problems of success rather than the problems of failure. If a new order in education is to be constructed it can only result from the preservation of the best which that past has embodied. We Americans are all too efficient at tearing down beautiful and elegant old buildings only to replace them with a nondescript functionalism which does not function.

The essays in this book were written during those years of educational collapse through which we have all just lived. Their continuing validity, I believe, resides in the fact that they were not simply efforts to shore up the existing system. They were critical of that system at a moment when it seemed only elementary good sense to come to its defense. Their continuing validity also resides in the fact that they anticipate a better future and they discuss what must be done if the great promise of American education is ever to be realized. And they attempt not only to identify what is wrong but to define what is right in education, either in spirit or in concrete form.

The mood of education at present ought to be hopeful rather than apprehensive. It is a time not unlike the moment of defeat in Prussian history, when after the Napoleonic debacle Wilhelm von Humboldt undertook the total reform of Prussia's educational system. It has been convincingly argued that von Humboldt's reforms created the possibility of Prussia's greatness in the nineteenth century. America's greatness, indeed America's survival, is dependent on a reform at least as thoroughgoing. The moment must be seized now, when the vested interests and the old ways together with the bankrupt demands of the radicals have all been repudiated. We may not soon again have such an opportunity.

While it is important when change comes that it be systematic and pervasive, it is equally important that there be a plurality of solutions to particular educational problems. The solutions which von Humboldt provided for Prussia were uniformitarian in character. We should seek diversity while at the same time insisting upon uniform standards of performance. At the moment there is increasing uniformity accompanied by a decline in standards. The state ought not to concern itself with methods and curricular details. It should show itself to be intensely interested in the actual performance of students and in accreditation based upon performance.

We must not let ourselves be persuaded to wait until the inevitable further studies and more elaborate experiments have been made and yet more commissions have been appointed and still more commission reports have been filed. It is important to act on the basis of what we now know. Further research has too often in the past served as a method for postponing action.

Nor must we postpone reform until we feel that the problems of the cultural crisis have been solved. It is tempting to argue that until the civil rights crisis has been resolved, that until the problems of ethnic and cultural pluralism have been met, until the decay of values has been arrested, we shall do nothing in the schools. These vexing questions do pose enormous problems for education. We cannot, however, permit them to deter us from action. We must foster, through education, not one set of values, but many competing values.

Nor ought we to view the problems of diversity as unmitigated evils. In another but analogous context, St. Paul, lover of diversity, wrote: "Do not stifle the utterances of the Spirit, do not hold prophecy in low esteem. Put all things to the test: keep what is good, avoiding every kind of evil." (Thess. I, 19-22) We shall all be made richer by diversity of viewpoint and method. Our children will be better educated in terms of their gifts and needs, and society will be better served if we can choose from a wide variety of schools and educational objectives. The state ought not to go beyond the establishment of standards and the testing of competences both in basic skills and in professional and vocational training. How competence is achieved and what curricular content may be should be a matter of studied indifference on the part of the state. No doubt much that is genuinely retrogressive would, under such a system, be offered the public in the effort to achieve some higher cultural or religious goal. But just as certainly we shall see extraordinary results, not simply in the development of new and more skillful techniques but in the creation of variety within the common culture.

Ultimately the reforms we seek and the educational and cultural values we wish to preserve are all dependent upon the withdrawal of the state from any active educational role. The role of the state ought not to go beyond that of certification and the equitable distribution of tax revenues to competing private educational initiatives. In the whole area of education it is vital for the state to take those steps which will encourage private initiative and lead to the reestablishment of genuine diversity. It is wrong to suppose that state enterprise, which cannot even efficiently manage the postal service, can effectively satisfy the diverse and complicated educational needs of a population of hundreds of millions.

But even here we cannot afford to wait until the state has voluntarily withdrawn. Those who are anxious about current educational practice must do the only things they can. They must support to the absolute limit of their resources private schools and private educational initiatives. Beyond this they must insist that the private schools offer educations which are genuine alternatives to those provided by the state.

There have been few such moments in our past when the demand and the opportunity for change have come at the same time. Unless we avail ourselves of the opportunity now we may never again be able to redefine what we mean by education and restructure our institutions to achieve our goals.

Stephen J. Tonsor
March 10, 1973   The Hoover Institution

I. Images of Society

Modernity, Science and Rationality

In a brilliant essay, "The Importance of Cultural Freedom,"[1] Richard Weaver observes that "a poet who cannot show that he has felt the disillusionment of his own time as poignantly as other people cannot speak to his time." If one applies this dictum to the topic under discussion one must assume that any exploration of the antinomian, anti-rational and anti-scientific movement, which is so markedly an aspect of modernity, should come from someone who understands and at least shows some sympathy for the attitudes and arguments which mark the so-called "cultural revolution." If we are unable to bring to our topic that initial understanding we will be able neither to speak to our contemporaries nor overcome those anti-cultural and anti-rational forces which lodge not only in our society but are an important element in our own natures.

Let us begin by agreeing with Robert Frost when he wrote:

> Something there is that doesn't love a wall,
> That sends the frozen-ground-swell under it,
> And spills the upper boulders in the sun;
> And makes gaps even two can pass abreast.

Robert Frost was uneasy about walls, boundaries, rules, analysis and order, fearing their impact on himself and on his world. He knew, of course, as we know that life is impossible without all of these elements though just where one should strike a balance Frost was uncertain and his poetry is a long discussion of freedom and constraint. And we too are uneasy and troubled at the iron necessity of law, ineluctable order, the need for instinctual renunciation, the thought of a world in which all passion has given way to calculation and all feeling has become analysis. We all fear the loss of our humanity and think it just possible that the most important choices of our lives may be made somewhere outside ourselves on the basis of knowledge and information unknown to us. Worse still we fear that we will be lamed in our vitality, that spiritually and physically we will find ourselves robbed of our potency and creativity; reduced to shadowy functionaries serving the mechanical necessities of a sterile robot culture.

Behind these well-founded fears and at a deeper level of our existence, unconscious but powerful, lies the human drive to anarchy and immediate, complete instinctual gratification. We want what we want when we want it and what we want is nearly always to be had only at the expense of society and by endangering our own futures. The criminal, the con-man, the delinquent are all men who have chosen what all of us are tempted to choose. "Each of them," Jacob Bronowski writes[2], "is protesting against something in society which constricts him, and each of them wants to be a man after his own heart; yet each act of protest is more commonplace, and each conspiracy more uniform, than the society they would like to despise."

"Something there is that doesn't love a wall" and yet the walled city, the walled garden, the enclosure made by the four walls of a house, all these are the very symbols of the exclusion of chaotic and anarchic nature. They are the ways by which men secure themselves and order their existences. Beyond the wall lies the insecurity and the violence of a world where the rules and purposes of civilized life do not apply. In myth and legend those anarchic and threatening forces outside the wall are depicted as dragons, Minotaurs and sphinxes. But they have allies in the city, allies who give them the power which they possess to work destruction on the city. Those allies are no less than the citizenry of the city who in their divided natures and wishes seek the destruction of order at the very same time as they desire its preservation. It is for this reason that the Minotaur is kept at bay by human sacrifice; a part of mankind, a part of human society is surrendered to him. Seven youths and seven maidens were sacrificed each year to the half-man, half-beast monster that lived in a labyrinth cunningly constructed by the first of the great technicians.

The image of the city with its protecting wall is more than the image of community life. It is the image of all order. That order is threatened by what lies outside the city wall, but the city is in even greater danger from what lies within. The Trojan horse of unreason, the lust for lawlessness and disorder, and the impiety of Alcibiades and his drunken friends are all a greater threat to the life of the city than the enemy outside. Order is bought at a great price. It is always provisional and unstable and it is always enforced at the expense of individual men and their fondest desires. Law is necessary in all those instances where the common advantage is not coincident with the advantage of the individual. The theory of anarchism supposes that altruism and voluntary association will enable men to live without the law or the ordinary structures of organized community. But law exists and community exists precisely because the individual, left to his own devices, sees advantage in disorder and the triumphant will of the strong individual. Whatever the truth or the untruth in terms of historical accuracy of Sigmund Freud's exploration of the development of community in *Totem and Taboo, Moses and Monotheism,* and *Civilization and its Discontents,* his essays possess a profound mythic truth in their acknowledgment and affirmation of the drive to immediate instinctual gratification, their awareness of the social dimension of all culture and their insistence that culture is created in the ceaseless war against nature and through instinctual renunciation. Man in his human rather than his animal dimension is a cultural creation. His hold upon order and civility is always precarious and threatened both by the natural exterior and by his own anarchic and ego-involved interior. Nature outside the gates and man inside both do not love a wall and would have it down.

But why, precisely, is that wall so important and why is order so essential to any human activity? It is a fact that the very structure of our humanity is dependent upon the ordered world of symbolic thought. Language, numbers and the objectification of experience in art are all ways of ordering and structuring. Outside the world of symbols there is and can be no humanity.[3]

Even were we to discount the value of our humanity and assume that an unspoiled and unfettered animality was preferable to the world of culture we men would still find ourselves trapped in the world of the distinctively human. As animals we are terribly ill-prepared, aside from our superior intellectual capacity, for the unremitting struggle with nature which is the essential condition of the non-human world around us. It is precisely the ability to order, to symbolize, to organize, to deny present gratification in order to gain a distant or long-term advantage which enables the "naked ape" to succeed in this hostile and unfriendly universe. Were he to abandon this single advantage man would cease to be the most successful biological organism on earth and would very possibly disappear altogether. The choice has been made. We may reject its implications. We may balk at the demands which the choice entails but unless we are willing to hazard extinction there is no turning back.

Nor, indeed, are many other than the satisfied and satiated classes of the Western World, going to be willing to turn back. Some time before ecology became fashionable and antinomian irrationality became the vogue among the well-heeled cognoscenti in our society, C. P. Snow made his point very ably. He wrote:[4]

> For, of course, one truth is straightforward. Industrialization is the only hope of the poor. I use the word "hope" in a crude and prosaic sense. I have not much use for the moral sensibility of anyone who is too refined to use it so. It is all very well for us, sitting pretty, to think that material standards of living don't matter all that much. It is all very well for one, as a personal choice to reject industrialization—do a modern Walden, if you like, and if you go without much food, see most of your children die in infancy, despise the comforts of literacy, accept twenty years off your own life, then I respect you for the strength of your aesthetic revulsion. But I don't respect you in the slightest if, even passively, you try to impose the same choice on others who are not free to choose. In fact we know what their choice would be. For, with singular unanimity, in any country where they have had the chance, the poor have walked off the land into the factories as fast as the factories would take them.

More recently Peter Drucker made the same point in his impressive study, *The Age of Discontinuity*.[5]

It does not even matter greatly whether the developed countries would prefer to call a halt to technological change and economic growth. There is no sign that mankind is ready to forswear economic growth and with it technological change. There is no sign that the majority of developed countries live in great wealth. Not only are the developing nations desperate for economic advancement; other developed nations, especially Western Europe and Japan (not to mention Russia), are eager to catch up with the United States and to push economic growth as fast as it can be pushed.

Science and technology, economic growth and industrialization are, however, perhaps only the most obvious aspects of the revolution against reason and order in the modern world. There can be no doubt that science and technology themselves have too often been caught up in the pursuit of irrational and anti-human goals and objectives; that science has too often confined itself to the realm of means rather than to the analysis of ends. Suffice it to say that the problem is not simply the rejection of science and technology but rather the rejection of rationality altogether.

Daniel Bell has explored at considerable length[6] the cultural consequences of the triumph of the will over reason. He regards the current wave of irrationalism in our society as a major cultural crisis. One need not be as pessimistic as Bell in order to recognize this development as a movement of major consequence to ourselves.

Although the development of rationality is a process which antedates the appearance of man, and although the technical manipulation and mastery of the environment is as old as man, the self-conscious employment of science, technology and all the processes of rationalization do not extend back over a period of time longer than Europeans have been present in significant numbers on the North American Continent. The really major changes in the organization of society, the growth of knowledge and the mastery of the environment through science and technology which mark off "modernity" from the past have nearly all come since 1600. The decisive changes produced by these cultural and intellectual forces are even more recent. The process has been an accelerating one. You are all acquainted with the statistic that 90 percent of all the scientists who ever lived are alive at the present moment and those of you who have browsed in the work of the "futurologists" know

7

that further dramatic technical and social changes lie in the immediate future, indeed are already well under way.[7] Indeed, if we look back over that comparatively short time span since 1600 in comparison with the totality of human history we will recognize that it accounts for greater changes in man's world and in humanity itself than any brief time span since the Neolithic revolution.

How are we to account for this enormous speedup in the rate at which change impinges upon us and in the manner in which events of world historical importance pile upon us? It sometimes must seem that history is rather like a motion picture; that vast stretches of it are in slow motion, (some societies, even today, live in this world of slow motion). But about the 12th Century the projectionist began to speed up the picture until today the figures dance a mad and uncoordinated jig; run about confusedly like the participants in certain well-known television commercials.

Why has this enormous speedup taken place? What is the driving force behind the transformation of Western history since 1600? We know that Western society in that time span was unique; that no other society in history has exhibited such dynamism and such revolutionary energies. Indeed, all the non-Western societies we know are traditionalist—or were until the West touched them with its transforming energies. Many of them were stagnant and changeless, caught and encapsulated in the past as fossil flies are caught in amber. Or change occurred in them in a random, meaningless fashion. The notion of progress, unidirectional linear time, development and process, are distinctively Western ideas. These days there is a great deal of discussion of the impact of the non-Western world on the West. There has been a return to the cult of *ex Orient lux,* that curious belief that the failed societies of the so-called third world have some special humanity and spirituality which the Western world is lacking, and that we ought to renounce our rationality and science for the primitive but pure life of non-technical society. No one can deny the tremendous influence which non-Western societies have exerted on the West nor the value of non-Western culture to contemporary Western man, but the fact remains that it was and is the West which opened up the world and both destroyed and energized the traditionalist non-

Western societies. Still, the question remains: why has the West been the changing, aggressive, energetic, innovating society it is? Why has history speeded up for us and why, finally, does it appear, as Spengler, Toynbee and others have pointed out, that our culture is in a state of dissolution and decay?

Max Weber in his introduction to *The Protestant Ethic and the Spirit of Capitalism*[8] points out that "only in the West does science exist as a stage of development which we recognize today as valid." He goes on to insist that in every aspect of Western life a long term and unique rationalization exhibits itself; in philosophy, religion, art, government and, in short, the total structure of culture and the organization of life. Weber recognizes that implicit in Western culture was an anti-traditionalism, a rationalism, a calculating spirit which constantly and with ever-increasing momentum transformed Western life. The motive power of Western history, as Weber saw it, was the vision of a rationally ordered life which called forth an energetic and unremitting pursuit of its goal and which eschewed all magical escapes.

The Spirit of Western man, far from being the product of the material environment and dominated by the mode of production, as vulgar Marxists insist, transforms and revolutionizes through its persistent quest for rationality in this material environment and the mode of production. The history of medieval society is the story of the slow process of the rationalization of that society and the displacement and destruction of traditional institutions and ideas or their amalgamation with more rationalized forms and modes.

This rationalization of all the aspects of Western life has involved a successive elaboration of techniques and methods, and the creation of attitudes which can best be described as professional. Technique is a rational method applied to a particular problem. The problem may be totally intellectual or spiritual or it may be manipulative or mechanical. What in each case it involves is the employment of rational means to achieve rationally conceived ends.

Now the essential characteristic of modernity is not that it is "the most recent," and certainly not that it represents a period of Western history which began in 1492 or 1600. The modern age rather is the period of Western history marked most decisively by the process of rationalization. If we are attempting to define an institution or an idea as modern we will not inquire into its date but will simply ask to what extent its orientation is traditional, *i.e.*, rooted in customary behavior, poses for itself non-rational objectives, and acts through non-rational methods, or to what extent it is a rational system. Custom, fear, unpredictableness, anxiety and magic are the marks of the older, traditional and especially the non-Western cultures. To be modern is to seek, in so far as possible, the solution to practical and intellectual problems through the employment and expansion of rational means.

Essential to these developments is the professionalization of life; the increasing bureaucratization of every aspect of human existence. For professionalization and bureaucratization are among the most important techniques by which life is rationalized. The substitution of known procedures which are indifferent to the status or the influence of the person for arbitrary actions by government, teachers, or doctors; these are all a part of the general development of professionalism and bureaucracy.

It is, of course, tempting to see the rational innovating forces of our society as always on the side of progress—tempting always to approve of revolution if it is made in the name of reason; forever to transform without thought of consequences; to believe that reason is always right and that the heart, whatever its reasons, is always wrong.

But obviously not all of life is subject to rational manipulation; nor is the spirit exclusively rational. We are all aware, or at least I hope we are, that important areas of life are not so much irrational as arational. That is to say they lie outside the purview of rational systems and rational methods. When rationalism becomes too exaggerated in its claims these aspects of life which lie outside reason, beyond it, revolt and take their revenge upon rational systems. And that too is a part of the history of the recent past.

It is the fear of a totally rational society and its constraining and deadening impact upon human behavior which led Max Weber to the gloomy and pessimistic passage with which he closed his essay on *The Protestant Ethic and the Spirit of Capitalism* in 1920:[9]

10

No one knows who will live in this cage in the future, or whether at the end of this tremendous development entirely new prophets will arise, or there will be a great rebirth of old ideas and ideals, or if neither, mechanized petrification, embellished with a convulsive self-importance. For the last stage of this cultural development, it might well be truly said: "Specialists without spirit, sensualists without heart; this nullity imagines that it has attained a level of civilization never before achieved."

But this is not the only and is perhaps not the most important problem involved in the processes of rationalization and technological mastery. Surely one of the most threatening aspects of technology and bureaucracy lies in the separation of rational techniques from a rational spirit. The consequence of this separation is that rational means, of a highly sophisticated nature, are employed in the pursuit of totally irrational objectives. The processes of dehumanization and alienation are the direct effects of the pursuit of irrational ends. If the ends of life go unexamined and only the means are considered by our society; if we assume that everything is allowed so long as it is technically possible, then we condemn ourselves to a sophisticated barbarism.

[1]Richard Weaver, "The Importance of Cultural Freedom" in *Life Without Prejudice and Other Essays* (Henry Regnery Company, Chicago, 1965), p. 36.

[2]Jacob Bronowski, *The Face of Violence* (Meridian Books, Cleveland, 1967), p. 5.

[3]Peter L. Berger and Thomas Luckmann, *The Social Construction of Reality*, A Treatise in the Sociology of Knowledge (Doubleday, New York, 1966).

[4]Sir Charles P. Snow, *The Two Cultures: And a Second Look* (New American library, New York, 1964), p. 30.

[5]Peter F. Drucker, *The Age of Discontinuity*, Guidelines to our Changing Society, (Harper and Row, New York, 1969), p. 71.

[6]Daniel Bell, "The Cultural Contradictions of Capitalism" in *The Public Interest*, No. 21, Fall 1970, pp. 16-43.

[7]Herman Kahn and Anthony J. Weiner, *The Year 2000* (Macmillan, New York, 1967). Victor C. Ferkiss, *Technological Man*, The Myth and the Reality (New American Library, New York, 1970). Peter F. Drucker, *The Age of Discontinuity* (Harper and Row, New York, 1969). New York, 1969).

[8]Max Weber, *The Protestant Ethic and the Spirit of Capitalism* (Scribner's, New York, 1958), p.15.

[9]Max Weber, *The Protestant Ethic and the Spirit of Capitalism* (Scribner's, New York, 1958) p. 182.

The Iconography of Disorder:
The Ruined Garden
and the Devastated City

Henry Adams began his famous autobiography with a charming picture of the ancestral household at Quincy. His great-grand-father, President John Adams was the central figure of that household. Here is the way Henry Adams describes it:

> He [Henry] hung about the library; handled the books, deranged the papers, ransacked the drawers; searched the old purses and pocket-books for foreign coins; drew the sword cane; snapped the traveling pistols; upset everything in the corners, and penetrated the President's dressing-closet where a row of tumblers, inverted on the shelf, covered caterpillars which were supposed to become moths and butterflies, but never did. The Madam bore with fortitude the loss of the tumblers which her husband purloined for these hatcheries; but she made protest when he carried off her best cut glass bowls to plant with acorns or peach stones that he might see the roots grow, but which she said, he commonly forgot like the caterpillars.

It is the captivating picture of a boy and a great-grandfather con-spiring together in horticultural projects.

> . . . his grandson [Henry Adams added] was saddened by the sight and the smell of peaches and pears, the best of their kind, which he brought up from the garden to rot on his shelves for seed. With the inherited virtues of his

Puritan ancestors, the little boy Henry conscientiously brought up to him in his study the finest peaches he found in the garden, and ate only the less perfect. Naturally he ate more by way of compensation, but the act showed that he bore no grudge.

But by the penultimate chapter of *The Education*, a chapter Adams entitled, "A Law of Acceleration (1904)," the tone and texture of the life he is describing have shifted completely. The bucolic mood has vanished together with the certainties and all that remains is movement, undirected and catastrophic.

Adams observed:

> A law of acceleration, definite and constant as any law of mechanics, cannot be supposed to relax its energy to suit the convenience of man. . . . If any analogy whatever existed between the human mind, on one side, and the laws of motion, on the other, the mind had already entered a field of attraction so violent that it must immediately pass beyond, into new equilibrium, like the Comet of Newton, to suffer dissipation altogether, like meteoroids in the earth's atmosphere. If it behaved like an explosive, it must rapidly recover equilibrium; if it behaved like a vegetable, it must reach the limits of growth; and even if it acted like the earlier creations of energy—the saurians and sharks—it must have nearly reached the limits of expansion. If science were to go on doubling or quadrupling its complexities every ten years, even mathematics would succumb. An average mind had succumbed already in 1850; it could no longer understand the problem in 1900.

However, the law of acceleration had only just begun to exert its most profound effects in 1900. One wonders what Adams would write in 1973.

Not everyone, of course, had the penetration of intuitive insight which Adams possessed nor did many combine, as Adams did, keen powers of analysis and a first rate historical mind. The uneasy weight upon the human spirit of rationalization, technique, science and bureaucratic order has been reflected most clearly in the last and in the present century by the poets, in imaginative literature, and by the artists and architects. Over and over again they have articulated the mood of revolt and despair, have reflected on decadence and yearned for rejuvenation. Even the avant-garde which has come to seem so meaningless and anarchic has its roots in social and metaphysical anxieties which cannot be divorced from the history of the past two centuries.[1]

In the course of the 19th century the world became an uneasy habitation for mankind, and the images through which the Romantic artist expressed his unease were the images of the ruined garden and the devastated city. It is difficult to understand at first glance just why the notion of ruins had such appeal to 18th and 19th century Westerners. No previous era in history has been so endlessly constructive; none has ever left such monuments to its dynamic energies. And yet, from 1750 onwards there is a steady drumfire of books and essays which analyze the problem of decadence.

Even more fascinating is the fact that ruin and apocalypse are associated with the processes of nature, a nature which until the beginning of the eighteenth century had been described as wholly beneficent and which had been depicted in the image of a mother suckling her children at her breasts. Time's erosion, which darkens every fair prospect and brings low every high hope is seen, after the middle of the 18th century, as a totally natural and organic process. Until then decadence and regeneration were processes seen to be outside the ordinary scope of natural processes. Time might be overcome by religion, or by magic, or by a repetition of an archetypal creative gesture. Natural process is seen after the beginning of the century as an ineluctable cycle from seed-time to harvest, from spring to winter. History and mankind's hopes were doomed, after a short time of flowering, to death and decay to which all organic things are subject. The rationalistic, analytical, and mechanical-scientific ideas of the seventeenth century were in their implications deeply optimistic but once nature was conjoined with the sense of history and the images of ruin, the human universe darkened. Whatever else may be said of it, Darwin's "tangled bank" was not the seedbed of a new and dynamic faith or a sense of overriding optimism. "Darwin's bulldog," Thomas Henry Huxley said in the Romanes Lectures of 1893, "I know no study which is so saddening as that of the evolution of humanity as it is set forth in the annals of history. . . . Man is a brute, only more intelligent than other brutes," and "even the best of modern civilizations appears to me to exhibit a condition of mankind which neither embodies any worthy ideal nor even possesses the merit of

15

stability." Still, we must ask ourselves again and again to explain the source of the aesthetic pleasure which men derived from the prospect of ruin, decay and apocalypse. Why was the image of the ruined garden so extraordinarily appealing to the Romantic mind?

One can find many examples of the images of the ruined garden. Here is one chosen nearly at random, and literary rather than an example chosen from representational art. The passage is from Nathaniel Hawthorne's *The House of the Seven Gables*. The description is of the garden of the decaying Pyncheon seven-gabled house.

> After an early tea, the little country girl [Phoebe] strayed into the garden. The enclosure had formerly been very extensive, but was now contracted within small compass, and hemmed about, partly by high wooden fences, and partly by the outbuildings of houses that stood on another street. In the center was a grass platt, surrounding a ruinous little structure, which showed just enough of its original design to indicate that it had once been a summer-house. A hop vine, springing from last year's root, was beginning to clamber over it, but would be long in covering the roof with its green mantle. Three of the seven gables either fronted or looked sideways, with a dark solemnity of aspect, down into the garden.
>
> The black, rich soil had fed itself with the decay of a long period of time; such as fallen leaves, the petals of flowers, and the stalks and seed-vessels of vagrant and lawless plants, more useful after their death than ever while flaunting in the sun. The evil of these departed years would naturally have sprung up again, in such rank weeds [symbolic of the transmitted vices of society] as are always prone to root themselves about human dwellings.

Of course, the images of the ruined garden and the devastated city are much older than the Romantic movement. As with so many of the furnishings of the mind of Western man they are Christian and primevally mythical in their origin and if one is to accept Freudian and Jungian explanations of symbolic forms, they are characteristic representations of the ruined mind. Dante's *Inferno* is filled with alternating symbols of the garden which has been ruined and the perverse, tormented and devastated city.[2] Still, the overriding emphasis which these symbols receive at the hands of the Romantics sharpens the question.

The garden is perhaps the central and controlling image of Western thought. Over and over again it has served as a shorthand symbol for nature perfected by science and art. Shakespeare used it as the symbol of the well-ordered kingdom, and the idea of the "king's garden" as the symbol of both political and cosmological order is at least as old as the Babylonians.[3] The garden was, until the middle of the 18th century, a part of nature set off from the primeval wilderness by a wall and ordered by the hand of man. The garden as an enclosed space subject to order, moreover, always carried in itself a freight of transcendental symbolism. It is the symbol of nature perfected; of nature refined by science and harmonized by art, and is seen to be a foretaste of the perfection of nature through grace at the end of time; an anticipation of the great restoration. The Garden of Eden shall then be God's grace and perfect order in all its aspects. St. Paul wrote in the Epistle to the Romans, "Yet there was this hope: that creation itself would one day be set free from its slavery to decay, and share the glorious freedom of the children of God. For we know that up to the present time all of creation groans with pain like the pain of childbirth."

There was a revolution in garden architecture in the 18th and 19th centuries, and these new gardens, no less than the old, pointed beyond themselves. As Hans Sedylmayr observes in *Art and Crisis*, "Even then, however, it was still felt that gardens should awaken in the beholder memories of the Garden of Eden, of Arcadia, of Milton's Paradise, of Elysium and of the idylls and the fairyland of poetry."[4]

The garden, moreover, did more than serve as a simple reminder of the lost Eden. Efforts to restore time and history, to end the cycle of decay and to renew life centered on the notion of a return, while yet on this earth, to Paradise. These efforts find their culmination in the landscape architecture and the revolution in biological science which ushered in the 18th century. Men began to assume that the very act of living in a totally "natural" landscape would infuse a fallen and corrupted race with virtue and primal strength. The myth of renewal through a return to nature was born.

The new landscape architecture of the 18th century is a direct rejection of the garden art of the 17th and earlier centuries. Sedylmayr remarks that " . . . The landscape garden was something much more than a new kind of garden. It implied a wholly new relationship between man and nature and a new conception of art in general."⁵ To an even greater extent than Sedylmayr implies, however, the new landscape architecture of the 18th century was a revolutionary art. Indeed, some commentators have suggested that it corresponds directly to the triumph of Whig politics in England. The garden architecture of the 17th century had been a garden art of mechanical, geometric perfection. The garden had been conceived architecturally, the areas of the garden as rooms of a house or palace extended into nature. The object of the gardener was totally to order nature according to mathematical and mechanical design, or at least to confront nature, as at Versailles, and overpower it with the ordered constructions of man. The consequence was a garden devoid of rapture; pretty without being beautiful; a nature which was splendid without being awesome.

Sir Kenneth Clark has said that "the idea that appreciation of nature can be combined with a desire for intellectual order has never been acceptable in England."⁶ Whether or not such is the case it is true that the new school of landscape architecture developed quite suddenly in England. To be sure, there had been anticipations in the growing cult of ruins, the preoccupation with mortality as evidenced especially in the graveyard school of poets, in the preoccupation with transience and organic process, in the quest for origins and primitive purity, and most especially, in the nature poetry of James Thomson. Alexander Pope had done much by way of anticipation both in his poetry and in actual garden design to usher in the new era.⁷ But it was William Kent, working from the 1720s to the time of his death in 1748 who banished from garden architecture⁸ the bilateral symmetry, the geometric design, the simplicity, regularity and uniformity which had been the chief characteristics of Baroque garden architecture, especially as practiced by the great French garden architect of Versailles, Le Notre. Kent sentimentalized the garden and associated it, not with order, but with a humor psychology and a heavy emphasis upon death, mutability and the seemingly contingent and accidental. What

William Kent succeeded in creating was a garden design from which the rational and analytical style, as it was conceived in the 17th century, had disappeared.

It is impossible to mistake the clear intention of the new school of garden architects. They intended to destroy the previous image of nature, and although a great many painters and viewers in the new Romantic style assumed a larger, organic harmony to reside in the natural, it clearly lay beyond the powers of rational or scientific analysis and could only be perceived through the powers of intuition. Most importantly, however, the new garden architecture presupposed human nature and rationality to be a part of the organic processes of the landscape and the endless flow of time. The geometric gardens of the past which were little more than extensions of the house or the palace into the landscape, had sought to demonstrate, on the contrary, man's mastery over nature. There are few better examples of the psychological impact of the new attitudes toward nature and time than Goethe's novella, *Elective Affinities* (*Die Wahlverwandschaften*). In this novella the psychological relationships, organic and tangled as a Celtic illumination from the *Book of Kells*, reflect the subtle organic harmonies of chemistry, the landscape and primeval time.[9] The novel, like much of Romantic thought, depended for its power on the theme of a hidden harmony revealed; a harmony which lay beyond the power of rationality in its ordinary sense.

However, at least a considerable amount of the aesthetic pleasure men got from the new conception of the garden lay in the appreciation of the images of order being overthrown by the processes of nature. Time's erosion and the dissolving powers of nature are among the dominant symbols of the romantic sensibility. The ruined garden and the works of man brought down by the forces of nature, whether in the devastated city or the ravaged and ruined mind, are the themes of poet and painter alike. Ruin is the mood of Shelley's "Ozymandias":

And on the pedestal these words appear:
"My name is Ozymandias, King of Kings:
Look on my works, ye Mighty, and despair!"

19

Nothing besides remains. Round the decay
Of that colossal wreck, boundless and bare
The lone and level sands stretch far away.

The iconographic equivalents are to be found in nearly every major Romantic painter. Eric Newton in *The Romantic Rebellion*[10] writes, "It [a flash of lightning] is a symbol of a new relationship between Man and Nature which was to become commonplace enough in the early years of the following century, but which, when it was first experienced, seemed to deserve a new name. According to the intensity with which the hostility to nature was stated [in the 17th and early 18th centuries] it could be either 'picturesque' or 'sublime.' In both cases the intention was the same. Its purpose was to point out that Man was sensitive and civilized, nature unruly and untamed. What man had created nature could destroy. But whereas the earlier half of the [18th] century had regarded such destruction as in every way undesirable and disgusting, the new Romantic attitude began to find it impressive and, given the correct, the sensitive attitude to it, admirable."

The "sensitive attitude" which the new sensibility required was an altogether understandable one. It was the consequence of the anxiety which order produces. It is not altogether accidental that the century which dreamt of inventing a perpetual motion machine would fall in love with ruins and mutability.

By the end of the 18th century apocalyptic themes are extremely common in both art and literature. The cosmic disorders depicted by John Martin, the apocalyptic visions of Benjamin West, the roar of disordered elements which figure so prominently in the works of Turner all illustrate this growing vogue. At first the themes are cast in terms of biblical and historical events. By the end of the 18th century, however, the apocalypse has been naturalized, and holds out no meaning larger or more transcendent than time's erosion and nature's dissolution.

The greatest historical work of the 18th century, Gibbon's *Decline and Fall of the Roman Empire* had its inception in Gibbon's interest in the physical ruins of ancient Rome. Giovanni Battista Piranesi (1720-78) celebrated those same ruins in the most splendid and remarkable set of etchings which the 18th century produced. These etchings are justifiably famous even though one tires of seeing them on the walls of every pretentious hotel and motel room in America.

Less well known are the etchings created by Piranesi in which he depicts fantastic prisons modeled on a monstrous Roman architectural scheme. It is as though Piranesi, in his conjunction of ruins and rationally calculated but nonetheless fantastic prison scenes, is seeking to convey the futility and the absurdity of any rational and ordered construction. He says, in effect, that such constructions serve as prison houses for the human spirit and are eventually, no matter how grand, overthrown by time. "The Dream of Reason brings forth Monsters," Goya wrote beneath one of his "Los Caprichos." That madness was somehow associated with a mechanical and monstrous rationality was sensed by the artists and writers of the 19th century. Their fascination with madness is an analogue of their interest in the ruined garden and the devastated city.

The Romantics had ceased to conceive of order and analysis as beneficent and saw them as folly and horror. Horror, however, was a mood not much prevalent in 18th and early 19th century thought. When it appears it is decked out in the stage-designer's costumes and in a theatrical setting. Horror is still a poetic fiction, and apocalypse, divorced from its religious matrix, a kind of fantastic make-believe. The chilling raptures of the Romantics were up to the end of the 19th century still a source of amusement and aesthetic titillation. Goya was, in fact, an anomaly. It remained for the 20th century to turn the artist's dream and the poet's vision into workaday reality. If sentimentality may be defined as having an emotion without paying the price for it, then 19th century Romantic art is sentimental without being genuinely horrible. No one has accused the apocalyptic art of the 20th century of sentimentality."

Nonetheless, the basic symbols of contemporary art had been invented and the modern sensibility had been created by the Romantics. The most emphatic preoccupation of that sensibility was the problem of order, particularly as order expressed itself in rational technique and in the harmony of nature. If order is the key then disorder, tumult, and primal anarchy serve to underline and to denominate an order which has been lost and a humanity which is alienated. The earthly paradise, so often the symbolic focus of art, literature and politics in the 19th century, is in part credible because of an earthly hell.[12]

Until recently two of the greatest of the Romantic painters, Joseph Mallord William Turner (1775-1851) and Caspar David Friedrich (1774-1840), have received only a tithe of the attention which they deserve. Nearly exact contemporaries, they drew upon the same iconographic symbols even though they expressed themselves in very different artistic idioms. They set themselves to depict a world of unmastered and irrational primal energies. In the works of each, man is swallowed up and defeated by natural forces which can not be contained, regulated, or even understood. Apocalypse is secularized and translated into avalanche, storm and the slow decay and ruin occasioned by the passage of time.

No doubt Turner is the greater of the two painters, considered only in aesthetic and formalistic terms, but Friedrich displays an equal perception of what the modern sensibility has believed to be man's predicament. In Friedrich's paintings the joy in ruins is everywhere discernible.[13] These ruins are not only the physical remnants of time-eroded gothic buildings and monasteries. Friedrich is at his most impressive best when he presents a ruined and blasted nature frustrated by time's ability to dissolve. Death and the ruined garden are, for both Turner and Friedrich, demonstrations of the ultimate irrationality of man's existence. In Turner's paintings even the energies released by the industrial revolution meld and blend with the demonic forces of nature. The rational, in short, is absorbed by the irrational, and purpose and order vanish in a pyrotechnic display of light and color.

The sea has always been the symbol which stands most in contradiction to the garden. "Why," asks Herman Melville in *Moby Dick*, "is almost every robust and healthy boy with a robust healthy soul in him, at some time or other crazy to go to sea? Why upon your first voyage as a passenger, did you yourself feel such a mystical vibration, when first told that you and your ship were now out of sight of land? Why did the old Persians hold the sea holy? Why did the Greeks give it a separate deity, an own brother of

Jove? Surely all this is not without meaning. And the still deeper
meaning of that story of Narcissus, who because he could not grasp
the tormenting mild image he saw in the fountain, plunged into it
and was drowned. But the same image, we ourselves see in all rivers
and oceans. It is the image of the ungraspable phantom of life; and
this is the key to it all."

The mystery and awfulness that answers to this "why?" is
suggested later by Melville when he speaks in praise of the whale.
"Of all divers thou has dived the deepest. That head upon which
the upper sun now gleams, has moved amid this world's foundations. Where unrecorded names and navies rest, and untold
hopes and anchors rot; where in her murderous hold this frigate
earth is ballasted with bones of millions of the drowned; there, in
that awful water land, there was thy most familiar home. Thou hast
been where bell or diver never went; hast slept by many a sailor's
side, where sleepless mothers would give their lives to lay them
down . . . "

In Melville as in Turner and Friedrich it is the sea that becomes
the ultimate symbol of nature. It is a disordered force from which
man's cunning and his reason receive their final and certain frustration. It is the realm from which order has either been expunged or,
alternatively, replaced by a mysterious and magical order beyond
fathoming by reason. W. H. Auden in his brilliant but rather
formless lectures, *The Enchafed Flood or The Romantic
Iconography of the Sea*,[14] makes the same point. Auden writes:

> The sea, in fact, is that state of barbaric vagueness and disorder out of
> which civilization has emerged and into which, unless saved by the effort of
> gods and men, it is always liable to relapse. It is so little of a friendly symbol
> that the first thing which the author of the Book of Revelation notices in his vi-
> sion of the new heaven and earth at the end of time is that *"there was no more
> sea."*

The use of the symbol of the sea is more complicated still by the
fact that it is offered as the diametric opposite of the garden. Auden
perceives the relationship of the symbol of the garden to that of the
sea although he does not develop this antithesis. He points out[15]
that, "When society is normal the image is the City or the Garden.
That is where people want and ought to be. As to the sea, the

classical authors would have agreed with Marianne Moore. 'It is human nature to stand in the middle of a thing; But you cannot stand in the middle of this.' ''

Only one symbol lies beyond that of the sea in the intensity of its absurdity. That symbol is the image of the frozen ocean, absolutely and totally inhospitable to man and his purposes. It is the whiteness of ice that is the color of the whale and which evokes from Melville the justifiably famous passage, Chapter XLII on ''The Whiteness of the Whale.'' Friedrich's most famous painting *''Die verungluckte Hoffnung''* (The Wrecked Ship Hope), (Hamburg, Kunsthalle), takes as its iconographic theme a shipwreck in an arctic sea; the ship, appropriately bearing the name Hope, crushed by the huge blocks of ice randomly and crazily thrust upon one another by the chaotic forces of an absurd nature.

Shipwreck is a common theme of the Romantic painters. Delacroix had tried his hand but his effort is pale and unconvincing when compared to Theodore Gericault's ''The Raft of the Medusa.'' It has been described as the greatest single painting of the Romantic era, though this honor must surely be held by Delacroix' ''Death of Sardanapolis.'' Gericault depicts a raft filled with the survivors of the shipwrecked Medusa. The living have cannibalized the bodies of their dead. They are caught in the angry and destructive motion of an empty, implacable and stormy sea. Gericault's contemporaries read into the painting a message of hope but that surely is mistaken.[16] It is clear that the irrational expectation of salvation held in spite of the hopelessness of the situation and in the midst of death, fill the painting with contradiction and a mood of delusion. The French historian Michelet wrote of this painting, ''It is France herself, it is all our society which is embarked on the raft of the Medusa.'' And so the ruined garden has its analogue in the symbol of a ruined and overwhelmed humanity.

Although these symbols of disorder are first evidenced in the treatment by the artist of nature, they are soon extended to man. Gericault was the first modern painter to study madness and to treat it both naturalistically and symbolically. He banishes exaggeration from his paintings and lets the agonized confused and ravaged faces of madmen speak for themselves. The beauty of deformity, the structures of inverted and perverted order,[17] the drugged rapture and the sadistic pleasure are the commonplace themes of Romantic and contemporary literature. The ruined landscape of the human spirit was found to be as entertaining and as exciting as the landscape of the ruined garden. The charm of these symbols of ruin lies in the sense of relief from order and calculation which they provide, lies in their ability to titillate the sensibility without reckoning on the consequences. It is only when the poet's image is translated into waking reality that the full horror of a disordered world becomes apparent.

The images of the garden and the city have been fused, at least since the Renaissance. Dante's great rose image in the *Paradiso* combines the two so skillfully that they merge and become one symbol of perfected order. Those same painters and artists who discovered the ruined garden also exploited the image of ultimate disorder in the theme of the ravaged and devastated city. At first the theme is developed in slightly biblical terms. The disordered city is Nineveh. The theme of the collapse of Empire is not, until the middle of the 19th century, specifically Roman. The distance between artistic competence and artistic genius is nowhere clearer than in a comparison of John Martin's "The Fall of Nineveh" and Eugene Delacroix' "Death of Sardanapolis." Delacroix' painting is the Romantic vision of the city besieged and on the point of surrender. It is the moment of the final no of disorder, conquest and destruction. It is the moment when lust and death reign supreme.

Thomas Cole, the American Romantic painter, traces in his cycle of paintings, *The Course of Empire,* the growth and destruction of empire through the image of the imperial city. The echoes of Claude and the pastoral myth of the golden age are apparent in "The Savage State" and in "The Arcadian or Pastoral State" but the paintings entitled "The Consummation of Empire," "Destruction and Desolation" strike a new note. They rely on models provided by John Martin and echo the profound distrust of imperial greatness which characterized not only American republicanism but 19th century European thought generally. Thomas Couture's "The Romans of the Decadence" explores the same theme though without the artistic integrity of Martin, Delacroix and Cole. By the middle of the 19th century the notion of the decay of imperial grandeur and the decline of cities and states into the lawlessness and hedonism of decadence was fast becoming an intellectual cliché.

We have become accustomed to thinking of revolutions as historic events which take place in the realm of public life; in the streets and in the noisy assemblies of legislators. We fail to recognize that every revolution which reaches the streets has first been made in the minds of men. Those minds are not the minds of a howling mob made up of the proletariate. They are the minds of men who possess a cultivated and sophisticated sensibility. Revolutions are first made in the world of the spirit, and in that world art and literature are more effective revolutionary instruments than guns.

The images of reason cut adrift and order overthrown are universal symbols of enormous and compelling power. Each of us sees in the dethronement of discipline and order an immediate personal advantage. Even when we are reluctant to turn our fantasies into overt action we still dream of a world in which instinct rather than reason is dominant and in which anarchic freedom rather than ordered restraint is the permanent condition of human existence.

It is important to remember, however, that we are capable of resisting the siren songs of anarchy only when the demands made by order are compatible with our lowly humanity and only so long as order is directed to thoroughly rational ends, and the rewards of order are apparent and immediately enjoyable, in some degree, by the whole of our society. The Romantics and the neo-Romantics of the present time have found the image of order overthrown so attractive and compelling precisely because the benefits of order were not widely recognized, and the costs of order, especially the psychological costs, were so keenly felt and so widely known.

---

[1]Renato Poggioli, *The Theory of the Avant-Garde*, translated from the Italian by Gerald Fitzgerald (Harvard University Press, Cambridge, 1968).

[2]A. Bartlett Giamatti, *The Earthly Paradise and the Renaissance Epic* (Princeton University Press, Princeton, 1966).

The Iconography of Disorder

[3]Thomas Finkenstaedt, "Der Garten des Konigs" in *Wandlungen des Paradiesischen und Utopischen, Studien zum Bild eines Ideals* (Walter De Gruyter & Co., Berlin, 1966).

[4]Hans Sedylmayr, *Art in Crisis, The Lost Center*, (Hollis and Carter, London, 1957), p. 18.

[5]Ibid., p. 16.

[6]Kenneth Clark, *Landscape Painting*, (New York, Scribner's, 1950), p. 70.

[7]Maynard Mack, *The Garden and the City, Retirement and Politics in the Later Poetry of Pope, 1731-1743*, (The University of Toronto Press, Toronto, 1969).

[8]Margaret Jourdain, *The Work of William Kent*, (London, Country Life, 1948). See also, Derek Clifford, *A History of Garden Design*, revised ed. (Frederick A. Praeger, New York, 1966), Edward Hyams, *Capability Brown & Humphry Repton*, (Scribner's, New York, 1971) and Christopher Hussey, *English Gardens and Landscapres, 1700-1750*, (Funk and Wagnalls, New York, 1967). For the background of the revolution in garden architecture see, H.V.S. and M.S. Ogden, *English Taste in Landscape in the Seventeenth Century*, (The University of Michigan Press, Ann Arbor, 1955).

[9]Goethe, Johann Wolfgang von, *Die Wahlverwandtschaften*, (*Elective Affinities*), translated by Elizabeth Mayer and Louise Bogan, introduced by Victor Lange (Chicago, Henry Regnery Co., 1963).

[10]Eric Newton, *The Romantic Rebellion* (St. Martin's Press, New York, 1962), p. 105.

[11]Max Peter Maass, *Das Apokalyptische in der modernen Kunst, Endzeit oder Neuzeit, Versuch einer Deutung* (F. Bruckmann, Munchen, 1965).

[12]Werner Hofmann, *The Earthly Paradise, Art in the Nineteenth Century*, translated from the German by Brian Battershaw (George Braziller, New York, 1961).

[13]William Vaughan, Helmut Borsch-Supan, Hans Joachim Niedhardt, *Caspar David Friedrich, 1774-1840, Romantic Landscape Painting in Dresden* (The Tate Gallery, London, 1972).

[14]W. H. Auden, *The Enchafed Flood or The Romantic Iconography of the Sea* (Random House, New York, 1950), pp. 7-8.

[15]Ibid, p. 8.

[16]Lorenz Eitner, *Gericault's "Raft of the Medusa"* (Phaidon, London, 1973).

[17]Mario Praz, *The Romantic Agony*, translated from the Italian by Angus Davidson (Meridian Books, Cleveland, 1956).

The Poet
Against the Machine

In a recent discussion of the city in literature[1] Irving Howe asserts that "We may destroy our civilization, we cannot escape it." One notes immediately that Howe used the term "civilization" and not the word culture precisely because Howe believes that our culture is a culture of cities, that it is, indeed, civic. Howe's awareness of the civic nature of Western culture is an awareness which he shares with almost the whole of Western intellectuality. The city has been the basis in our society from ancient times onward, of a life of amplitude, freedom and reason. Even Thoreau at Walden Pond would have been unthinkable aside from the context of nearby Cambridge.

However, the truth of Irving Howe's assertion must be underlined. Our culture is civic and without the city, life as we know it would be quite unthinkable. The city is, in fact, the central node of rational endeavor. It is the home of science, bureaucracy, capitalism and procedural technique. In a sense, the city is more than simply a highly organized community characterized by extreme division of labor and extraordinary social complexity. It is the preconditioning factor for the development of modernity in all its aspects. It is the city which represents analytical and rational ordering in its highest and most complete expression. Of course it is quite possible for us to destroy our civilization. Those intellectuals who have fallen in love with the images of the ruined garden and the devastated city may accomplish their objective of a society from which order has been expunged and in which anarchic freedom takes the place of the restraints of order. Those who have visited New York City recently, or perhaps have spent some time in Washington, D. C., are aware that this possibility is not remote or far-fetched.

But we cannot, as Howe says, "escape our civilization." We cannot, in short, return to a pastoral existence, to an "organic community" based on the soil. We cannot survive by joining a commune and living on vegetables and cereals produced without the help of chemical fertilizers and pesticides. We surrendered that option long ago. For the fact is clear that we are either going to become totally barbarous or increasingly urban. There is no middle ground of pastoral natural communities in which the difficulties of the rational life are avoided.

If such is the case how does it happen that the poets, the philosophers, the spiritually creative and the political thinkers in our culture have been, almost without exception, opposed to the city. The landscape of our Christian mythology bears this out. Paradise is a primeval garden, hell is the city of dismal night. Sin is something peculiarly associated with cities and virtue almost the monopoly of the countryside. "I saw you luring the boys under the gaslights," Carl Sandburg writes of Chicago, but he was simply echoing a cry so old that it was a cliché when Herodotus said the same thing of Babylon. General von Moltke, looking down on conquered Paris in 1870, predicted that it would be the cancer of which France would perish and a host of observers of Berlin in the Weimar era echoed von Moltke's prediction in expressing their fears of what would happen to Germany.

It is important that we examine the pastoral ideal and raise the question of the source of its perennial attraction.[2] Why have Western intellectuals been so willing to retreat, at least in theory, into an idealized pastoral landscape when the city which is the very home of rationality has been so obviously the *sine qua non* of productive intellectual existence?

Pastoral poetry has, I believe, a political purpose. That purpose is nearly always disguised, or latent. Here is an example. I am quoting from William Empson's *Some Versions of Pastoral.*[3]

> Gray's "Elegy" is an odd case of poetry with latent political ideas:
>
> Full many a gem of purest ray serene
> The dark, unfathomed caves of ocean bear;
> Full many a flower is born to blush unseen
> And waste its sweetness on the desert air.
>
> What this means, as the context makes clear, is that eighteenth century England had no scholarship system. . . . This is stated as pathetic, but the reader is put into a mood in which one would not try to alter it . . . By comparing the social arrangement to Nature he makes it seem inevitable, which it was not and gives it a dignity which was undeserved. Furthermore, a gem does not mind being in a cave and a flower prefers not to be picked; we feel that man is like the flower, as short-lived, natural, and valuable and this tricks us into feeling that he is better off without opportunities. . . .

The pastoral poet may achieve any one of a number of goals but they all have as their ultimate purpose the adjustment of the individual or his society to conditions which are either unbearable or which, given common sense and human ingenuity, ought not to be borne. The purpose of pastoral literature may be a slick and satisfied justification of stagnation, impoverishment and a generally low level of existence. Marie Antoinette and her court playing shepherds and milkmaids at the Petite Trianon revealed the very pastoral values which make the indefensible beautiful by falsifying its nature. The love affair contemporary intellectuals are conducting with primitive peoples and primitive technologies has a similar character.

A second, and perhaps more important achievement of pastoral literature is its ability to shift men out of a landscape filled with tension and conflict into an imaginary landscape from which tension has been eliminated and unavoidable conflict removed. Aggression, conflict and all the horrors of social violence in one form or another are the very conditions of human existence. Conflict is exacerbated by the complexities of rationalization, urbanization and industrialism. The pastoral poet does not attempt to resolve the con-

31

flict by the application of reasoned technique to the problem at hand. Rather, he proposes that we evade the problem by shifting the location of human existence away from the conflict-ridden environment to an imaginary landscape where, by definition, no conflict is possible. Many of the ecological enthusiasts of the present day are in fact attempting to retreat from the effort to solve the major problems which confront us. Their method is the method of the pastoral poet; they retreat into an imaginary landscape in which conflict is impossible.

Finally, the pastoral poet insists that the landscape itself regenerates fallen man. Man's morals are not improved by conversion and repentence, man's character is not improved by the technical mastery of the environment but he is made good simply by living in nature raw and unimproved.

I quote Thomas Jefferson's response to Query XIX in his *Notes on Virginia* at length because of the clarity with which he expresses this pastoral proposition.

> Those who labour in the earth are the chosen people of God, if ever he had a chosen people, whose breasts he has made his peculiar deposit for substantial and genuine virtue. It is the focus in which he keeps alive that sacred fire, which otherwise might escape from the face of the earth. Corruption of morals in the mass of cultivators is a phenomenon of which no age or nation has furnished an example. It is the mark set on those, who not looking up to heaven, to their own soil and industry, as does the husbandman, for their subsistence, depend for it on the casualties and caprice of customers. Dependence begets subservience and venality, suffocates the germ of virtue and prepares fit tools for the designs of ambition. This, the natural progress and consequence of the arts, has sometimes, perhaps been retarded by accidental circumstances: but generally speaking, the proportion which the aggregate of the other classes of citizens bears in any state to that of its husbandmen, is the proportion of its unsound to its healthy parts, and is a good enough barometer whereby to measure its degree of corruption. While we have land to labour, then, let us never wish to see our citizens occupied at a workbench, or twirling a distaff. Carpenters, masons, smiths are wanting in husbandry: but for the general operations of manufacture, let our workshops remain in Europe. It is better to carry provisions and materials to workmen there, than bring them to the provisions and materials, and with them their manners and principles. The loss by the transportation of commodities across the Atlantic will be made up in happiness and permanence of government. The mobs of great cities add just so much to the strength of the human body. It is the manners and spirit of a

people which preserve a republic in vigour. A degeneracy in these is a canker
which soon eats to the heart of its laws and constitution.

Notice that the source of corruption lies not only in urban life but
in industrial production. It is what William Blake called "the dark
Satanic mills" which both destroy the landscape and corrupt the
man. However, Blake went even farther than Jefferson. The
machine is not only unnatural and morally vicious but beyond that,
the rationalization which the machine represents has its expression
even in science and philosophy. "To his mind," Jacob Bronowski
writes,[4] "the machine became one with the mechanics of Newton
and the mechanical society of Locke. The Satanic Wheels and the
Satanic Mills are symbols for the planetary orbits and the laws of
gravitation which govern and constrain them, filling 'the abstract
voids between the stars' with the machinery of Newton's
astronomy. Blake saw in these laws symbols, in their turn, of an
abstraction, and in human society of constraint. Although the symbols are whimsical, what they say is simple: that the machine was
becoming master, in the theory and in the practice of science—a
giant orrery or planetarium 'to turn that which is Soul and Life into
a Mill or Machine.'

> I turn my eyes to the Schools and Universities of Europe
> And there behold the loom of Locke, whose
>   Woof rages dire,
> Wash'd by the Water-wheels of Newton:
>   black the cloth
> In heavy wreathes folds over every Nation:
>   cruel Works
> Of many wheels I view, wheel without
>   wheel, with cogs tyrannic
> Moving by compulsion each other, not as
>   those in Eden, which
> Wheel within wheel, in freedom revolve
>   in harmony and peace.

Blake clearly perceived that urbanization and industrialization,
the world of the city and of the machine do not stand alone but are
bound up with the whole of the rationalization of Western society.
He determined, therefore, to attack not only the rationality of the

machine but rationality in religion together with the science of Newton and the politics of Locke. Like the pastoralists, Blake seeks to build the New Jerusalem in England's green and pleasant land.

The pastoral quest accorded well with the intellectual superstitions of the 19th century. These superstitions dictated that men attempt to recreate community and society on the organic biological model, that they reject analytical and rational political forms in favor of "natural" politics and that the ideal of community be based upon notions of love, ethnicity and moral obligation rather than contract theory. Those political ideals which emerged in the 19th century, consequently, were the folk state with ethnicity and nationalism at its core and the "natural" peasant community living on the land, its institutions without the benefit of ratiocination, uncorrupted by capitalism and the cash nexus. Of course, the ideal, the dream was totally in contradiction to the realities of 19th century life. That reality was the triumph of capitalism, rational order, contractual forms, democratic government, science and bureaucracy. The new Europe was not, and could not be, the landscape of which the poet and the dreamer approved. They worked out of a deeper and older level of the human consciousness. They borrowed their symbolic language and their mythic structures from a prerational and a pre-scientific era. They saw quite clearly that either poetry must transform itself and learn a new language or the poet must undertake the task of shifting the human environment back to a condition in which the impact of rationalization will be, at the very least, diluted.

The evidence is overwhelming that this was the case. In the poets' revulsion at the city it is perhaps most clear, though the poets were nearly as hostile to capitalism and to science. Dickens' vision of London is typical. London, fascinating and mysterious as Dickens found it, was always in his novels the locus of sin and the scene of human corruption and degradation. David Copperfield learns how to be a "fine, firm fellow" in the countryside home of Aunt Betsy Trotwood and in the provincial towns. However, much the same could be said of nearly all the Dickens novels. However, Dickens is only the most important of the writers in English who took the city as his problem.

Nor can we say that the attack upon modernity came exclusively, or even chiefly, from the left. In fact the left has been aesthetically and culturally unimportant for most of the past two hundred years. The dominant ideas during that time are the statements of men who ideologically were far more at home on the Right. In many of its most important aspects and expressions the attack upon modernity, the hostility to science, the revulsion at the city, the rejection of reason, the running war with industrialization have been the work of self-proclaimed members of the Right. So much is well established and one has only to look at such things as George Steiner's "Eliot Lectures" or the more thorough and systematic treatment of this topic by John R. Harrison in his 1967 book, *The Reactionaries, A Study of the Anti-Democratic Intelligentsia*. Few modern writers have exhibited, for example, such envenomed hostility to nearly every aspect of modernity as Ezra Pound. Our present state, says Pound, is all the fault of industrialization (Canto 50).

> The first folly was planting factories for
> wool spinning in England and Flanders
> then England kept her raw wool, so that
> camped down the exchanging
> the arts gone to hell by 1750.

That statement is not entirely coherent but clarity was not an obsession with Pound. *The Waste Land* by T. S. Eliot is clearer and more specific in its attack upon the soul-destroying aspects of modernity.

Still the most concerted and the most typical attack made on modernity is not to be found in the work of those poets of the Right, William Butler Yeats, Wyndham Lewis, Ezra Pound, T. S. Eliot, and Roy Campbell. Rather it came from an apolitical man, D. H. Lawrence, who is important to our discussion not only because he is symptomatic of the poets' war against the machine but because he has found such a profound and universal response in contemporary culture. If one really wishes to understand contemporary morality, the intellectual superstitions of the present moment and the puzzling behavior of our contemporaries, one can not make a better beginning than by reading Lawrence's novels, particularly *The Rainbow* and *Lady Chatterley's Lover*.

D. H. Lawrence grew up in England's industrial midlands at the end of the last century. His father was a coal miner, his mother a sensitive and upwardly mobile woman who drove Lawrence on to success and implanted in him his desire to leave the dirty and circumscribed world of the collieries. That however involved problems, for in Lawrence's world the adolescent male became a man, proved his virility and masculinity by going down into the mines, by doing a man's work and playing a man's role at the pub and in the sordid sexual encounters of that mean world. It is difficult to understand the link between sexuality and Lawrence's detestation of industrialism in all its aspects until we realize that Lawrence could not accept the conventional circumstances by which his contemporaries proved themselves as men. Over and over again he attacks industrialism as taking men's sexuality away from them. What he is saying is that he could not become a man in the conventional circumstances which his situation imposed on him.

For Lawrence reason, instinctual renunciation, capitalism, urbanization, industrialism and science form one complete unit. It stands between modern man and his fulfillment, particularly in his creative and his sexual dimension. However, Lawrence's solution was not total revolution—and a retreat into barbarism. In fact, like so many of the members of the youth culture, Lawrence was not a revolutionary. Rather Lawrence sought, like all the other pastoral poets before him, to retreat into a middle ground in which conflict would be impossible and fulfillment certain. We must be fair to Lawrence. He did not seek to reject reason wholly. He wrote in the *Fantasia of the Unconscious*, "We know we cannot live purely by impulse. Neither can we live solely by tradition. We must live by all three, ideal, impulse and tradition each in its hour . . . Man always falls into one of three mistakes. In China, it is tradition. And in the South Seas it seems to have been impulse. Ours is idealism."

Still the great weight of Lawrence's work is on the side of impulse rather than on tradition or what he denominates "idealism" and I would call reason. The great theme, then, in nearly all Lawrence's work is not, as one might suppose, sexuality and its expression, for Lawrence was rather a Puritan as Mark Spilka has pointed out so well in his book, *The Love Ethic of D.H. Lawrence*.

36

Rather, Lawrence took as his theme, even in the travel books such as *Mornings in Mexico, Etruscan Places* and *The Sea and Sardinia*, the problem of man's inability to fulfill himself in our modern rational and machine culture.

The Rainbow, perhaps Lawrence's most successful novel from a literary standpoint, begins with the sentence, "The Brangwens had lived for generations on Marsh Farm, in the meadows where the Erewash twisted sluggishly through older trees, separating Derbyshire from Nottinghamshire." It is interesting to note at the outset that Lawrence's novels are set in the countryside. He had absolutely no feeling for the city and could not even take pleasure in the adventure and mystery the city afforded while abhoring its corruption and degradation, ·as was the practice with so many 19th century novelists.

These Brangwens "felt the rush of the sap in the spring, they knew the wave which cannot halt, but every year throws forward the seed of begetting, and, falling back, leaves the young-born on the earth, sunshine drawn into the breast and bowels, the rain sucked up in the daytime, nakedness that comes under the wind in autumn, showing the birds nests no longer worth hiding," etc. In short the Brangmen live in loving organic wholeness with nature. Their lives have been a pastoral idyl. The problem of modernity asserts itself when the machine intrudes into the bucolic landscape. It is the problem, as Leo Marx so aptly puts it of "The Machine in the Garden."

In both *The Rainbow* and in *Lady Chatterley's Lover* one of the central characters is the man committed to the machine; the heartless man of reason; dead from the waist down, dreaming his dreams of power and mastery and turning the proud and vital drive of sexuality into the demonic energies of a mechanized world. Gerald Crich in *The Rainbow* and Lord Clifford in *Lady Chatterley's Lover* are both men who have sacrificed sex to power, and vitality and organic relationship to mechanism and reason.

Here is the way in which Lawrence describes Gerald Crich:

> He saw the stream of miners flowing along the causeways from the mines at the end of the afternoon, thousands of blackened, slightly distorted human beings with red mouths, all moving subjugate to his will. . . . They were all

subordinate to him. They were ugly and uncouth, but they were his instruments. He was the God of the machine.

If the impact of the machine on the master was heightened aggression and the pursuit of power, its impact on the men who served the machine was dehumanization.

"The joy went out of their lives, the hope seemed to perish as they became more and more mechanized. And yet they accepted the new conditions . . . They were exalted by belonging to this great and superhuman system which was beyond feeling or reason . . . Their hearts died within them but their souls were satisfied . . . It was the first great step in undoing, the first great place of chaos, the substituting of the mechanical principle for the organic, the destruction of the organic purpose, the organic unity, and the subordination of every organic unit to the great mechanical purpose. It was pure organic disintegration and pure mechanical organization. This is the first and finest state of chaos."

The solution Lawrence offers is to develop phallic consciousness, turn away from the machines and flee into the countryside. Some critics have hinted that Lawrence was a crypto-fascist. That, it seems to me, pays Lawrence's political consciousness too large a compliment. He was simply a confused and frustrated neo-Romantic who had had an extremely difficult time growing up.

In *Lady Chatterley's Lover* the same theme is developed with even greater explicitness. Connie, the heroine, is married to Lord Clifford, the colliery owner. Lord Clifford had lost his manhood as a consequence of a wound he had received in the war and on his return he put all of his energies into the exploitative processes of mining coal. He becomes the very epitome of the reasoning machine. Lady Chatterley discovers nature, organic and undefiled, however, in the person of Mellors, the gamekeeper on the Clifford estate and together they hatch pheasants. It is Daphnis and Chloe, and all the other pastoral clichés, and their adulterous relationship is elevated by Lawrence to the level of a sacramental mystery because it is sanctioned and approved by nature.

In an edition of *Lady Chatterley's Lover*, the so-called *Second Lady Chatterley*, Mellors, the gamekeeper sketches out what he believes the behavior of the miners should be in contrast with what it is.[5]

> If you could only tell them that living and spending isn't the same thing! But it's no good. If only they were educated to *live* instead of earn and spend, they could manage very happily on twenty-five shillings. If the men wore scarlet trousers, as I said, they wouldn't think so much of money: if they could dance and hop and skip, and sing and swagger and be handsome, they could do with very little cash. And amuse the women themselves, and be amused by the women. They ought to learn to be naked and handsome, and sing in a mass and dance the old group dances, and carve the stools they sit on, and embroider their own emblems. They wouldn't need money. And that's the way to solve the industrial problem: train the people to be able to live, and live in handsomeness, without needing to spend. But you can't do it. They're all one-track minds nowadays, whereas the mass of people oughtn't even to try to think, because they *can't!* They should be alive and frisky and acknowledge the great god Pan. He's the only god for the masses, forever. The few can go in for higher cults if they like. But let the mass be forever pagan.

Lawrence seems to have been smoking the same water pipe as Charles Reich, and were I called upon to diagnose his case I would say it was a matter of premature greening. Written in the midst of the great depression in the English collieries and the mass misery it occasioned, Lawrence's solution to the problems of modern industrial life would surely have seemed cruel to the miners who might have read it. It sounds just as unthinking and as unheeding of real needs and genuine desires as much of the phony baloney coming at us at present from our better university faculties.

Still we cannot put Lawrence and the other poets aside so easily. They have put their fingers on some powerful discontents even though they have not said much that is sensible about them. What I take the poets to be saying is that the machine has not made men better or happier but rather more corrupt and more degraded than they were before they surrendered themselves to its power. This I think is manifestly untrue. It does not follow, however, that the human condition in an age of science, technology and industrialization leaves nothing to be desired and while I cannot imagine that we shall ever be the inhabitants of a paradise restored, a new Jerusalem where alienation has been abolished and all conflict harmonized, still I do believe that men are capable of living more grandly and amply than is the common experience at the present time.

How is that objective to be achieved? Of course I have no blueprint but I do offer a suggestion. At the very close of *Space, Time and Architecture,* one of the most important books of the past three decades, Sigfried Giedion writes:

> . . . The social disorder delivered to us is an inheritance from the Industrial Revolution. To restore order in this unbalanced world we must alter its social conditions. But experience shows us that this is not sufficient. It would be a fundamental mistake to believe that today's maladjusted man, the product of a century-long rupture between thinking and feeling, would disappear as the result of socio-political change. The unintegrated person is today multiplying everywhere and in every class; he is to be found equally among employers and employed, among high and low. His acts reflect his inner division. . . . [And Giedion tells us what the source of this disintegrative process is:] factual knowledge has not been reabsorbed and humanized by an equivalent feeling.

Were we to successfully create a garden we would need to consider three elements, nature, science and art. There are no great gardeners who can create harmonious order with only two of these elements. In art the feelings are reconciled both to reason and to nature and a balance is struck between the legitimate demands and needs of each. Nature alone will result in primitivism and chaos. Reason alone will result in mechanical sterility; art alone is too often the hysterical and empty gesture. If we are to succeed as individual men, as a society and as a species, we must know what we are, we must move with reason and calculation to the fulfillment of our natures and we must do all with the grace and beauty of art. That art should be the expression of our better self: too deeply felt for analysis, too certain for rational demonstration, too harmonious for mechanical reproduction. Art should lead us into wholeness and life and point beyond itself to complete fulfillment. It should make the tragic meaningful and the comic understandable and should reconcile us to existence without robbing us of our courage and our venturesomeness. With art we shall not become gods but we will be able to discern once more these things the gods have done.

Poet Against the Machine

[1]Irving Howe, "The City in Literature" in *Commentary*, Vol. 51, No. 5, May 1971, p. 68.

[2]See especially Leo Marx, *The Machine in the Garden, Technology and the Pastoral Ideal in America* (Oxford University Press, New York, 1964.

[3]William Empson, *Some Versions of Pastoral* (Chatto and Windus, London, 1950), p. 4.

[4]Jacob Bronowski, *William Blake* (Penguin Books, Harmondsworth, 1954), p. 128.

[5](1928) ed. D. H. Lawrence, *Lady Chatterley's Lover* (Penguin Books, New York 1946), p. 258.

Science, Technology
and the Cultural Revolution

If we are to believe the electronically amplified clucking of certain Luddite intellectuals and the outpouring of printed materials which dwarfs even the annual production of Bibles, America and indeed, the whole Western world is in the midst of a great cultural revolution. The invention of bell bottom trousers and rock music are happy inspirations on a level with Newton's formulation of the laws of universal gravitation and Gregor Mendel's inspired pea sorting; and hair, with which women have perennially been unable to do a thing, has suddenly become the visible sign of life renewed and spirit infused. America has "greened" we are told and Consciousness III has abolished, repealed, and repudiated not only war, alienation, hatred, and envy but even the basic factum which makes economic science possible, that old devil, scarcity. The Puritan ethic, it is said, has vanished and the work ethic has disappeared to be replaced by a noncompetitive era of indulgence in which the only pollution will be the healthy sort; the mountains of fecund literary manure which will fertilize the "greening."

America, whether spelled with a "c" or a "k," if we are to take certain of our intellectuals and many of our students seriously, has moved in the brief period of twenty-five years from the position of the "arsenal of democracy" to the "cesspool of plutocracy." One is tempted to say the "cesspool of technology" for in the thinking of these neo-primitives it is difficult to discern just which elements they believe to be chiefly responsible for our current fall from grace; wealth and affluence or science and effluence.

Closer examination of the rhetoric of ecological and cultural apocalypse reveals, however, that this movement of ideas and imagination has taken far less than a quarter of a century to occupy the dominant place in the house of horror many intellectuals assert is contemporary American society. Indeed, it would seem, the preoccupation with pollution and the revulsion shown toward science, technology and rationality is of very recent origin. Only a decade ago science and technology stood at the apogee of their power, and although, as C. P. Snow recognized in his essay of 1959, *The Two Cultures,* literary intellectuals were mounting a determined counter-attack, science still carried the day and dominated the intellectual and cultural scene. Now, if one is to believe the slick and middle-brow literary monthlies and the soap opera intellectuality of "in depth" television analysts, scientists are in nearly as desperate a shape as generals, parents, university presidents, policemen, Richard Nixon, and even good old God.

The apologists of the counterculture, the youth culture, or the apostles of greening have basically a simple position. It is that the "adversary culture" (to use another of these clever Madison Avenue-like terms which left intellectuals are fond of inventing for themselves) seeks to transform American society through a retreat from the world of science, technology, bureaucracy, rationality and organization. The position of the counterculture represents what one of them has described as "the great denial," a revolutionary act which will by transforming consciousness take us back to the age before the wheel, the atomic bomb and the urban crisis. Writing in the February, 1971 issue of *Fortune* Magazine, Lawrence Lessing described this intellectual syndrome in the following terms:

> The most visible embodiment of these philosophies is in the new youth culture, or counterculture, which turns away from hard science to the softer, still forming social sciences, the arts and handicrafts, the primitive and a

44

return-to-nature à la Rousseau—and ravels out in astrology, drugs, and those Eastern mysticisms that for centuries have held whole continents impoverished . . . Avowedly anti-science, its culture rests squarely on those electrical sciences that power its amplifiers, electric guitars, and stereo rigs and on the pharmacopeia of chemical agents that give it instant visions. Its communes are never far from the supermarket, that base of modern food technology, and it does not eschew motorcycles or motorcars. It accepts in other words, the science and technology that pleases it, and would destroy those that do not.

But science is indivisible, a seamless web of accumulated knowledge, and to destroy a part would rip the whole fabric.

The leaders and followers of the movement which describes itself as a counterculture say that it is new, that it is revolutionary and that the impact of the changes it would introduce would be wholly beneficial. I believe each of these claims is false. The position of the counterculture is not new, indeed it is as old as technology itself and a similar position was probably elaborated by hunters when in the course of the Neolithic revolution, the domestication of plants and animals took place. It is not revolutionary in any sense and especially in a Marxian sense, and if we were to systematically follow the advice of Charles Reich, the author of *The Greening of America*, the United States would, within a year's time, be the scene of pandemic disease, famine and complete social dislocation. Let us examine each of these claims in turn and analyze the available evidence.

I find the claim of novelty among the most interesting. A defective sense of history and little or no knowledge of the historic past enable the so-called youth culture to assert that their position, their values and indeed their cultural morphology are wholly new and radically different from anything that has happened before, that they are in fact "cultural mutants." Historically this claim, especially with respect to the specifically youthful aspects of the movement we are discussing, is simply false and betrays an appalling lack of historical information. Lewis Feuer, Walter Z. Lacqueur and Fritz Stern have all recently pointed out in detail the remarkable similarity between the contemporary youth culture and that other youth movement, the pre-Hitlerite youth movement of Wilhelmian Germany which ended in anguish and catastrophe in 1933. From my own very extensive investigations I categorically assert that there is not one value, not a single slogan, not a posture or costume, not a technique or political or cultural position which was not manifested in that earlier movement. The only difference lies in the increased silliness of the American version. That, I suppose, is wholly in keeping with the dictum of Marx that history repeats itself. The first time it is tragedy; the second time it is enacted as farce.

But let us consider the anti-technological, anti-scientific and anti-rational aspects of the movement more closely. Far from these being novel, they represent the commonest grist of the anti-intellectual mill for the past two centuries. From the middle of the 18th century onward there has been a steady procession of movements and ideas whose aim is the restoration of what certain elements in Western culture have mistakenly believed to be the lost paradise of pre-industrial society. Their recommendations have been various; the abandonment of the plow for the spade, the abandonment of refined and processed foods (witness, for example, the enthusiasm for graham flour which characterized the reformers of Thoreau, Hawthorne and Emerson's generation), the abandonment of clothing or the substitution of a uniform nondescript garment (witness the effort to popularize the bloomer in the 1840s), the campaign against the railroad as a polluter and poisoner of the countryside, the campaign against immunization, and finally the pervasive distrust of and hostility to urbanization and industrialization. Any historian who has read more than a few pages in the sources of 19th century social history can tell you the same story.

However, the element which makes this derailment of the Western spirit all the more poignant is the assertion on the part of its missionaries that it is boldly revolutionary, and that it is the most important contribution the intellectual and political Left has to make to the contemporary world. In fact this view is starkly reactionary, has always been associated with satiated classes and societies and in the recent past has far oftener been advocated by the extreme Right than the Left.

Whittaker Chambers, the 20th century's greatest convert from communism; a man who refused to describe himself as being a conservative and who preferred to call himself "a man of the Right," wrote, "for, of course, our fight, as I think we said, is only incidentally with Socialists or other heroes of that kidney. *Wesentlich*, it is with machines." Chambers described Senator Robert Taft as a liberal rather than a conservative because he did not say to farmers, "Farmers, back to horses and the hand plough; smash your tractors and buy no more." What Chambers intended, what he meant was that technology is an essentially revolutionary instrument and that it transforms not only the mode of production but society and politics as well.

Chambers, of course, was not alone in this perception. One of the first books published by Henry Regnery, the distinguished and erudite Chicago publisher who has contributed so much to the current neo-conservative movement in the United States, was *The Failure of Technology* by Friedrich Georg Juenger, (1949). Friedrich Georg Juenger is the brother of Ernst Juenger, the German poet, essayist, and man of the Right. Friedrich Georg no less than his brother subscribes to an aristocratic, conservative humanism and *The Failure of Technology* must be seen as a most persuasive document in the revolt against modernity. One is tempted to say that the New Left might have learned a great deal from the Old Right had their literary and historical education been a bit more thorough. Juenger's work is a long and systematic denunciation of the evils and the anti-humane character of technology. I quote him at random: "No human invention could possibly abolish the reciprocity between mechanical progression and elemental regression." Or, "The Gods manifestly do not love man the maker; they oppose him violently at times, while at other times they suffer him as a half-burlesque figure by their side, like Hephaistos. They beat down the revolt and presumption of the Titans." Or still again, "What will spell the end is rather the total character of those losses which include the human beings within the technological organizations. It becomes constantly more evident that the sum total of the technological efforts and investments overtaxes human capacities, that the sheet weight of the mechanical burden is getting too heavy, that once technology has reached perfection, it will not be long before modern man collapses."

In an introduction written for *The Failure of Technology* in 1956 by Frederick D. Wilhelmsen, whose ideology is romantic Spanish integralism, Wilhelmsen lapses into a tone which might easily be confused with that of the New Left. Wilhelmsen writes: "Juenger insists that as technology approaches [perfection] it purges nature of life and man of humanity. It perverts the state by turning politics into an order of technical problems rather than an exercise of moral judgment. It destroys the profit motive by subordinating the good of both the capitalist and laborer to the good of the machine; thus the technician," writes Wilhelmsen, "drove the craftman from his hand loom and forced him to become an operator in a mill, a proletarian. In this act his intent was not to enrich the capitalist at the expense of the factory worker, but he accepted this consequence without compunction. He was interested above all in developing the technical mechanism, and not at all in who profited by it. And we can hear Orwell's O'Brien," Wilhelmsen adds, "admitting casually that the vision of constantly increasing power has its own consolations, even if they bring with them the victory of the robot. 'If you want a picture of the future, imagine a boot stamping on a human face—forever.' "

One might lengthen the list of men of the Right who have seen in technology the most revolutionary and dehumanizing force in the modern period. Certainly both D. H. Lawrence and Henry David Thoreau belong in this company of bourgeois radicals who have seen the machine as mankind's chief enemy. How are we to account for this attack from the Right which seems to have so much in common with the New Left? Is it simply another instance of the congruence of the extremes, the tendency of the extreme Right and the extreme Left to come to the same conclusions and to employ the same tactics? I do not believe this to be a satisfactory explanation.

It is not a satisfactory explanation because the Old Left, genuinely revolutionary, clearly recognized, and recognizes today, the essentially revolutionary dynamic of science and technology and is at least theoretically more completely committed to science and technology than is the free world. Marx saw clearly the relationship of capital to technology and science as forces destined to transform the world in a revolutionary fashion. He wrote:

> Pursuing this tendency, capital has pushed beyond national boundaries and prejudices, beyond deification of nature and the inherited, self-sufficient satisfaction of existing needs confined within well-defined bounds, and the reproduction of the traditional way of life.
>
> It [capital] is destructive of all this, and permanently revolutionary, tearing down all obstacles that impede the development of productive forces, the expansion of needs, the diversity of production and the exploitation and exchange of natural and intellectual forces.

What strikes one immediately in the anti-rationalism, the anti-science, the anti-technology and anti-productionism of the New Left is its non-Marxian and non-revolutionary character. Both capitalism and Marxism are dedicated to the revolutionary transformation of society through a changing productive technique. Pre-capitalistic aristocratic ideologies, on the contrary, because they are the expression of a satiated and threatened class, seek to check technological transformation or to turn it from the production of consumer goods to the production of amusement and illusion. Moreover, it should not strike us as odd that the New Left is ideologically so closely allied with the Old Right. They are both satiated groups. The revolutions such groups make are revolutions of satiety rather than revolutions of deprivation. They seek to change without transforming and their aspiration is to secure for all time a status and a condition which they sense to be, at best, transitory.

Peter and Brigitte Berger, distinguished Rutgers University sociologists, sensed the fact I have observed above when they wrote recently:

> The "greening" revolution is not taking place in a sociological vacuum, but has a specific location in a society that is organized in social classes. There are enough data now to pinpoint this location. The cadres of the revolution are, in overwhelming proportions, the college-educated children of the upper middle class. Ethnically, they tend to be Wasps and Jews. Ideologically, they are in revolt against the values of this class—which is precisely the class that has

been running technological society so far. But the essentially bucolic rhetoric of this rebellion goes far beyond a radical (in a leftist sense) rejection of American class society and its allegedly evil ways. The rhetoric intends a dropping out of technological society as such.

What the Bergers suggest is the point I have just made. The anti-science and anti-technology of the New Left is not revolutionary; it is, indeed, a retreat to traditional society from which for more than a thousand years Western man has been struggling to free himself through the employment of reason, science and invention.

Richard L. Rubenstein, professor at Florida State University, probably put the whole matter most succinctly when he said recently, "Technological civilization has made it possible for millions of European and American young people to enjoy a moratorium from the adult world of conflict, competition and power. We call that moratorium the youth culture; Charles Reich has recently called it Consciousness III."

What makes the youth culture even more fascinating as a social phenomenon is its attempt to turn a moratorium into a permanent condition by biting the robot hand that feeds them. Far from being members of the revolutionary Left, these "greened" scions of the upper middle class are very close to the attitudes and values of the old aristocratic Right and their orientation is to a society not too unlike the traditional society which our ancestors struggled to transform in the early medieval period.

Robert Scalapino, professor of political science at the University of California at Berkeley recognized this when he distinguished the different meanings the word "revolution" has in Western society and in the non-Western world at the present time. In the Western world the revolutionary attack is an attack on production, on science and technology, on rationality and affluence. The ideal which the revolutionaries hold out to us is the ideal of traditional society: ill-organized, ill-fed and clothed, sick and uneducated but pure in motive and rejoiced by the mystical inward vision. The revolutionaries of the non-Western world seek just the opposite. For the most part they live in traditional societies which they are seeking to transform. They value political order, good schools and universities and the benefits of modern sanitation and medical science. Their proudest achievements are increases in industrial and agricultural production. Their heroes are engineers and industrial managers. This is the case because they know real poverty and genuine ignorance. They cannot afford the luxury of a pseudo-primitive existence made possible by a governmental food stamp plan.

But finally, the counterculture will not succeed, cannot succeed, because it runs counter to everything we know about human behavior. The anti-rationalists, and anti-technocrats anxious to restore a barter economy, introduce a vegetarian cuisine, give themselves over to free love and non-competition, or perhaps more modestly simply desirous of destroying capitalism, or the "gold bugs," are doomed to frustration. There has never been, short of an all-encompassing disaster, a voluntary return to a primitive technology once that technology has been replaced by one more sophisticated; one which gives man a better command of his environment and arms him more effectively for the battle against want, disease and discomfort. From the neolithic revolution to the hydrogen bomb, ideas and technology have steadily revolutionized society and mankind has welcomed each change, each social transformation, no matter how disrupting its social consequences, enthusiastically. And they have done so because each change has brought with it the promise of a more abundant and satisfying life. The quantitative and qualitative quest for life is the story of every religion, every political system, every social order. It is, quite simply, what history is all about. This quest is a quest intrinsic to man and most especially to Western civilization. We are all revolutionaries. We cannot, even were we to wish to do so, renounce the course upon which, not ourselves alone, but the whole of mankind has determined.

Let us make no mistake about this important matter. If we Americans renounce our leadership in science and technology and abandon the course upon which we are set, we cannot expect the remainder of the world to follow in our footsteps. While we "green" the remainder of the world will turn red. Even if we simply follow the pattern in science and technology which we have set during the past few years it is quite possible we shall be within a

51

decade a second-rate state displaced by both Japan and the Soviet Union. Recently Dr. John S. Foster, Jr., director of defense research and engineering, Department of Defense, testified before the Senate Armed Services Committee. He pointed out that one reason for Soviet research success is the growing number of Soviet researchers. The United States had 142,000 graduates in engineering and the natural sciences in 1970, he said, while the Soviet Union had 247,000. He anticipated that in 1976, the United States would have 181,000 and the Soviet Union 359,000.

But it would be wrong to define a position and defend a principle solely on the basis of the Soviet challenge, however grave and however important that challenge is. Ultimately, the defense of rationalism, science and technology is one which is rooted in the total predicament of contemporary man. The price of survival is not less reason but more science. It is not less technology but more technology. Long ago Alfred North Whitehead, the great mathematician-philosopher, put it most clearly and succinctly when he said, "In the conditions of modern life, the rule is absolute: the race which does not value trained intelligence is doomed." I believe it may safely be asserted that either we shall drive on to the solution of our problems through rational-technical-scientific means, or mankind, defeated and overcome by the forces of nature and the disorder of his passions, will be forced to relinquish his mastery of the planet and will have to content himself with the very nearly paleolithic existence characteristic of the mountain dwellers of New Guinea.

Speaking before the American Association for the Advancement of Science, Dr. Philip Handler, president of the National Academy of Sciences said:

> I deny that my life has been made wretched or my freedom reduced by science. Rather do I believe that technology has made the lives of about three-quarters of all Americans richer, more comfortable, more enjoyable, and more healthy, than that of humanity in any other period of history. The challenge is to extend those boons to the remaining quarter. While recognizing the dangers ahead, I believe that, with judicious use of applied science, these dangers can be averted and humanity freed as never before for what Norbert Wiener called "the human use of human beings." To be sure, we have been dangerously exploiting the planet's natural resources and too rapidly despoil-

ing the environment. But only by much improved technology can we avoid the first danger and prevent the second, far preferable to returning to the good old days that never were.

The so-called cultural revolution is a retreat from reality, a vacation from genuine relevance. But these despairing gestures are not the actions by which a new world is made or even a new consciousness called into existence. They represent, not the future, but the heavy hand of the dead past, the stupidities of status quo contentment and the rigidities of behavior oriented to a thoughtless traditionalism. Certainly we need a science which is cognizant of human ends and purposes. Clearly we need a reevaluation of much of our technological effort in order to make certain that it serves to enlarge rather than to diminish our humanity. But this cannot be achieved by know-nothing Luddites whose only claim to moral superiority is that they belong to the current smart-set. It can only be achieved by humanists who have a deep understanding of science and scientists and technologists who have an equally deep understanding of our humanity. Together we shall redress the past and ransom the future.

Foundations
and the Public Interest

It is a common and understandable error that many confuse
destruction with reformation. When institutions which have served
men well are found wanting society ought to strengthen and clarify
the institutions' central purpose rather than impose destructive and
punitive measures. Reform is possible only when that central purpose is identified and obstructions to its fulfillment are removed.

This basic confusion of destruction with reformation is nowhere
more clearly evident than in the current discussion concerning the
role of the foundations in American society and proposals recently
made to reform their activities. It is evident from the character of
several of these proposals that the purpose of the foundation has
been misunderstood. It is even more evident that these proposals,
far from aiding the foundations successfully to fulfill their function,
would hamper their activities, distort their objectives and corrupt
their operations.

Of course all institutions should be subject to evaluation and constant testing, and the scrutiny foundations are currently undergoing
is long overdue. Those who have observed foundations at all closely
over the last twenty years have become increasingly convinced that

their actions are frequently arbitrary, their operations characterized by personal and political cronyism, their great resources employed for the political aggrandisement of their directors, and their role in American life has been more and more connected with political activism and social revolution. The facts are so irrefutable that it has become clear that foundations have lost a substantial measure of the trust the American people reposed in them.

To admit that the foundations have not been the instruments of unmitigated good which the American people thought them to be should in no way detract from either their achievement or their potentiality. Few institutional forms are more distinctively American in either inspiration or intention than the foundation, which seeks to accomplish for society through private initiative those things which government does poorly or cannot do at all. Perhaps, if the foundations and the American people understood this, a great deal of the present difficulties of foundations would not have eventuated. For when foundations assume partisan political postures or attempt to do the work of government they nearly always corrupt both society and themselves.

It can be argued, however, with some justification that the activities of foundations have become increasingly politicized, not because foundations have been infected by politics but rather because big government has usurped many of the fields in which foundations have, in the past, been legitimately active.

Ideally the foundation reflects in innovative philanthropy the risk, venture and creativity which resulted in the accumulation of these great capitals. It is a philanthropy which can afford to take chances and is not afraid to gamble. It has been able to champion the eccentric, to support the unpopular, to investigate the unlikely and generally to resist the pressures of social, intellectual and cultural conformity which de Tocqueville saw, more than a century ago, as an inherent weakness in American society. The foundation, at its best, has been able to achieve this because by its nature it has tended to create, reward and increase diversity, whereas the tendency of government at every level is toward centralization and bureaucratic uniformity.

56

Foundations acting as patrons can foster and reward invention and discovery in those areas where patent and copyright serve as ineffective stimuli. They have served to institutionalize and disseminate a "high" culture. Those cultural forms which were and are in other societies the prerogative of a privileged elite or dependent upon the generosity of the state have become commonplace enthusiasms of the American masses and are uncorrupted by state patronage. The variety and vitality of American culture is, consequently, not the product of state action but rather the result of a diverse and private initiative. Finally, the foundations, at their best, have sought new solutions to the age-old problems of social, economic and spiritual deprivation. Their ameliorative experiments are uncommonly effective because for the most part they have been private endeavors, small in scale, local in character, and individual in application. Foundations have pointed the direction welfare activity must take in an era when the failure of massive governmental welfare programs has become apparent.

"Make the advocacy of radical causes sufficiently remunerative, and the supply of advocates will be unlimited," Milton Friedman has observed. There is some evidence that our larger foundations have attempted to discover how many radicals per acre campus projects will produce when fertilized by foundation dollars. Although this is undeniably the case and has resulted in some of the public's disenchantment with foundations it should be recalled that advocacy and even dispassionate investigation from any perspective other than that of the current orthodoxy is a very expensive undertaking. Society preserves its stability in part by making radicalism costly. (Here I use "radicalism" broadly to mean any idea which deviates significantly from accepted theory or practice.) It is precisely because creative dissent is so costly that a society such as ours, which is so heavily dependent upon reasoned change, must view non-governmental patronage as one of its most important sources of freedom and innovation.

Few individuals possess the economic resources necessary to challenge settled public opinion, whether it is the opinion of the scientific academy or a prevailing economic doctrine. Wealth and a principled resistance to meaningless and destructive conformity are only occasionally united in one person. The creative individual of modest means is usually dependent upon patronage for the opportunity to realize his vision. Men are free only insofar as they can afford to be free, and without patronage few would be able to challenge either the power of the state or those pervasive biases which threaten every culture with conformist mediocrity. The role of the foundation as patron produces its severest critics and provides it with its proudest boasts.

Liberal democrats, whether left, right or center, all subscribe to the idea that numbers of advocates or believers are no pragmatic test of the validity of an idea. It may be regrettable that foundations in the present decade have been such ardent supporters of the left liberal orthodoxy, but all the support in the world will not make a wrong idea functional. So long as there is patronage for ideas which challenge orthodoxies (and in the present instance the liberal orthodoxy most needs challenging), the foundations will have served the needs of American democracy well. That such anti-establishment ideas are expressed through foundation support is beyond questioning. That these ideas have had a decisive impact on our society within the last decade is a demonstrable fact. Ideas in a democratic society need meet only one test and that is the test of the marketplace. The function of the foundations as a group is not that of testing ideas but rather of getting them into the marketplace.

If the larger purposes of the foundations are the maximization of diversity, the exploration of alternatives and the steady enlargement of freedom, will current suggestions for reform aid the foundations in the achievement of their objectives? Two recently proposed reforms clearly will not provide incentives to foundations to strengthen their most socially relevant functions. Indeed, one arrives at the unshakable conviction that the purpose of these so-called reforms is not reform at all but punishment. These two alleged reforms are the effort to tax foundation earnings and the attempt to prevent foundations from making direct grants to individuals.

It is a truism that the power to tax is the power to destroy. It is unimportant that the proposed tax will probably be fixed at a relatively insignificant five per cent of annual income. The enactment of any tax establishes the principle that the judgment of the politician as to the expenditure of foundation income will be wiser and more socially beneficial than the judgment of foundation officers. No experience we have of government leads us to believe that this will be the case. It is an odd argument which says that because some foundations have used their funds politically all foundation funds should be subject to political expenditure.

It must be said again and again that foundation funds are not public funds though they are expended in what is deemed to be the public interest. The foundation stands at the intersection of private beneficence and public interest. Its great strength lies precisely in the fact that it is not a part of the public sector and at its best is not subject to political considerations and social pressures. The fruitful diversity of foundation interests will disappear once political judgment and political motives supersede the interest of donors and the traditions of enlightened patronage they establish. The expropriation of endowments by the state is an ancient chapter in the history of European civilization. Its results have always been a lowering of the cultural level of the state in which the expropriation takes place and an absolute decline in freedom.

The attempt to prevent foundations from making direct grants to individuals is only slightly less ill-advised. It is ill-advised in the first place because it will not accomplish what it sets out to do. Supposedly, were foundations unable to make grants directly to individuals, situations such as the Fortas and Douglas scandals would have no possibility of developing. Universities or some other intermediate institutions standing between the grantee and the foundation would, it is argued, serve to reduce the possibility of collusion and corruption. It is to be noted that Justice Fortas received a $15,000 fee from George Washington University, ostensibly to conduct a summer session seminar. It is also to be noted that both President Goheen of Princeton and Robert M. Hutchins, past president of the University of Chicago, serve on the board of directors of the Parvin Foundation. Those who assume that universities per se practice a higher morality than foundation officers are inexperienced innocents. Unfortunately, universities have not been exempted from the corrupting effects of original sin by an immaculate conception.

Although the abolition of direct grants to individuals will not prevent collusion and corruption, it will seriously impair some of the most socially and culturally creative aspects of foundation activity.

Federal and state budgets for pure and applied science now run into the billions of dollars annually. Federal and state patronage of the sciences and technology in one form or another is, moreover, as old as the Republic. At the same time, federal and state appropriations for individual research and publications in the humanities and in many areas of the social sciences are virtually nonexistent. One need only look at the present condition of the National Endowment for the Humanities to recognize the truth of this observation.

It is not altogether unfortunate that artists, writers and scholars must turn to private foundations for support. For the most part science is value-free and non-political. In any highly-charged political situation certain ideas in the social sciences and humanities would be excluded from support or neutral scientific projects would be chosen instead.

Many colleges and recently established universities have little or no endowment to cover academic leave for research, furnish funds for travel or provide facilities for research. These needs in the humanities and the social sciences must be provided by direct foundation grants to individual scholars. Foundations such as Rockefeller and more especially Guggenheim have distinguished themselves by the quality of the awards they have made solely on the basis of artistic and scholarly promise. But to name these two great foundations is not to exclude the hundreds of smaller and lesser known ones which have done the same thing.

Let us suppose that all direct foundation grants to individuals were abolished and that hereafter colleges and universities would have the privilege and problem of allocating such grants. There is absolutely no guarantee that colleges and universities would allocate the money as it is now spent. A high percentage of grant money would be diverted directly to the colleges and universities as so-called overhead. Most professors would agree that outside organizations are more objective than university committees in making evaluations or grants. In fact, most departments demand outside evaluation in such matters as promotion. More importantly, if one were turned down by the research committee of his college there would literally be no place to turn. Under present circumstances one can apply to a number of foundations representing diverse cultural, social, religious and economic interests. Simply by increasing the number of possible grantors the possibility of diversity is multiplied. It is absolutely essential to diffuse patronage rather than concentrating it. This, of course, is particularly true in the arts, humanities and social sciences, though a good case can be made for the diffusion of patronage in the natural sciences.

Let us assume that the applicant is a professor at a small and little known college. At the present time he is able to apply directly to a foundation for assistance. Should direct foundation grants be abolished it is unlikely that he would ever receive a grant. Foundation money would be lavished on the major universities and the prestige colleges, but no matter how worthy the applicant, were he to have the misfortune of teaching at a small school, it is unlikely that his school would have received foundation support.

America is the land of experimentation. Indeed our polity itself is a great and continuing experiment. It is a curious fact, however, that this dedication to experimentation is coupled with a horror at failed experiments. We seem always to be saying, "Go ahead and make an experiment—but don't make a mess." Unfortunately, the price of success in innovative endeavors is failed experiments. How many enterprises over the long run fail in the process of discovering that particular combination of ideas, skills and services which lead to success? We ought not to take foundation failures too seriously and we ought to judge them against the background of their magnificent successes.

Few citizens, and perhaps fewer academicians, would question the desirability of foundation reform. However, the object of such reform should not be punishment, but the return of the foundation to its primary role of enriching, diversifying and liberating American life.

61

governed that those who govern do not act in their interest, are not responsive to their needs and are contemptuous of their aspirations. Increasingly ordinary men and women have come to believe that violence, deception, fraud and absurdity carry the day. They have come to believe that the halls of justice are places where the criminal is exonerated and the righteous punished; that the processes of legislation were devised for rewarding the thriftless, the indolent, the feckless and the immoral at the expense of the industrious and the temperate; that love of country is a crime and that treason is genuine patriotism; that to bear the glorious burden of citizenship is stupid and that the genuinely intelligent always lets someone else pay.

What in practical political terms is the consequence of this massive disillusionment and alienation? Stewart Alsop, one of the most astute political observers in the United States, recently wrote, "When the Lower Middle gets angry enough to defy the law, those famous limousine liberals have reason to fear for their limousines and, just conceivably, for their lives. . . . 'You don't need a weatherman to know which way the wind blows,' wrote Bob Dylan. Indeed you don't. It blows, hard and strong, toward the right. It could be blowing toward some peculiarly American version of Fascism."

Of course, you say, that is the opinion of Mr. Alsop but all of that really can't happen here. I advise you not to let your complaisance outrun your good sense. Let us look for example at the last election figures. In a study of voter behavior in the last presidential election a team of University of Michigan political analysts offers the following interesting evidence. One out of every seven votes cast in the last election was cast for Wallace. There was a massive political shift to the right. "A full 40 percent of Nixon's votes came from citizens who had supported Lyndon Johnson in 1964." The Wallace vote was drawn mainly from the Democratic party, that stronghold of traditionally liberal political values. But not only was the Wallace vote large, it was surprisingly young. Wallace captured less than 3 percent of the vote of people over age 70 outside the South, but 13 percent of those under age 30. The report of these analysts adds a dramatic and little known fact: "Although privileged young college students angry at Vietnam and the shabby treatment of the Negro saw themselves as sallying forth to do battle against a corrupted and cynical older generation, a more head-on confrontation at the polls, if a less apparent one, was with their own age mates who had gone from high school off to the factory instead of college, and who were appalled by the collapse of patriotism and respect for the law that they saw about them."

Finally the report concludes that "It is obvious to any 'rational' politician hoping to maximize votes in 1970 and 1972 that there are several times more votes to be gained by leaning toward Wallace than by leaning toward McCarthy."

Perhaps, you will remark, voter behavior has changed since 1968 and these conclusions can no longer stand. You are, of course, correct. In a recent poll conducted by Sindlinger and Company, a national marketing and research agency, the voting public by a margin of 5 to 3 asserted that they would prefer a conservative to a liberal candidate for the United States Senate. This Sindlinger poll is borne out by the results of a Gallup poll which were published April 15. That poll establishes that at the present time Americans by a 3 to 2 margin identify themselves as conservatives rather than liberals.

A satisfactory explanation of this major political shift seems to me a matter of importance both to the scientific observer and the political participant. Why has it happened and what ought we as citizens to learn from it?

In an important recent book, *The Emerging Republican Majority*, Kevin P. Phillips offers what I believe to be the explanation of this massive shift to the right: "Back in 1932, the Democratic Party took office with a popular mandate to develop a new governmental approach to the problems of economic and social welfare which the Depression had brought into painful focus. Basically, Roosevelt's New Deal liberalism invoked government action to deal with situations from which the government had hitherto remained aloof, i.e., the malpractice of corporations, unemployment, malnutrition, lack of rural electricity, collapsed farm prices and managerial intolerance of organized labor. But in the years since 1932, federal interventionism has slowly changed from an innovative policy into an institutionalized reflex. . . ." The programs of the New Deal have been fulfilled and more than fulfilled. Liberal politicians have ceased to project attractive political aspirations and call for actions not only acceptable to but yearned for by the rank and file. Their dreams are shopworn, their solutions are ancient and, above all, they have stopped listening. The message of the Wallace vote and much of the Nixon vote was not a message of confidence in either Mr. Nixon or Mr. Wallace. It was simply a rejection of tired political hacks, passé programs and politicians who are unable to listen.

Are you listening? But if you do listen what can you expect to hear? What are the American people saying? What is the content of their dreams and hopes? What are their fears? What are the purposes they propose for government and why are they so opposed to the purposes government proposes for them?

We must be clear about one thing at the outset. The problems of American society at the present moment are not the problems of scarcity and poverty; they are not the problems of unemployment and hunger. Indeed those problems belong to the past and many politicians who have learned to live with them and have developed certain pat responses would like to continue to live with the crisis of 1932 rather than the reality of 1970. All of which is not to say that poverty and hunger and exploitation have ceased to exist. They do indeed exist and they must be dealt with; they can be dealt with, but they are not the fundamental problems of our time.

Those problems are not material, they are spiritual. Americans, right, left and center want to be called to belief and dedicated action, a belief which goes beyond themselves and the petty concerns of self and an action that is large, grand and generous in its inspiration. We want national leaders who do not tell us we are sick, but who affirm the purposes of health, dedication and goodness. We want intellectual leaders who do not, as President Fleming of the University of Michigan recently did, tell us we are suffering from cancer, but who project a believable and desirable image of humanist intellectuality, men who believe in something, if it is only themselves; men who act to obtain an objective not because of fear or compulsion but because the objective is right and good. We want, in short, men in leadership and public life who have some vision of the American dream and some knowledge of our history and who are capable of seeing the difference between revolutions of principle and revolutions of nihilism. We have asked our spiritual and governmental leaders for bread and repeatedly they have given us a stone. And when men go to the bakery to buy bread and are given a stone they soon stop going to the bakery.

Today we are being overwhelmed by a tidal wave of filth. Every tarnished and disreputable motive, every despicable and ignoble action, every degraded and perverted sentiment, every vulgar and ugly view is paraded and praised in the press and from the pulpit, in the halls of the legislature and from the endowed chairs of the university. When has anyone within memory raised his voice in praise of virtue or extolled self-sacrifice, manliness and simple patriotism? If these virtues are dead in our society they died by the assassin's hand. They were murdered by the gutter press, the licentious intellectuals, the lying politicians and the craven and self-deceiving liberals.

And it is precisely those who believe in nothing who will stop at nothing in pressing their claims upon society and in forcing their will and their purpose upon their fellow men. They substitute sentiment for principle and conviction, and the weaker their reasons the more violent and destructive their behavior. And who can deny that they have been successful? In the past five years we have all been educated in the uses of violence. We, at the University of Michigan, have been taught by no less a schoolmaster than the president of the university, that the peaceful and defenseless majority must bow to the armed mob and that after we have been abused and deprived of our rights we must masochistically proclaim our guilt. President Fleming, after the degradation and humiliation of bowing to the mob, then proclaimed that the mob won not by unchallenged power but by virtue and superior morality. But President Fleming is not alone in his supine acceptance of this inversion of the order of society. Mob rule has been substituted for the rule of law and orderly procedure in our courts, on our streets, in our schools, and even in our churches. And when these disgraceful intrusions of violence have occurred there have been Supreme Court justices, bishops, governors, mayors, school administrators and university presidents

67

to cheer on the felons, the arsonists, the revolutionaries and the disturbers of the peace. One can only wonder at a society which rewards its natural enemies with the badges of status and honor and the highest appointive and elective positions which it is in the power of the people to bestow.

It is understatement to assert that the American people are fed up with crime and violence but some legislators seem even now not to have got the point. In case that is true of anyone in this audience let me point again to the results of a recent Roper poll. In that poll 90 percent of those interviewed perceived law and order as our major political concern. The replies were so unanimous in this instance that the polltakers at first thought some sort of statistical error had occurred. We will have order. It will either be the self-imposed order of free men or the tyranny of a slave state. Nature abhors anarchy as much as it abhors a vacuum.

In the third place, the American people increasingly resent the growth of a newly privileged class which threatens to devitalize and destroy our society. This newly privileged class is the nonproducing consumers who insist that mere existence is a mandate for social and economic equality. This new class rejects the notion that rewards and status are in justice the fruit of labor and talent. They insist on confiscating what they will not earn, on appropriating positions and benefits which their talents and efforts do not permit them to achieve, on getting all they can and paying as little as possible. It is an insane society which taxes morality, virtue and industry in order to support the stupid, the vicious, the thriftless and the lazy. The notion is current, for example, that admission to the university should not be on the basis of talent and training but as a matter of right which is inversely proportional to qualities of intellectual excellence. Increasingly we have substituted need for ability. We have made bastardy a badge of honor and stupidity the mark of virtue.

I am not suggesting here that we deny assistance to the aged and the helpless in our society. Far from that. I am arguing that for the able and the strong, the young and the vigorous, public assistance ought not to go beyond the extension of opportunity and that we ought to do everything possible to prevent reproduction at the public expense. It is time for a thoroughgoing reassessment of our welfare programs, a reassessment which is not afraid of discovering that under the present liberal philosophy we do ill to ourselves and above all to the poor in the name of doing good.

I have argued that in three major areas government has failed to a shocking and disastrous degree. In the first place, those in positions of leadership and authority have failed to project a vision of political life and a set of social objectives which will tap the energies and enthusiasms of the American people. Secondly, our leadership has educated a generation in violence by rewarding the violent and by penalizing the orderly and law-abiding. And thirdly, leadership in America has increasingly insisted that in the name of equality we must ignore virtue, intellect, devotion and industry and distribute the goods of society indiscriminately and without any attention either to the results of achievement or the conditions imposed by nature.

Lest you imagine that my diagnosis of the problems of our society is an eccentric vision, permit me to quote at length from an essay appearing in *The Times* of London's *Literary Supplement,* one of the most distinguished cultural organs in the Western world.

The anonymous author writes in the February 19, 1970 number: "Violence rules now in many recently secure fields: in societies on both sides of the Iron Curtain, as in newly formed independent nations; in the cities of Britain as elsewhere. When all law and order, when Parliament and its members, when school and university and all other disciplines (including those of the family and sexual and other human relations) are brought into open contempt as 'establishment'; when Parliament, press, radio and television fall over backwards to advantage the criminals and law breakers, when excellencies, pay differentials or distinctions between one man or group and another are almost universally treated (though not in communist countries) as anti-social and morally wrong . . . every good rationalist will blench. Lesser mortals will read Professor Hugh Seton-Watson's letter to *The Times* (Dec. 10, 1969), describing 'the pogrom against culture in this country' or the Warden of All Souls's letter to the same paper (December 31, 1969) citing 'the sense of alienation not only from government, but from Parliament itself, now becoming widespread among the electorate,' and wonder how far we in Britain have already slipped down the slope taken by the Weimar Republic. The overpowering sense of the 'antis' being able to 'get away with it' all along the line grows, and leads to a despair among our governors and institutions as perilous as it is paralyzing to decent citizens of all ages. Which makes matters worse still—corrupting the best is the worst corruption."

There you have it. Translate what this Englishman has said is true of England into the American idiom and you will have an exact description of the state of our society at the present moment. I might have chosen instead of this Englishman's essay a dozen equally strong statements by citizens of the United States. I did not do so for it would be all too easy for the uninformed and the paid liberal liars to charge the statements with racism. That charge can not be brought against an Englishman who stands aloof from the current political cant popular in American liberal circles. What I have said has nothing to do with black and white. It does have a great deal to do with sanity, culture, morality, authority and order.

What I have been saying in a general way about our society is concretely in evidence at the University of Michigan. It is an institution led by men without vision or a sense of America's future. It is racked by violence and disorder. It rewards felons and penalizes the orderly. It bestows its benefits on the basis, not of ability, not even on the basis of a color-blind equality, but on the basis of an irrationally conceived demand on public largess. It is a sad fact that the university has lost its credibility in this state and is on the way to losing its intellectual stature in the nation because it is managed by craven administrative hacks who possess neither courage nor convictions. Their conduct is symptomatic of the unresponsiveness of American institutions, governmental, educational, ecclesiastical and informational, an unresponsiveness which has done so much to alienate the great masses of the American people and foster doubt, mistrust and the pervasive sense of "having been had."

I have said that the deepest and most important problem besetting American institutions at the present time is a loss of vision, the disappearance of any sense of design, purpose or commitment and above all the pursuit of objectives which flatly contradict the traditional values sheltered and promoted in the past by the institution and in conflict with public expectations with respect to the institution. The University of Michigan and its leadership afford us an excellent example of such a heartless, mindless, gutless institution.

When President Fleming had first come to the university as its new executive officer he was invited to speak on January 8, 1968 from one of the most prestigeous public forums in the state, the Economic Club of Detroit. It was an opportunity without equal for the president to discuss with the people of Michigan the educational mission of the university and its role in the life of the state. Indeed, he might have been expected on that occasion to have informed us of his own educational philosophy. What was his topic on that splendid occasion? Believe it or not, it was the question of out-of-state enrollment; it was a plea to permit out-of-state residents to continue, in spite of their inflated numbers, as students even though their attendance reduced the number of qualified in-state students who could attend. That is known in liberal circles as educational statesmanship.

And as if to drive home the total inanity and vacuity of his "educational philosophy" the president concluded his remarks with this statement: "I make this final comment. Clark Kerr once said that, 'the job of the university president is to provide football for the alumni, parking for the faculty and sex for students.' I have said that my only comment on his observation is that I sometimes wish students would go back to their old interests."

The university administration did not know then and does not know now what a university is all about. For twenty years now our universities have become the dumping grounds for all our unsolved educational, social and political problems and university administrations have welcomed the development of this concept of the university as a public dump. Do you have an urban problem? Take it to the university. Do you have a psychopathic son or daughter? Send him to the university. Do you have a felon on probation? The university is just the place for him, indeed it's likely the administration will put him on the payroll counseling students. Do you have people with reading skills which make them semi-

71

literate? The university is the place to improve their basic English. Do you wish to employ the research talents of the university rather than its commitment to training and teaching? Our university administrators will welcome your suggestions. In short, our universities have become gigantic conglomerate messes with no central purpose, no pervasive philosophy and no identifiable commitments. The present administration is ideal for such an institution.

One might imagine, for example, that all views would be heard on the campus. One might believe that in the reasoned debate which is supposedly the chief occupation of university professors, religious, political, methodological, social and educational differences would be built into the very faculty. The university administration is shocked that there are not more black professors, and so am I. But I am shocked, too, that there are not more Roman Catholic professors in the Literary College where only a handful of senior professors are Catholic after a century and a half of the university's existence. I am shocked, too, that in the humanities the right of center and the center, in terms of political position, are so poorly represented. In my own department of history with over fifty faculty members less than five are Republican. The situation in the other departments of Humanities and Social Sciences is equally unbalanced. When young people come to the university they hear only one side of any question. There is no debate; there is no attempt at a fair and open discussion of the issues. The university administration seems not to worry about this destructive imbalance. It does not worry because it sees advantage in the present situation for the partisan political and social views it espouses.

The situation of ROTC at the university is indicative of the genuinely partisan position which the administration has adopted. It did not defend ROTC or the rights of the professors to teach in ROTC or the rights of the students to take ROTC because distrust and dislike for the military was widespread in the administration and the faculty. Laxity in defending the courses and buildings of the ROTC program from destruction and disruption contributed measurably to the rise of violence and lawlessness on campus. Like former President Grayson Kirk of Columbia University, these men can not really defend academic freedom because their bodies are on one side of the barricades while their minds and hearts are on the other side.

The administration has often argued that it can not resist violence, coercion and lawlessness because the faculty will not support it. That assertion is palpably false; it is demonstrably false nationally. In a survey of 60,447 university and faculty members recently conducted by the Carnegie Commission on Higher Education and published by the *Chronicle of Higher Education* 80 percent of the respondents held that "campus demonstrations by militant students are a threat to academic freedom" and more than 76 percent agreed either strongly or with reservations that "students who disrupt the functioning of a college should be expelled or suspended." Has anyone been expelled from Michigan? Not on your life! Interestingly enough, in terms of recent events at the university, less than half the faculty interviewed believed that "more minority group undergraduates should be admitted (to the respondent's particular college or university) even if it means relaxing normal academic standards of admission." Almost three-quarters disagreed that "the normal academic requirements should be relaxed in appointing members of minority groups to the faculty." The administration has a clear mandate to protect both the peace and the standards of the university.

It seems obvious to me that we cannot ask students to subscribe to the idea that reason and analysis should be fundamental to the life of the scholar when the courses and the faculty are politically and ideologically weighted in favor of one position over another and when violence is rewarded.

Let me rehearse what has happened recently on the campus of the university. Those events had been in the process of development for some time. For the past two years the mood has changed perceptibly from day to day. There have been bombings, destruction of property, disruption of classes and a breakdown of civilized behavior as weekly, almost daily, occurrences. The recent troubles did not occur suddenly and unexpectedly. They came only after concession after concession had been made to the disruptive, the violent, the disorderly.

Lest it be thought that my description is colored and weighed I wish to quote the report of Dean Allen of the University of Michigan Law School to the students, faculty and staff of the Law School concerning the events of March 25-27: "On Thursday, Room 100 was taken over by the striking group without, so far as I have been able to determine, having requested or received permission to use the room from anyone in authority in the Law School. At approximately 1:45 the meeting concluded and demonstrators in numbers of 200-300, many carrying clubs as on the previous day, roamed through Hutchins Hall. Room 150 was invaded while a class was in progress; that and the following class scheduled for the room were disrupted; faculty members were pushed and jostled; chairs were broken; glass was destroyed, tops of newly refinished desks were materially damaged by the pounding of chairs on them. Persons identified as university staff and faculty members were seen in the corridors and in Room 150 cheering the other demonstrators on. All four floors of Hutchins Hall were invaded. Bulletin boards containing notices of job opportunities were torn from the walls and cards strewn on the floor. Plaques were thrown from the walls and damaged. Stink bombs were exploded. The library reading room was also invaded and its proper use disrupted; property was damaged and destroyed, and serious violence between students seeking to study and the demonstrators was narrowly averted."

Nor was the violence of those days limited to the Law School. Similar scenes, some of them even more violent, were enacted all across the campus. And day after day while the administration "negotiated," it refused to call the police, refused to grant ordinary students the protections guaranteed them by the Constitution and the ordinary decent usages of our society. That was an education in the uses of violence.

And the consequences of the negotiation were as disheartening as the violence which preceded the so-called agreement. Though disadvantaged whites outnumber disadvantaged blacks three to one, we have now singled out a particular group and have assured them a percentage quota of places at the university based solely on the fact that they are black and disadvantaged. The agreement is quite simply discriminatory in the worst sense and I doubt that it possesses even the color of legality. Its effect will be to make a world-famous university into a gigantic community college.

All this might in some highly ironic way be the source of laughter. It is high comedy when men who talk about quality, fairness, justice, innovation and imagination exhibit so little of the ideals to which they pretend. It might become the subject of some sweeping satire were not so much at stake. For not only a great university is threatened but our society itself is jeopardized by these events.

Do not believe that what has happened at the University of Michigan is not of importance to the remotest hamlet in the state. It is not only that what has happened at Michigan will have a harmful effect upon the education and future success of the next generation. That, to be sure, is a grievous matter. But even more important, these events have demonstrated that the central citadel of rationality is incapable of withstanding the pressures of unreason and of violence. The consequences of that lesson are fearful to contemplate.

A Fresh Start:
American History and Political Order

Stephen Vincent Benét wrote in his uncompeted *Western Star:*[1]

> Americans are always moving on.
> It's an old Spanish custom gone astray
> A sort of English fever, I believe,
> Or just a mere desire to take French leave,
> I couldn't say. I couldn't really say.

The poet's perceptions are usually better than his explanations and we cannot fault Benét if he is unable to tell us why we have always moved on to the fresh start; to the primeval landscape, regaining in our adventurous movement our lost innocence and our betrayed virtue.

Geographic mobility, no doubt, has been a major factor in our history, making the fresh start possible. Over and over again we have moved on in quest of that perfect place. Having failed, we move down the road to the next city, take the steamboat up the river and start over, take the train to the coast or change our names and our churches and invent a status for ourselves which only success as easy as our failure can justify. We have been a nation of transients, moving from choice as much as from necessity. Social status, institutions and communities have all possessed in our New World that mercurial changeableness which some observers have ascribed to our continental climate and others have attributed to necessity. We have been a nation "on the road" and mechanisms of long distance transportation from the steamboat to the space ship have been the most characteristic of our technological creations.[2]

This restless temper, however, was not simply the product of geography, of distances and space and the machines American men created in order to conquer them. Nor was it simply climate, or the understandable desire to improve one's lot. The experience of the New World was above all else a desire to escape history, an attempt to throw off the burden of the past and make a fresh start.

Thoreau, the very archetype of the contemporary anarchist-individualist expressed it with complete insight and awareness when he wrote in *Walden:*[3]

> . . . Furniture! Thank God, I can sit and I can stand without the aid of a furniture warehouse. What man but a philosopher would not be ashamed to see his furniture packed in a cart and going up country exposed to the light of heaven and the eyes of men, a beggarly account of empty boxes. . . . I could never tell from inspecting such a load whether it belonged to a so-called rich man or a poor one; the owner always seemed poverty-stricken. Indeed, the more you have of such things the poorer you are. Each load looks as if it contained the contents of a dozen shanties; and if one shanty is poor, this is a dozen times as poor. Pray for what do we move ever but to get rid of our furniture, our *exuviae;* at least to go from this world to another newly furnished, and leave this to be burned? . . . I look upon England today as an old gentleman who is traveling with a great deal of baggage; trampery which has accumulated for long housekeeping, which he has not the courage to burn; great trunk, little trunk, band box and bundle. Throw away the first three at least. It would surpass the powers of a well man nowadays to take up his bed and walk, and I should certainly advise a sick one to lay down his bed and run. . . .

I have quoted this passage from *Walden* at length for in it Thoreau fuses completely the image of the immigrant on the road struggling with the accumulation of the past with the image of a society burdened by its history. To both the individual and the society Thoreau offers a simple and easy solution, "lay down or burn down your burden; escape the past." In a perceptive and tell-ing essay[4] Richard Weaver clearly identifies the antihistorical tendency in Thoreau and links it to his contempt for politics and his anarchic individualism. Indeed, Weaver virtually gives us the dic-tum that where there is no history there can be no politics.

The present perennially recognizes itself in some moment or movement glimpsed from the past. Thoreau speaks with such authority because he voices an enduring American theme. That the New Left seeks once more to escape from history should not sur-prise us and demonstrates, if demonstration were necessary, that the student radicals of the 60s were far closer to native American populism and knownothingism than they were and are to the orthodox certainties of Marxism. In this flight from history the stu-dent radicals are joined by the main tradition of American culture. Primitivism and nativism accord, as Leo Marx in his great critical essay, *The Machine in the Garden*[5] recognized, with a particular conception of history:

> Like all primitivist programs Gonzalo's plantation speech [in Shakespeare's *The Tempest*] in effect repudiates calculated human effort, the trained in-tellect, and, for that matter, the idea of civilization itself. It denies the value of history. It says that man was happiest in the beginning—in the golden age—and that the record of human activity is a record of decline. . . .

It is accurate to observe that the pastoral ideal which has pro-vided so many of the symbols and themes of American literature constitutes an effort to escape into a landscape in which conflict and the ambiguities of the historically conditioned life are absent. In American literature, as in America, the geography and technology of mobility are wedded to the myth of the pastoral golden age, and the notion of a fresh start takes on the proportions of a national purpose. David W. Noble has viewed all of American history as dominated by this theme.[6] He argues that American history has been dominated by the world-view of the English Puritans who came to Massachusetts. In its secularized form in 18th century enlightened thought, in 19th century democratic romanticism and in progressivism the continuity with the Puritan ideal was preserved. This view, more than any other factor, determined the way in which Americans viewed the past. As Noble puts it:[7]

> The American people believe that their historical experience has been uniquely timeless and harmonious because they are the descendants of Puritans who, in rejecting the traditions and institutions of the Old World, promised never to establish traditions and institutions in the New World. If history is the record of changing institutions and traditions, then by definition there can be no history in a nation which by Puritanical resolve refuses to create complexity. And the American historian is the Chief Spokesman for cultural tradition. . . .

And nearly every powerful American experience fed into and augmented the drive to eliminate and expunge history. The immigrant experience was such as to encourage the immigrant to strip off his European institutional and cultural past and to become a new American man. The evangelical Protestant conversion experience with its emphasis on a decisive break with the past encouraged the ideal of personal and cultural novelty. It would be difficult to overestimate the total impact of these cultural forces, but at their minimum they created a myth of American novelty and simplicity, virtue and harmony which is constantly threatened with corruption and confusion from the forces of high culture and history.

But above all the Jacobin element in American life has been unremittingly hostile to history. Speaking of the temptations confronting English democracy in the 19th century Matthew Arnold wrote in *Culture and Anarchy:*

> Other well-meaning friends of this new power are for leading it, not in the old ruts of middle-class Philistinism, but in ways which are naturally alluring to the feet of democracy, though in this country there are novel and untried ways. I may call them the ways of Jacobinism. Violent indignation with the past, abstract systems of renovation applied wholesale, a new doctrine drawn up in black and white for elaborating down to the very smallest details a rational society for the future—these are the ways of Jacobinism.

The revolutionary component which Arnold identified by the shorthand of Jacobinism would like to abrogate history and with it previous culture and politics because these all stand in the way of the transformation of mankind. It does not matter whether the revolution is American, French, Russian or Maoist; many of its partisans attempt the improvement of the future by the destruction of the past. At the present moment, no doubt that Jacobin attack upon the past is of equal importance with the more traditional American desire to let the dead past bury the past.

History, however, is not so easily disposed of. In the midst of the frustrating and gloomy opening years of the Civil War, President Lincoln in his Annual Message to Congress, December 1, 1862, said, "Fellow citizens, we cannot escape history." He meant, in the context of that message that what Congress did would determine the future and how the future viewed the past "to the latest generation." But Lincoln's view of the impact of the burden of history upon a later generation, its life and its politics, was even more tragic. I recall his Second Inaugural in which Lincoln dwells at some length on the subject of national sin and its punishment in subsequent generations. He, more than most men, was aware that wishing does not make it so and that a fresh start is made possible, not by an abrogation of the past, but rather through acceptance, charity and reconciliation.

Lincoln is the outstanding example of the American statesman with a sense of history, but whatever the symbols of American literature and the clichés of American political life, he was far from being the only statesman with such a sense. *The Federalist Papers* exhibit an encyclopaedic knowledge of the history of the past. Hamilton, Madison and Jay do not see history as a burden from which the new Republic must escape but rather as a source of political norms and experience concerning human behavior. Sir John Seely's dictum that "history is past politics, and politics present history" is a dictum they would have understood and approved.

However much by inclination and tradition we are tempted to jettison the past and to make a fresh start, we as pragmatic political men ought to ask ourselves whether this is, indeed, a possibility or whether, as President Lincoln assured us, we will find that we cannot escape history. Our emotions and our wishes are all on the side of the visionary, the revolutionary, the young. We too would like to reorder and reconstruct human existence by destroying the past or at least inventing for ourselves a past which is more in keeping with our ideal of what we would like to be than the very tarnished and rather discouraging record of what we have been.

I do not believe that the past can be either abrogated or reconstructed. The past as we 20th century men perceive it is so closely related to our humanity and consequently to our politics that its abandonment or its reconstruction would result in depriving us of those very qualities which make us fully men.

No one dares challenge the basic proposition that it is speech which gives man his distinctive human character. Without speech man would in fact resemble all the other primates, bound to the iron necessities of nature by instinctual fiat. But speech and the world of symbols which it embodies is history. We cannot escape history because we are creatures of language and language is always conservative and traditional in its influence. It is for this very reason that revolutions seek to strike at the cultural continuity that any linguistic formulation represents. George Orwell's vision in *1984* of a language debased and transformed to meet the needs of ideology is only a most extreme case of all revolutionary efforts to transform human behavior by changing the language. These efforts, however, are doomed to failure. Man cannot jettison history because he cannot evade language.

Stephen Spender pointed this out some time ago when he wrote:[8]

> Language of its own nature repudiates a complete break between past and present. A "revolution of the word," in the sense of words changing completely their sense and becoming something else, is one kind of revolution that is impossible, a revolution in human nature being perhaps another. Dictionaries contain the material with which writers work, and they are overwhelmingly traditional. It may be theoretically possible to discover an entirely new form in which a poem might be written, but form is only one aspect of a poem, and its unprecedentedness would only make a superficial break with the unavoidable continuities of grammar and usage.

Language is the repository of history. In order to abrogate history it would be necessary first to destroy language. It is not sufficient that language be corrupted and barbarized; it must, in fact, be destroyed. However, the effects of corruption of language give us some insight into the nature of language and its relationship to history and politics. Dante lodges these corrupters and falsifiers in the tenth bowge of hell because they strike at the very order which makes society possible. Dorothy Sayers writes:[9]

The Valley of Disease is at one level the image of the corrupt heart which acknowledges no obligation to keep faith with its fellow men; at another it is the image of a diseased society in the last stages of its mortal sickness and already necrosing. Every value it has is false; it alternates between a deadly lethargy and a raving insanity. Malbowges began with the sale of the sexual relationship, and went on to the sale of Church and State; now, the very money is itself corrupted, every affirmation has become perjury and every identity a lie; no medium of exchange remains, and the "general bond of life and nature's tie" (Canto XI) is utterly dissolved.

Language is historical in nature. Its symbols are the distillation of man's experience. It orders and classifies all later experience and makes the raw data of experience capable of assimilation. It is for this reason that our humanity is so completely a product of language and history and that all subordinate ordering systems (political order, for example), are dependent upon the experience of order in history and the distillation of that order in the symbols of language.

The distinction between the world of man and a human world is a fundamental one. The concept of man is biological. The concept of the human is cultural. All of these characteristics which pertain to man are grounded in the necessities of nature. In the realm of nature there are no obligations and there can be no politics. The process of becoming human, however, is one through which culture is appropriated and superimposed upon biological development. Man belongs to the world of nature and instinct. The human world is the creation of culture and the product of social experience. Cleanth Brooks made the distinction between these two worlds, the world of nature and the world of culture, clear recently while discussing Robert Frost's poem, "Stopping by Woods on a Snowy Evening." Frost's horse, Cleanth Brooks remarked, had his own reasons, instinctive ones, for wishing to resume the journey. They were not Frost's reasons, "promises to keep." The horse had no obligations, no promises; those distinctively human preoccupations which are the ground of all politics belong to the world of culture.

Culture endows experience with meaning. Purpose in a human rather than a natural sense is a social creation. It is important to recognize, however, that this socially constructed world is not an arbitrary creation. In the measure that it is arbitrary it is useless or even destructive to human purposes. When the socially constructed world of culture serves human purposes best it is in agreement with the objective experience of the environment.[10] The world of culture is, above all, the world of order. The booming, buzzing confusion of raw sense data is subjected to a *nomos* or a meaningful order. The multiplicity of individually experienced worlds is given by culture a common meaning and it is on the basis of this common meaning that politics in both its broadest and its most circumscribed sense, is possible. Meaningful order (*nomos*) within the society and the culture is always related to a wider order in the *cosmos* and is perceived as congruent with that order.[11] That is to say, the central images and symbols of any culture are religious in nature and these "tyrannizing images" (Richard Weaver) impose their forms, or seek to impose their forms, on the totality of experience.

Order in its broadest sense expresses itself in language and is related directly to the cosmological quest for meaning. This quest for meaning gave rise in the experience of primitive man to the great cosmological myths. In the Western tradition, conditioned by Hebrew-Christian revelation, those "tyrannizing images" do not derive from cosmological processes but rather are related to historical experience. Consequently, not only is language the ordinary tool of nomization, historical in structure and impact, but the cosmic images which it mediates are historical in nature. Buried in the structure of our language and in the fabric of our thought are those elements which make it impossible for us to make a "fresh start." Any order which is not arbitrary, any meaning which is not a trifling fiction or an inverted cosmos is rooted in a total cultural reality which is historical in nature.

It is because of this that the precondition for overcoming history and for the transformation of the human predicament is not anomie or amnesia but increased and deepened historical understanding. It will not be by leaving the past behind us that we will discover our humanity and usher in a new, a better era. Great political orders and cultural eras are born, not in unconsciousness and barbarism but in the full light of historical understanding. The past is a burden only so long as it is not forced to pay its own way.

Language and art are objectifications of order. The order, however, is not an arbitrary or subjectionist creation but a response to existential reality. While the symbolization of order is always time-bound, historically contingent and because of this, "relativistic," the quest for that order is permanent. As Eric Voegelin has recently expressed it in an unpublished paper, "Equivalences of Experience and Symbolization in History," "What is permanent in the history of mankind is not the symbols but man himself in search of his humanity and its order." Men encounter order and participate in that order in the areas of existence: in the individual human spirit and its relationship to the transcendent, in the nature of experiential reality, and in the structure and experiences of human society. Consequently, revelation, natural law and historical experience all possess a common commitment and are engendered by a common center.

While language and art are the objectification of order they may and indeed, often do, obscure and conceal the order they originally illuminated. The full meanings of words and symbols once divorced from their engendering experience are lost to succeeding generations or prove impenetrable even to contemporary minds. The experience itself, however, lives on and continues to exert its impact on later human behavior. Men act out of a past which is submerged below the level of consciousness. History as a living and dynamic force continues to exert its sway whether or not its symbolism is understood by a later generation and whether or not its creative forces are perceived at the level of consciousness by later actors in the drama. Far from being able to jettison history, it is most active in the affairs of men when they are least aware of its dynamism. It is precisely those who live in the eternal present who are most completely the butt of those buried historical forces which constitute the eternal order of justice.

The function of the historian and the function of the political scientist is to bring the buried but active past into the full light of consciousness where its meaning can be apprehended and its consequences dealt with. Sir Lewis Namier touched on this problem when he wrote in 1952:[12]

> A neurotic, according to Freud, is a man dominated by unconscious memories, fixated on the past and incapable of overcoming it: the regular condition of human communities. Yet the dead festering past cannot be

85

eliminated by violent action any more than an obsession can be cured by beating the patient. History has therein a "psychoanalytic" function; and it further resembles psychoanalysis in being better able to diagnose than to cure: the beneficial therapeutic effects of history have so far been small: and it is in the nature of things that it should be so. Science can construct apparatus which the user need not understand: a child can switch on the electric light; nor does surgery depend for its success on being understood by the patient. But psychoanalysis works, if at all, through the emotions and the psyche of the individual; and history, to be effective, would have to work through those of the masses. . . .

Namier had a profound insight in this passage into the role of the historian. But he leaves us with a puzzle and a problem. How, Namier asks, can political order be joined to history in such a way as to overcome history not by abrogating historical experience but through its transformation?

I believe that the answer lies in the role of the historian and the political scientist as political rhetoricians. The invention of political rhetoric, the formulation of the symbols of community, is the paramount task of those who explore political order, past and present. It does not take an age when the poets are silent or speak only in broken, corrupted and ravaged dialects of a diseased and disordered culture and polity to recognize that "the poets are the unacknowledged legislators of the world." They and they alone can give to the dumb and the inchoate a voice and can enable men to see into the mystery of their existences.

To know the symbols which the past has created and the experiences which engendered those symbols is not enough. They must be made vividly present to this generation and their meaning must be translated into the experience of this present moment. When that act of understanding and reflection has taken place the past will indeed be overcome and its yoke will be sweet and easy to bear. But where political rhetoric is either wanting or is dominated by the symbols of what Eric Voegelin calls "deformed existence," the truth of the verse in *Proverbs*, "Where there is no vision the people perish," is all too apparent.

[1]Stephen Vincent Benét, *Western Star* (Farrar & Rinehart, New York, 1943), p. 3.

[2]George W. Pierson, "The M-Factor in American History," *American Quarterly*, Vol. XIV Summer, 1962, pp. 275-289; George W. Pierson, "A Restless Temper . . ." *American Historical Review*, Vol. LXIX, No. 4, July, 1964, pp. 969-989; Daniel J. Boorstin, *The Americans, The National Experience* (Alfred A. Knopf, New York, 1965), especially "The Transients," (pp. 49-57).

[3]Thoreau, Henry D., *Walden, or, Life in the Woods*, The Annotated Walden ed. by Philip Van Doren Stern (Clarkson N. Potter, New York, 1970), pp. 199-202.

[4]Richard Weaver, "Two Types of American Individualism" in *Life Without Prejudice and Other Essays*, edited by Harvey Plotnick and introduced by Eliseo Vivas (Henry Regenery, Chicago, 1965).

[5]Leo Marx, *The Machine in the Garden, Technology and the Pastoral Ideal in America* (Oxford University Press, New York, 1964), p. 55.

[6]David W. Noble, *Historians against History, The Frontier Thesis and the National Covenant in American Historical Writing Since 1830* (University of Minnesota Press, Minneapolis, 1965); *The Eternal Adam and the New World Garden, The Central Myth in the American Novel Since 1930* (George Braziller, New York, 1968); *The Paradox of Progressive Thought* (University of Minnesota Press, Minneapolis, 1958).

[7]David W. Noble, p. 4.

[8]Stephen Spender, *The Struggle of the Modern* (Hamish Hamilton, London, 1963), p. 191.

[9]Dorothy L. Sayers, *The Comedy of Dante Alighieri the Florentine*, Cantica, I, Hell (Penguin Books, Harmands-Worth, 1949), p. 256.

[10]Peter L. Berger and Thomas Luckmann, *The Social Construction of Reality: A Treatise in the Sociology of Knowledge* (Doubleday & Company, New York, 1966).

[11]Peter L. Berger, *The Sacred Canopy; Elements of a Sociological Theory of Religion* (Doubleday & Company, New York, 1967).

[12]Sir Lewis B. Namier, "History" in *Avenues of History* (Hamish Hamilton, London, 1952), p. 5.

II. The Crisis in Education

Liberal Education: Is it a Matter of Courses or Questions?

Every age gives itself over to certain intellectual superstitions, the object of which is to protect men from the painful process of thought and enable polite society to continue the endless exchange of banalities which pass for communication. These intellectual superstitions are the unexamined premises which are coined into action and opinion and which nurture the platitudes with which men paper over the cracks in their unexamined lives.

One of the most powerful of these intellectual superstitions at the present moment is the received idea that a momentous change has occurred in human life and the environment in which man finds himself, and that this change has been so great and so disruptive that the experience of the past is meaningless, if not indeed, harmful. It is argued that the rate of technological change has totally reshaped the human environment and that this alteration of the environment has transformed the human condition. Whether your guru is McLuhan or Marcuse you have heard the same assertion that there has been a radical disjunction in human history, that indeed there has been a mutation in the human species and that the past with all its experiences, its lessons, its rubrics and rules is no longer applicable to the new day; that in this bright new dawn of unconditioned freedom, of limitless abundance and chemical joy, the definitions of what the past held to be permanently human and those actions which the past held to be consonant with the human condition are no longer applicable.

This cliché has become so pervasive that history is no longer consulted or studied, and literature, which once took as its task the exploration of the human condition, has now become a report of meaningless, random and scattered events, spastic happenings not unlike the twitchings of an eviscerated frog.

In the light of this supposed break in continuity it is argued that education must also transform itself; that it must adapt itself to the supposed revolutionary situation which confronts contemporary man; that it must abandon an orientation to the past; that it must assist in the recasting of values and the transformation of institutions; that it must dare to be open, flexible, fluid and totally permissive. In short, the values inhering in liberal arts education are either inappropriate to the present time or they are even dangerously reactionary.

It is important that we examine this assertion and test its validity, for not only the continuation of liberal arts education but our whole notion of humanity depends on its refutation. For if we have indeed become a new kind of men, if we are no longer Adam's sons and if there is no strong family resemblance to all those sinners and saints, heroes and ordinary men whose composite lives formed the pattern of the past, then indeed we are in trouble.

It will not do to say that because the circumstances in which men live have changed men themselves have taken some sort of quantum jump which has radically transformed them. Aside from the fact that all nature is uniformitarian in character and is beyond the power of sudden and decisive transformation, all that we know of man in the past should lead us to doubt that any decisive change in the human essence is possible as a consequence of the material alteration of circumstances. Naive materialist explanations which seek to account for human behavior solely, or even largely, in terms of nonspiritual factors are notoriously inadequate. At bottom they all resemble the explanation that Napoleon was finally defeated because, prior to the battle of Leipzig he ate a green peach and his ensuing stomach ache made it impossible for him to fight the battle. What happens in history is far more a consequence of what men think; their hopes, aspirations, values, dreams, than what they have for dinner or do not have for dinner, the kind of advertising they read or even the television programs they watch.

Moreover, is it true that we live in an era of unprecedented change? To be sure, the changes which our society has encountered in the past two centuries have been very great but there have been other periods of intense change. Recall with me that in the 8th and 9th centuries of the Christian era Northern Europe was an underdeveloped subcontinent. Its inhabitants were barbarous and encountering for the first time a sophisticated high religion. Its gods together with its ancient mores were giving way, and from the standpoint of their primitive society even more revolutionary changes were being produced by literacy, changed legal and political systems, and those alterations which were due to the advent of an advanced technology. It is worth reminding ourselves that although Charlemagne could sign his name he was what is now called a functional illiterate and that the Merovingian kings found it impossible to sit still long enough even to learn to sign their names. The fact is that the human capacity for adaptation is greater than the capacity of the environment to transform itself.

Over and over again men have been thrown into strange and hostile landscapes or have been confronted by an advanced and perplexing culture. They have given way to confusion and agony of spirit but finally they have molded the new circumstance to ancient human needs and purposes. Pastoralists have become settled agriculturalists, pagans have become Christians, men who were born barbarians have learned to employ and live in the spirit of the most advanced technology and science. And this has not happened once, it has happened over and over again.

Of course, we are all tempted to see ourselves as unique and our circumstances as unprecedented. The chief merit of the past as we encounter it in men, books, and great art, is that it reaffirms our common humanity and enables us to recognize in the folly and the grandeur of other men living in vastly different circumstances our

93

own trivial and exalted natures. The only mutations which history records are those transformations of the spirit which enable men to rise above petty circumstance and convoluted selfishness to a higher and nobler humanity. Such mutations, I need not add, are not the consequence of technical or environmental innovation.

Far from man's new circumstances making his past experience and his past culture obsolete, these new circumstances make the close analysis of all that man is and all that he has been of increasing importance. The important question today is not how we can accommodate humanity to a technology which is in itself arational and demonic but how that technology can be accommodated to our humanity.

All great technical, cultural or civilizational changes reflect themselves in demands for educational change and no aspect of a society so exactly mirrors the society as its educational goals, techniques and institutions. The classroom is the society in microcosm. That is why the current disorder in American education must be taken so seriously. The disorder in the classroom reflects the confusions present in our society.

It behooves us then to ask why our classrooms are disordered. It would be easy to place the full responsibility for our current confusion at the doorstep of our desertion of what is called the liberal arts and our typical American devotion to vocationalism. It would be easy, but it would be as mistaken as it is easy.

All education worthy of the name is vocational education. The schools of Athens were vocational. Medieval universities trained lawyers and clerics. Nineteenth century German universities trained bureaucrats, and while Newman's Oxford pretended to— and did—train gentlemen, these gentlemen were those talented English amateurs who by the end of the 19th century made England the mistress of a world empire and its domestic institutions the envy of the civilized world. Cicero's study of the classics at Athens may have been what we today would describe as liberal arts education but it was, in fact, the rhetorical vocational education of the statesman. Luther at Wittenberg would have had little patience with our contemporary "pressed-flower" theories of liberal education.

It has been commonly held in the past few decades that only certain courses and only certain books qualify as material suitable to liberal arts education. Sometimes it is Mortimer Adler's "Great Books," sometimes the curriculum of St. John's College at Annapolis. There is a wide range of works and curricula but their common characteristic is that they concentrate exclusively upon certain particular books and programs. The rigidity of a program in liberal education so conceived has in recent years led to a retreat from the classical curriculum and an increasing emphasis upon new disciplines and programs which are thought to be practical. Does this, in fact, mean that the liberal arts are dying on the vine?

I do not believe that it does and I would like to consider with you what our intentions should be when we attempt to teach in the spirit of liberal education. It will help us to understand what liberal education should be if we return to one of the early formulations of its educational philosophy. In 1459 Battista Guarino, a leading humanist, pondering the educational debate between scholastics and humanists in his own day, wrote the following: [*De Ordine Docendi et Studendi*]

> . . . To each species of creatures has been allotted a peculiar and instinctive gift. To horses galloping, to birds flying comes naturally. To man is given the desire to learn. Hence what the Greeks called *paideia*, we call *studia humanitatis*. For learning and training in virtue are peculiar to man; therefore our forefathers called them *humanitas*, the pursuits and activities proper to mankind. And no branch of knowledge embraces so wide a range of subjects as that learning which I have here attempted to describe.

Education so conceived does not begin with a fixed curriculum. It is not confined to a particular set of courses or the parsing of a few great books. One of the merits of this definition is that it places the emphasis where it belongs, on the object rather than the specific content of education. Its object is "learning and training in virtue," that is, "the pursuits and activities proper to mankind."

The chief difficulty with classicism of any kind is that it forces new life into an old mold, in the belief, to be sure, that the old mold is innately superior to the new form. It may indeed be superior and if it has more of life and reality in it, then it has an immediate and direct claim on our attention. More often, however, the classic form

95

has been divorced from its engendering experience and has become empty. It is quite often the case that the classics leave us untouched and unmoved until we have found a way to relate our own experience to that of the classic writer and artist. It is for this reason that educational reform, renewal in the arts, yes, even liturgical reform is absolutely essential from time to time. These reforms aim at enabling us to feel once more the power of the engendering experience in the repeated symbol.

Consequently, liberal education must, at all costs, avoid the frozen world of classicism. Speaking of Goethe, the American philosopher, Santayana said in *Egotism in German Philosophy:*

> . . . This is only another way of saying that in the attempt to be Greek the truly classical was missed even by Goethe, since the truly classical is not foreign to anybody. It is precisely that part of tradition and art which does not alienate us from our own life or from nature, but reveals them in all their depth and nakedness, freed from the fashions and hypocrisies of time and place. The effort to reproduce the peculiarities of antiquity is a proof that we are not its natural heirs, that we do not continue antiquity instinctively. People can mimic only what they have not absorbed. They reconstruct and turn into an archeological masquerade only what strikes them as outlandish. The genuine inheritors of a religion or an art never dream of reviving it; its antique accidents do not interest them, and its eternal substance they possess by nature.

"The truly classical is not foreign to anybody," Santayana says and that is because Santayana means by classical those things which Guarino said are "the pursuits and activities proper to mankind." Let us study the classics so long as they speak effectively and persuasively to us, but when they do not, let us turn elsewhere for our intellectual and spiritual formation. Far better to read C. S. Lewis with understanding, than to stumble through the pages of Thomas à Kempis' *Imitation of Christ*. Robert Frost may speak to us more penetratingly than Edmund Spenser. Making something of the same point, a Catholic writer, Anthony Bullen, in a short meditation on "Listening to the Holy Spirit" said, "We speak of 'listening to the Holy Spirit.' Doing what the Spirit of Jesus tells us.

"This does not mean that we hear his voice whisper physically in our ears. The Spirit of Jesus speaks to us in various ways. You may remember that he appeared to the apostles as fire and wind.

"Sometimes when we listen to the advice of a friend, it may be that the Holy Spirit is telling us what to do. If we see someone in misfortune and we feel compelled to help, it is the Spirit who is speaking to us. An odd word said over the radio or TV, a paragraph in a book, an advertisement in a newspaper—the Spirit of Jesus may be invading our lives in all these different ways.

"But if our lives are to be guided by the Spirit, then we must be listening people."

We ought not to be afraid then of disciplines, courses and books which do not conventionally fall within the liberal arts curriculum. It is the spirit of that curriculum rather than the specific course content which is important. Walt Whitman wrote in his "Song of Myself":

> And to glance with an eye or show a bean in its pod
> confounds the learning of all times,
> And there is no trade or employment but
> the young man following it may become a hero,
> And there is no object so soft but it makes
> a hub for the wheel'd universe, . . .

"The pursuits and activities proper to mankind" leave us with an extremely wide field of study. How are we, if we accept such a definition, to protect ourselves from the anarchic, fragmented, and often meaningless experience which passes as education in so many of our colleges and universities? Is not the prescription of openness and curricular flexibility an invitation to intellectual and spiritual rootlessness?

It seems to me undeniable that there are grave dangers in curricular freedom as there are in any other variety of freedom. I do not wish to minimize those dangers. The chaos in higher education, however, is not a confusion resulting from free choice. Rather it is a confusion resulting from method and intention. That method is one which, regardless of the subject matter, the content of the book, or the discipline, is destructive of the spirit of liberal education. That intention is one of escaping hard problems by refusing to ask difficult questions. The method and intention now dominant in all fields of study are often and with great aptness described as "positivistic." Why are they called "positivistic" and why are they completely out of keeping with the spirit of the liberal arts?

In an essay called "Political Ideas in the Twentieth Century," Sir Isaiah Berlin makes the following observation:

> The central point which I wish to make is this: during all the centuries of recorded history the course of intellectual endeavour, the purpose of education, the substance of controversies about the truth or value of ideas, presupposed the existence of certain crucial questions, the answers to which were of paramount importance. How valid it was asked, were the various claims to provide the best methods of arriving at knowledge and truth by such great and famous disciplines as metaphysics, ethics, theology and the sciences of nature and man. . . . There were, of course sceptics in every generation who suggested that there were, perhaps, no final answers. . . . It was left to the twentieth century to do something more drastic than this. For the first time it was now conceived that the most effective way of dealing with questions, particularly those recurrent issues which had perplexed and often tormented the original and honest minds in every generation, was not by employing the tools of reason, still less those of the more mysterious capacities of "insight" and "intuition," but by obliterating the questions themselves. . . . It consists in so treating the questioner that problems which appeared at once overwhelmingly important and utterly insoluble vanish from the questioner's consciousness like evil dreams and trouble him no more. . . .

What Sir Isaiah describes here is the triumph of positivistic science. Comtean Positivism in the last century attempted to banish metaphysical problems from the world by the systematic application of the methods of the natural sciences to all problems, irrespective of their nature. Because at the pragmatic level natural science is an interest in what happens, in immediate or efficient causes, in definitions in terms of the process going on, it was believed that this method when applied to fields outside the natural sciences would yield the same dramatically utilitarian results. Such a system, it was thought would be value-free and non-teleological. It would be operational and instrumental in character. Its slogan was, "Just don't ask any big questions!" Its purpose was to subject human behavior and the realm of creativity to the easily manipulable methods which prevailed in the natural sciences.

The consequences, however, were disastrous. For it is precisely in the realm of value that all human activity takes its rise whether it is humanistic or natural scientific. That natural science deals only with immediate causes is one of those fictions with which unthinking men divert themselves. Natural science is as metaphysical in its basic assumptions as the humanities and when those metaphysical concerns have finally been eliminated rationality and science will have perished with them.

Nonetheless the illusion prevails in the schools that in science and the humanities we ought not to ask any questions of ultimate meaning; that we ought to postpone any consideration of value, that we should shy away from any discussion of purpose, that we should forgo any ontology. Every subject matter then becomes totally autonomous. Judgment and value in the humanities, of necessity, become matters of opinion rather than questions to be reasoned about, and the patient and dull elaboration of fact replaces the education of the heart and mind. Until the 19th century the object of study was to make big questions out of little ones, wholeness, integrity and larger truths out of the partial and the insignificant. For the last two centuries there has been a flight from meaning and an effort to retreat into the partial and the anarchic. The unreason of our times is no more than a reflection of the more basic confusion and irrationality which lie at the heart of contemporary intellectuality.

It is for this reason that I insist that the problem of the restoration of liberal education does not lie in the restoration of specific curricula or the study of particular texts. Such courses and texts may or may not prove useful dependent entirely upon the spirit which is brought to their study. The restoration depends upon the kinds of questions we bring into the study, the laboratory and the classroom. If we do not look for order we will not find it. If we do not seek value we will not perceive it. If we do not search out the good we shall not discover it. No doubt studying Homer is preferable to reading crime comics but Homer, too, may become a profitless exercise if our purposes are no larger than an analysis of Homer's catalogue of ships or other positivistic pastimes. Let us begin, then, the restoration of liberal education by putting questions back into the classroom, and by putting wonder back into our everyday encounter with the world. Our world is not nearly so troubled with wrong answers as it is by the failure to ask the right questions at the right time.

Education: Who Calls the Tune?

One of my favorite authors, Professor Milton Friedman, once observed in the course of a debate with Paul Goodman that there was really no basic disgreement between himself and Mr. Goodman as to the ends and objectives they wished to see realized in our society. "The difference," Professor Friedman declared, "is that you [Paul Goodman] do not know how to get what you want, and I do." To paraphrase his observation I have no basic disagreement with Mr. Morse as to objectives. Our difference is that he does not know how to get what he wants, and I do.

Let me first explore briefly the points of agreement between Mr. Morse and myself. But, as he recognized in his paper, this agreement is so general and pervasive in American society that it is, in fact, a basic element in our political and social credo. We both believe that every individual ought to be encouraged to improve not only his skills but his mind, though—as a sometime disciple of John Dewey—I find it difficult to draw a line between what one

---

°These remarks were presented as a response to a paper "Who Should Decide Who Goes to College" by the Honorable Wayne L. Morse at a meeting of American Association of Higher Education, March, 1970.

thinks and what one does. We both believe that the American dream of full political participation and social mobility is directly related to the easy availability of education throughout the lifetime of the individual. We both recognize that the educational crisis of our time is not simply of our colleges and universities, but a crisis which confronts all post-secondary education. I would go much further than Mr. Morse and insist that most young adults entering the labor market will be forced by technology or lured by personal choice to learn to use and employ completely new and different skills at least three times during their working lifetimes. We are agreed that we must see education as a lifetime undertaking, and not a set of courses to be crammed into a brief and circumscribed number of years. Finally, and perhaps most importantly, I believe we would agree, though Mr. Morse had not quite the courage to make the assertion I am going to make, that the only one who should decide as to whether or not the young adult should have more education is the potential student himself. To the question, "Who should decide who should go on to post-secondary education?" the only answer we can give in our democratic society is "let the student decide."

It is, however, at this point that Mr. Morse and I part company. I do not believe that his plan will permit him to achieve his objectives. Mr. Morse enjoys thinking of himself as a heretic. I believe him not nearly heretical and radical enough. What exactly is heretical about the notion that someone else should pay the bill, an idea which has been a favorite of politicians from the birth of the Republic to the present? I am going to make a radical suggestion. I urge both that money in the form of guaranteed loans be made available to every qualified student seeking post-secondary education and that every student be charged full-cost tuition.

What Mr. Morse did not say is that education is not a free good; that in fact, it is very expensive. Because of this it will be rationed; indeed, it must be rationed. It is absurd to believe that everyone can attend Harvard though Mr. Morse holds out as a substitute the offer of a diluted and diminished AB degree at Podunk Community College. For a good reason Mr. Morse did not discuss open admissions to Harvard. Open admissions would destroy Harvard and every other quality educational institution in the United States. I am as concerned as Mr. Morse with equality of opportunity, but I recognize, as he does not, that there are gross inequalities of talent and motivation. These are inequalities, moreover, which do not magically disappear even under the most inspired tutelage.

If it is true that post-secondary education is a scarce good and will be rationed—rationed under any circumstance, or at the very least, purchased at the expense of equally desirable alternative social goods—then we must ask ourselves just which system of rationing we wish to employ. It is possible to ration education on the basis of ability to pay, or on the basis of talent and achievement, or on the basis of deprivation and cultural retardation. In all of these rationing systems favored groups are admitted and less favored groups are excluded. Which of these methods of rationing a scarce good is most equitable? It seems obvious to me that the market mechanism is most equitable, but only if every potential buyer has some opportunity to make his demand effective. Why not permit the individual to measure himself against entrance requirements, performance standards, and real costs which enable him to judge whether or not he has the necessary qualities and is willing to pay the necessary costs in terms of a long-term loan?

How is it possible for me to argue that education at the post-secondary level is a more worthy objective of public expenditure than the alleviation of poverty? Or that education at the post-secondary level is a more worthy object of public expenditure than health care for the aged? Or that education at the post-secondary level is a more worthy object of public expenditure than national defense? And yet, these are the choices which confront us in the allocation of our tax monies. By the middle of the 1970s expenditures for higher education will be running about 40 billion dollars per year. That sum will provide education for less than one-half of our young adults over 18 years of age. Were we to expand our post-secondary educational opportunities to include all those in our society over 18 years of age who wish to improve a skill or enlarge a talent, I estimate the cost would run 80 billion dollars per year. I charge Mr. Morse not with thinking too big, but with thinking too small. The sums involved are enormous and even if they could be raised readily by taxation, and could be appropriated in the face of competing demands (one asks here, parenthetically, about the competing needs of elementary and secondary education), how could such sums be equitably distributed in an educational system as diverse and polymorphous as our own aside from the rationality of the market?

The expenditure of such money through state and federal agencies would drive private education to the wall. Much private education is already enthralled by the golden chains which bind it to the governmental bureaucracy. The net effect of such a program would not be diversity and experimentation but homogeneity and stagnation. Let us assume, however, that there is a wise and discriminating policy of grants on a per capita basis which are made directly to the institutions. Such a policy, attractive as it seems initially, will only increase institutional irresponsibility and sharpen the lack of relevance to the genuine educational needs of the student, which is characteristic of so much of higher education in America. It is only when the student possesses the ability to choose from among educational alternatives on the basis of his ability to pay that relevance and differentiation will be maximized.

Why not then simply make direct grants to students; grants as a matter of citizen right? I believe there are a number of reasons why such a system must end in failure. Let me begin the analysis by asking: at what point should education at the public expense end? Why should men be entitled to an AB degree and not a PhD? What will happen to the notion that men and women ought to be able to train at any time during their working lives for new vocations? I believe that post-secondary education will be realistic only when the recipient calculates the values, and balances those values against the actual economic costs to himself. No one can afford to think rationally about education so long as someone else always foots the bill. Moreover, so long as the costs of a college or university degree are not fully and clearly apparent to the individual student, the link between status and the AB degree will remain unbroken. We will revere the degree not because of what it enables us to do, but because of what it enables us to be. Were we better able to gauge the costs of alternative educations and measure the demands and renunciations characteristic of intellectuality against the rewards of alternative vocations, I am convinced our choices would better fit our individual needs.

We do not have too much education in America. We do have too much of the wrong kinds of education. We must plan for more rather than less education, but it must be education which is responsive both to the needs of society and the needs of the individual. Mr. Morse sees, if I am not mistaken, the goals of post-secondary education to be an expanded citizenship training program, a kind of remedial civics. He assumes that there is necessarily something tainted and narrow in vocational education. This accounts, I believe, for the great bias in his remarks favoring conventional college programs. All good education is vocational education. Its purpose should be to induct the student into the world of work. In addition, it should enable him to take an active and intelligent role in the political life of his community, and it should assimilate him into the adult world of responsible commitment. Indeed, that is what work is all about.

A college education which is not vocational, in the large sense of the word, is passé. The best kind of citizenship training I know is that education which enables its holder to perform his function in society well. The world of work and the world of citizenship are not separate entities; they are one and the same thing. Broadly liberal and humane sympathies are not incompatible with vocational specialization. The cloud-cuckoo politics of the nihilist left is, in my opinion, partially the result of the estrangement of the academy from the world of vocational reality. It is clearly evident that the intellectual spastics among the students do not come from the sciences, engineering, medicine, business administration, and the law. No, they are students who have been educated in the defunct tradition of the gentleman and in short, have been given a class education. They have come to believe that the world owes them something because they are students. I would like to give students the opportunity once more to owe something to their society; to feel responsible, to feel committed, and to feel obligated. To pay one's own way through an educational program which is intelligently vocational is one of the chief ways of achieving this objective.

105

There are many ways of keeping the poor impoverished—among the cruelest of them being the way in which we give the poor an inferior education in the name of granting them a boon. Whether he realizes it or not, that precisely will be the impact of the community college program of Mr. Morse unless that program is coupled to another which will enable the untapped half of our population, who cannot now avail themselves of post-secondary education, to get the very best when they are qualified. The experience we have had with the Negro college and the Negro university as bastions of academic mediocrity should have taught us our lesson a long time ago. Now, admittedly, an inferior education is better than no education at all. However, I do not believe that to be our choice. We must see that the potential student is enabled to borrow the full cost of his education, let the educational institution determine qualifications, and provide the student with a quality elementary and secondary education and vocational counseling and guidance through a federally funded program from elementary through secondary school. Such a program will enable talent to seek its own level. The community college program alone will simply preserve the educational inferiority which distinguishes so much of America's education of its poor. Under the program I have outlined, there will be institutional competition to raise the level of quality in education rather than a governmental incentive to lower it. We want the very best in plumbers, electricians, doctors, lawyers, philosophers, and historians. We do not want diminished minds and provincial talents who have been forced into mediocrity by finding that the local community college was the only post-secondary education available.

Education: Who Pays the Piper?

In human affairs the how of doing anything is usually less vexatious than the why. Once the community has decided that a particular policy is appropriate or that a particular program is essential, human ingenuity will speedily devise ways to achieve the purposes of the community. Therefore I do not propose to discuss the how of financing full-cost tuitions to be paid by the students of post-secondary educational programs but rather why it is both desirable and essential that the student pay his own way. By discussing the "why" we shall shift our attention away from the pragmatic to the ideal and it is in terms of the ideal that I wish to cast my argument.

There is a widely held view that programs financed by governmental resources are free programs which cost the recipients of these benefactions nothing. Anyone with a rudimentary experience of government should realize by this time that of all the ways of doing anything, having it done by government, whether local, state or federal, is absolutely the most expensive way of purchasing an equivalent service. This is especially true of education at all levels. Moreover, if education does, in fact, raise the earning capacity of those who receive it there can be no doubt that they will bear a disproportionate share of the costs of education relative to the general population. The higher earning capacities are raised through education, the higher will be the general tax levies paid by educated individuals. Consequently, the belief that the educated will receive a gift is simply nonsense. There is, however, one qualification to what I have just said. Only about 11 percent of the American people have attended a college or university, but all of them are invited to pay the costs of higher education. The affluent receive a disproportionate share of the education provided while the poor pay a substantial portion of the cost.

A number of studies have now been done on the income redistribution effects of higher education; that of W. Lee Hansen and Burton Weisbrod in California, Douglas Windham's study of the situation in Florida, and Judson Barker's study of the redistributive effects of higher education in Minnesota being the most notable. These studies all indicate that while subsidies in the form of lower tuitions benefit students from some low income families, the major effect is to transfer income from lower to higher income groups. Gains for the middle income groups are made at the expense of the poor and the disadvantaged. At the present time only one-fourth the youth in college are from the half of the families below the median income and the situation is not improving. Harold L. Hodgkinson, a University of California educator, pointed out recently in a study done for the Carnegie Commission on Higher Education that while colleges and universities have expanded the rainbow of ethnic groups to which their institutions are open they have not greatly expanded the number of the disadvantaged, lower class students attending college. This means, in many cases, more blacks and fewer white disadvantaged students. A sign painted recently on the corridor wall of a classroom building put the very embarrassing question, "Where are the recruiters for the white disadvantaged student?"

But let us assume that a totally equitable system could be worked out so that the poor would not in fact be taxed to pay for the education of the more affluent. Would there be other considerations which might lead us to advocate the payment of full-cost tuitions by those who receive the education?

There is, in the first place in America, the widely held prejudice that those who are capable ought to pay for the benefits they receive from the community. Philosophically, Americans still prefer opportunities to gifts and still believe that direct grants should go only to those who are incapable of assisting themselves. Now while it is true that those students in primary and elementary school are incapable of assisting themselves, nothing less accurately describes the young adult who enrolls in a program of post-secondary education. He is at the very peak of his physical and intellectual prowess. The future belongs to him, the world is his oyster, or at least so he was told regularly by commencement speakers until the Vietnam war crowded more germane matters out of the fatuous remarks most educators made on such occasions. Who is better able to assume debts and the responsibility for self-improvement? Surely we do not wish to tax the aged or penalize minors, the sick or the indigent, to pay for the education of young adults. And yet the massive allocation of tax dollars required for post-secondary education in America in the next ten years means that we will do just that unless we find an alternative method of financing the educational needs of young adults. Paul McCracken, the former chairman of the Council of Economic Advisors, has pointed out on a number of occasions that anticipated increases in tax revenues over the next decade are, in fact, already allocated to existing programs and that new needs can be met only at the expense of already existing programs. Can we assume that a public, only 11 percent of whom have attended a college or university, will be willing to allocate an additional estimated 40 billion dollars per year of scarce resources to post-secondary education? I believe that to assume that our public and our legislators will act in this fashion is indicative of a utopianism that I have supposed was not even to be found in the academy, that home of things fantastical. But I need not remind you that at the moment institutions of higher education are not in good repute either with the public at large or with state legislatures. The fashion today is to cut higher education budgets rather than augment them. It is a fashion which may persist for some years.

Shall we take the money from the sick, the aged, the impoverished, the hungry, the cities, the environment, defense, veterans, transportation, elementary or secondary education, or shall we take it from those most able to pay: the young adults who are the recipients of the education? I believe that I can confidently predict the behavior of legislators faced with such a set of alternatives.

Moreover, even middle income groups are finding it progressively more difficult to pay the bills of sons and daughters attending college or the university. Fathers and mothers with two or more children find it extraordinarily difficult even with a $15,000+ income per year to find the $15,000 and upwards now required to send a son or daughter through four years of college. It seems unfair that a young man or woman who has achieved physical and psychological maturity should still be dependent economically and absorbing resources which the family can ill afford to take out of ordinary patterns of consumption. The question must occur to many parents of the justice of mortgaging their future when the son or daughter might be able to assume the responsibility.

Post-secondary educational costs are rising now and will continue to rise. Are we to assume that, as is presently the case in some Ivy League schools, only the very rich and the very poor will be able to afford post-secondary education, or shall we create the opportunity which will enable every qualified student to finance his own way through school?

Stronger even than these arguments are those which anticipate the effect full-cost tuitions will have on the educational system and the students. The great fact of 1970 in the educational world is the impact increasing costs and inflation is having on private education. The private college or university is hardly better off than the private elementary and secondary school. It is not simply that the weak private colleges are going to the wall; even the strongest and most adequately endowed are in desperate financial condition.

Most of you are aware of the desperate plight of higher education. Let me refresh your memories by citing a few facts. Stanford University this year ran a $6,000,000 deficit. Columbia University has run a deficit in each of the past five years and this year [1970] the deficit totaled $11,000,000. Next year the projected deficit at Columbia will be $15,000,000. Those who are acquainted with requests to foundations from colleges and universities know that increasingly these requests are for money, not to add new programs or new buildings but, simply to pay last year's bills. A number of private schools are attempting to solve their problems by going public and becoming a part of the state system. But even that is at best a partial solution, because state legislatures have drawn the purse strings tighter. Nor can public giving to the private colleges and universities do more than alleviate their most pressing financial needs. Private giving does not constitute a long-range solution. In 1968-69, the year before the decline in the stock market, 1,013 institutions reported total voluntary support of $1,460,877,899. That seems a very impressive figure, but it comes to average support per institution of only $1,442,130. The fact is that post-secondary education can no longer afford to remain private.

Higher education in the past three decades has shown a marked and accelerating tendency to uniformity and homogeneity. The chief differences between many schools now is the speed or lack of speed with which their bureaucracies function, the inefficiency of their IBM machines, and the degrees of dullness which characterize their institutional food and housing. Curriculum, instruction, and even so-called experimental courses and colleges are monotonously alike. Even the community college movement threatens to be swallowed up in this sea of educational sameness. A recent study observed that "unless the community college can develop its own curricula, its own appeal to faculty, it may find it is simply at the lower end of the single academic totem pole rather than becoming a new kind of institution serving new societal needs with new forms of organization and reward and new definitions of status and achievement, badly needed in higher education."

If we genuinely desire variety, pluralism and non-conformity in post-secondary education we must reward it. It costs money and effort to be different. One wonders how much innovation there would be in the field of electronics if investment in that field were determined by state legislatures or congressional committees.

Innovation and pluralism are maximized when the purchaser of the good or service is able to make realistic choices between alternatives. Those who would be horrified at the effects of monopoly in

111

the auto industry face the reality of monopoly in education with complete composure and equanimity. If we wish to go beyond a hypocritical lip service to pluralism and diversity in our culture, let us insure the continued existence of the private post-secondary educational institution. If private education is, in the long run, to be genuinely private it must be totally independent from the state. Independence in the realm of finances is more important than independence elsewhere for it remains as true now as in the past that he who pays the piper calls the tune.

Placing power in the hand of the consumer will, moreover, transform the nature of education. In a recent study of the economics of education, *Academia in Anarchy* by James Buchanan and Nicos Devletoglou, the authors point out that university education viewed economically possesses the characteristics of a unique industry because the consumer does not purchase the product. The producer does not sell his services and those who finance higher education do not control it. Under such circumstances demand will always exceed supply, the quality of production will be poor and scarce resources will be invested in chaotic and irresponsible educational ventures. Can one imagine any other enterprise managed in such a fashion? (I can think of one, the facilities for the care of the sick, and they, like educational facilities, are in a thoroughgoing crisis.)

What are the effects of institutions and teachers who are not directly responsible to the customer? The problem is not a new one. Adam Smith writing in *The Wealth of Nations* at the end of the 18th century noted the consequences of the failure of the market system in education. "In other universities," Smith says, "the teacher is prohibited form receiving any honorary or fee from his pupils, and his salary constitutes the whole of the revenue which he derives from his office. His interest is, in this case, set as directly in opposition to his duty as it is possible to set it. It is the interest of every man to live as much at his ease as he can; and if his emoluments are to be precisely the same, whether he does, or does not perform some very laborious duty, it is certainly his interest, at least, as interest is vulgarly understood, either to neglect it altogether, or if he is subject to some authority which will not suffer him to do this, to perform it in as careless and slovenly a manner as that authority will permit . . . In the University of Oxford, the greater part of the public professors have, for these many years, given up altogether even the pretense of teaching" (Adam Smith, *The Wealth of Nations,* Modern Library Edition, pp. 717-8).

The most tragic aspect of this anti-economic behavior, however, is its impact on the individual consumer. When individuals do not count the costs they often choose that which is disadvantageous and are provided with items poor in quality or useless. How many students avail themselves not of what they want, vocationally and in terms of curricula, but of what they can get? The bloated enrolments in liberal arts colleges are a constant reminder of this situation. How many students, unable to purchase a quality education, must reconcile themselves to the intellectual inferiority of the local community college? How many students are encouraged literally to waste four years of their lives in a kind of penal servitude, relieved only by the amusements of orgy and violence, because they were unable to prepare themselves for the future in any other way? Force the student to count up the costs and reckon the advantages and disadvantages. It is only then that preparation for a vocational choice will be a rational and realistic operation.

In a study just published, *Education and Jobs: The Great Training Robbery,* the point is made, and made convincingly, that given a choice it would be preferable, in terms of national policy, to improve the quality of K-12 education rather than increasing the 34 percent of direct educational outlays now spent on higher education; and much as the self-interested proponents of higher education are reluctant to admit it, the argument is cogent and correct.

We must, above all, realize that higher education is not the only kind of post-secondary education necessary in our society. We must therefore devise a system which will enable the post-secondary student to secure whatever kind of training in the acquisition or refinement of a skill or the mastery of a discipline which will enable him to lead a more adequate and rewarding life. We must remember that a minority of the American people now take conventional

Student Autonomy
and Financial Independence
in American Education

Institutional reform usually begins because of a financial crisis; indeed revolutions are quite commonly the result of unbalanced budgets. The financial crisis in our colleges and universities, consequently, not only demands that we find more adequate support for higher education but affords us the opportunity of examining whether or not higher education is currently providing the kinds of talents and skills needed in our society and of rationally exploring educational issues in the hope that this exploration will lead to more adequate support of education both by its customers and the broader public.

Education always possesses implications and rewards for both the society and the individual. We know without being told that the price of intelligent political action in a democracy such as ours is widespread and effective popular education. We do not need to be told that there can be a direct relationship between a qualitative improvement in life and increased education, though we ought always to bear in mind the dictum of Uncle Remus that "being good and being smart ain't the same thing." And, finally, we know that every increase in skill and widening of abilities enriches not only the individual but enriches the whole society of which he is a part.

It has, indeed, been argued that because society benefits in such large measure from the education of the individual, the burden of the costs of education ought to be largely social rather than individual. Higher education at the present time is predicated in large measure on this assumption. Its contrary, that the benefits of education both cultural and economic are so great as to place primary financial responsibility upon the individual for his education, is even more clearly demonstrable.[1] It is impossible, in fact, to determine who benefits most from education, the individual or society in general. Consequently the mechanisms we employ to finance higher education should not be based on an attempt to establish some equitable relationship between costs paid and benefits received. More important than equity, where equity is so unclear, must be a concern with providing adequate education, of diverse kinds, in the quantities needed, open to all throughout their working lifetimes and made available in such a way as to increase the autonomy of the individual student and the institutional independence of the school.

I wish to argue that even were the social benefits of education beyond the secondary school level vastly to outweigh benefits to the individual, it would still be desirable to make the individual financially responsible for the education he receives in the adult years of life. For we must be quite clear that when we discuss education beyond the secondary school level we are talking about the education of adults. Colleges and universities have only reluctantly recognized this fact and at present give it only grudging and incomplete assent. Much of the *in loco parentis* debate derives from the failure to recognize that an eighteen-year-old is, in fact, an adult and that his majority ought to be recognized socially, politically and economically. He ought to decide about behavior for himself; he ought to vote and he ought to assume the full financial burden of his support and further education. It seems folly to ask, to require, men and women to behave responsibly until we do in fact make them responsible.

116

We cannot make men and women who have achieved physiological and sexual maturity responsible if we prolong their dependence and refuse to open up to them opportunities for calculated and rational choices. The sociologist Bennett M. Berger has pointed out that, "the problem of student unrest is rooted in the prolongation of adolescence in industrialized countries."[2] I believe it is a safe generalization that so long as our young adults are not politically potent in the conventional sense of exercising the franchise, are not identified with a social role which they intend to fill through socially meaningful work in their adult lives, and are not financially independent and responsible, we cannot expect them to combine their moral enthusiasms with any marked degree of political and social realism. Until, indeed, education is once more linked realistically to vocation and vocation becomes the calculated, unconditioned choice of the individual willing and able to pay the price for the life he wishes to lead in the future, our students will exhibit the same irresponsible and irrational behavior which characterizes all who find themselves in positions of dependency and inequality.[3]

It has not been sufficiently noted by either neo-conservatism or the New Left that higher education, and indeed the whole structure of middle class family life, provides the perfect paradigm of the welfare state, and it is precisely in these areas that the limitations of welfarism are most clearly evident. The adolescent child and the adult student are asked to postpone a meaningful role in the societies in which they participate. Their roles and identities are undefined, their responsibilities nonexistent. They are excluded from the present work of society and they are asked to prepare for a future not of their own choosing.

The chief purpose of any educational system ought to be the integration of the individual into the work and the cultural activities of the society rather than his effective exclusion from society. That work and those cultural activities must become the center and meaning of the life of the adult individual. The Peace Corps, Vista Volunteers and other such programs (which are at best a kind of outdoor recreation for the displaced young adults of the middle classes) are no substitutes for lifetime vocations which, at one and the same time, fulfill the individual and serve the society. Our educational system must teach our young adults to deal with the real world in terms of vocation and role, hazard and choice, cost and responsibility.

Not only must education be adult, but that very demand implies that the potential student must be able to make some rational choices concerning his education. He must be able to calculate in terms of rewards and costs, abilities and limitations, immediate and deferred rewards whether or not he will go on to any kind of education beyond the secondary school. More importantly, he must be capable of choosing among a wide variety of educations beyond the secondary school. The link between social status and the AB degree must be broken. While it is true that we cannot have too much education, we do, at the present moment, have too much of the wrong kind. We have increasingly penalized variety by creating educational monopolies, by rewarding so-called higher education at the expense of apprenticeship programs, craft, technical and semi-professional programs and skills learned on the job or in proprietary institutes and schools. It is the height of unreality to search for a solution to the problem of financing higher education without taking into account the educational needs of all adults. After all, those who go on to higher education now constitute, and probably always will constitute, far less than half of our secondary education graduates. How can we defend an educational system which will always be elitist in nature and which will guarantee the rewards of social mobility associated with education to what must always remain a minority of the total population? We must either decide to send every man to college or to permit every man to choose and pay for the education he perceives himself as needing and society as willing to recompense adequately. Consequently, any system for financing higher education must be capable at the same time of financing the total adult educational needs of the society.

Moreover, those needs must be seen as extending throughout much of the adult life of the individual. It is a truism that knowledge and skills in our culture have a very short half-life. To see education as a once-and-for-all-time process which the young adult is subject to between his 17th and his 25th year is to indulge in pure illusion. We must expect occupation change with increasing frequency as the result of technological innovation. We must also realize that in the past we have limited the social usefulness, the self-esteem and the earning capacities of many of our fellow citizens by foreclosing the possibility of their returning to training or to education except at prohibitive cost to themselves. Is it so un-reasonable to ask for an educational system which will continue to educate people so long as they are able to make a convincing case that society will reward them for deepening their capacities and enlarging their skills?

Increasingly the assumption has become "that only government can finance higher education."[4] This assumption has grown up because the costs of financing higher education alone, to say nothing of other types of adult education, have become so enor-mous. However, "the truth is that all the finance for education that has been increasingly channelled through government is private in origin. Higher education is financed by private businessmen who pay company taxation and by individuals who pay income, purchase and capital taxes. There is no necessary reason why their moneys should be channelled to the universities indirectly through governments, so that universities are accountable to politicians, and not directly by consumers of university teachings and buyers of un-iversity services, so that the universities are answerable to them as customers."[5]

The result of relocating the source of payment for the costs of higher education has, as the above quotation suggests, important implications for the reestablishment of institutional responsibility. All of us who are jealous of our liberties regret that our surviving private colleges and universities are increasingly becoming the thralls of the federal government. They stand now, cup in hand, waiting not only for agency largess but for agency decisions con-cerning educational philosophy and the conduct of their affairs. At the state universities and colleges matters are in even sadder shape. Dependent upon federal largess, these schools can no longer afford to deal independently with such vital and important issues as research, curriculum, and admissions. Questions in these areas are not resolved on the basis of a rational educational philosophy elaborated by the faculty and administration but are the product of federal bureaucratic fiat. We must, it seems to me, not only make the student responsible for and to himself but we must at the same time make the university and the college responsible to and for itself.

Foremost among the results of such a policy will be an almost instantaneous increase in the diversity of methods and ideas in higher education. The outstanding feature of contemporary higher education in America is its homogeneity. There is some justice for the call for the establishment of "free universities" by the New Left. Mistaken as I believe most of their assumptions to be, I think they are accurate in asserting that genuine debate and experimentation are not encouraged at present on our campuses. They are not encouraged because it is expensive to be different, and difference under present circumstances must be paid for by the institution and its faculty and staff rather than by its customers, the students.

Students should be able to choose between private and state educational institutions (on the basis of religious commitment alone, if for no other reason). Today, even those students fortunate enough to afford a college education are often not wealthy enough to afford to make an institutional choice. How many students would prefer a small, church-connected college but settle for the megalopolitan state university simply because of the marked differential in tuition? How many small schools have been forced to dilute their academic standards and their codes of student conduct in order, quite simply, to stay in business? The private colleges and universities which have had such a long and distinguished history in American education and which have made such important contributions to American life must once more be made competitive with the state institutions.

However, the quest for diversity must go beyond the elementary and simple question of supporting the private sector of American education without turning it into a fiefdom of the federal bureaucracy. Students ought to be able to choose from a variety of institutional forms, curricular models, and instructional methods. There should be available, based upon demand, alternative programs and educational experiences. Dependent upon the student's willingness to pay in the future, he should be enabled to seek out and enjoy the kind of education best fitted to his needs. Conversely, the institution will, under such circumstances, be able to discontinue the practice of being all things to all men. Any institution of higher education ought to be able to counsel the discontented and the dissatisfied student to go elsewhere, to seek in another setting the kind of education which will be for him genuinely relevant. Much of the unrest of the present hour, I believe, might be handled in just such a fashion. Such a program has the great merit of forcing men to pay the price for being different.

Society preserves its stability, in part, by making radicalism costly. (Here I use "radicalism" broadly to mean any idea which deviates significantly from accepted theory and practice.) Milton Friedman has observed, "Make the advocacy of radical causes sufficiently remunerative, and the supply of advocates will be unlimited." But it is precisely because creative dissent is so costly that a society such as ours, which is so heavily dependent upon reasoned change, must view non-governmental patronage as one of its most important sources of freedom and innovation. I believe that full cost tuitions paid by the student would increase diversity among institutions and improve the quality of debate.

One of the most interesting analyses of students from poverty backgrounds makes the following striking observation:[6]

> Despite their apparent similarity and readiness with respect to ability, motivational characteristics and values, the *Severe Poverty* students seem to end up at institutions of lower academic standing than the more comfortable students. Our data show a sizeable relationship between family income and academic standing of *both* the schools the students ever considered and the schools they subsequently attended. . . . Yet with respect to their goals and other motivational characteristics, these poverty students would seem ready to handle the highest quality education available, certainly the same quality as other income groups. This disadvantage is highlighted by the fact that certain

of the highest ranking schools, which are apparently less available to poverty students, send disproportionately large numbers of students on to graduate school. So. to be poor means both less chance for the highest quality undergraduate education and less likelihood of getting advanced training and education.

The authors of this study confess an inability to explain these facts. The explanation, I believe, is simple. Poor planning, when it exists at all, is never completely rational. Aspirations are conditioned and hedged around by a thousand qualifications. The poor know that too often opportunities do not match abilities and that the margins dividing success and failure are much narrower for them than those more advantageously placed. If the child of poverty could assure himself that his educational future was in his own hands and that the choice of the school he was to attend was completely dependent on one factor only, his ability to perform, I believe the phenomenon which Gurin and Epps observed would disappear. The behavior of the disadvantaged student is not too different from the behavior of the impoverished shopper. He shops wastefully because he cannot afford the rationality of his middle class counterpart.

Broadening educational choice, then, is one of the most important aspects of any program for financing adult education. But, again, I must insist that "educational choice" must be construed to mean all kinds of education, from vocational crafts and skills through professional and graduate education.

It is quite clear that the American people long ago identified education as the most important single avenue in our society for social mobility. Those of us who have come from backgrounds of poverty know that it was education which made the big difference in our lives. There is general agreement that we must have more, rather than less, education of all descriptions in the years immediately ahead. Our educational achievements are the most demonstrable evidence of the success of the American dream and it is for this reason that the crisis which faces the whole of American education is so important to America's political and social future.

It is interesting to note that when the public was polled as to whether we should solve the problem of rising costs and inadequate institutional facilities by adopting a policy of limited enrollments or by building more colleges so that more students could attend, 79 percent of those questioned choose the course of building more colleges.[7] To be sure, these same people were quite uncertain as to how the costs of these additional colleges were to be met. In a sense then, the future of adult education has been in part decided. It is going to grow in quantity and scope. The issues which are undecided center on quality, variety, independence, and accessibility.

To assume that either the state or the federal government can provide the enormous sums necessary for this expansion of the educational program seems to me unrealistic. It is unrealistic, in the first place, because more politically attractive programs in the welfare area compete now and will compete more effectively in the future with educational budgetary needs. Education is, for example, less popular politically than medical programs. It must be remembered, too, that new taxes, either state or federal, are apt to be levied upon those who already find their salaries so low that they cannot afford to send their children to college or take time and money to improve their own skills. It is a cruel myth to believe that tax support for higher education derived from those who earn less than $10,000 per year constitutes any social advantage to them.

It must seem manifestly unjust to many people, in spite of the social utility of improved skills, that the costs of an education which benefits the individual in a very measurable fashion (medical and dental school, for example) should be passed on to the general public. W. Lee Hansen and Barton A. Weisbrod in their study, *Benefits, Costs, and Finance of Public Higher Education*, make this point more than adequately.[8]

> Nationally, a larger percentage of low than of high-income youngsters drop out of high school and so are not eligible to receive any higher-education subsidies. Those low-income students who are eligible to go to higher educational institutions most often wind up at institutions where the education subsidy is lowest. And they are more likely to drop out before graduation. For these and other well-known reasons, the cards are stacked against low-income youngsters. Yet because tax revenues are used to support higher education, the anomalous result is lower-income families not only do not receive significant amounts of public higher-education subsidies but actually pay a larger fraction

of their income in taxes to support higher education than do more affluent families. At a time when pressures are mounting to reduce disparities between privileged and disadvantaged, it is clear that something has gone awry. The mythology of equal educational opportunity for all is just that: mythology.

The demands of both equity and social mobility can be met only if every student is enabled to assume the financial responsibility of educating himself in a school, apprenticeship, technical institute, college or university of his choice.

Any program which enables the student to pursue such diverse alternatives and any system which rewards increments of ability and skill as lavishly as does ours must be predicated on a national rather than merely a statewide system of finance. Students must be able to choose from the entire range of educational opportunities available to them in the United States; indeed, with such a program one could make a perfectly good case for use of borrowed money to study abroad. Finally, we must not create a situation where every state which increases its educational opportunities without being able to assess costs against the individual educated would find it had a "brain drain." The English economist Colin Clark has ascribed Britain's "brain drain" to precisely such conditions.

These "radical" thoughts are not nearly so radical as they may at first seem. They lack, indeed, even the distinction of novelty. Nor are they distinctively the product of the ideological right, though market economists have played a leading role in developing them. That ideas are given serious consideration on the left as well as on the right is attested by the article, "Paying for the High Cost of Education, A National Youth Endowment" by James Tobin and Leonard Ross in the May 3, 1969 *New Republic*.[9] The program has been widely studied in both the United States and Great Britain[10] and certainly does not suffer from a deficiency of literature on the subject.

It seems to me that the only feasible program is a nationwide program of loans (what Hansen and Weisbrod describe as a "fixed payment" system),[11] made directly to the student for study in accredited schools and training programs, to be repaid as a tax, or installments, assessed against future earnings once the earnings of the recipient have reached a certain agreed level. The tax form of repayment has the great merit of ease of collection and might be tied either to the income tax or social security systems.

Note, however, that this is a loan plan for the repayment of the precise amount borrowed together with interest. The economics of such a program, particularly the economic justification of the program, has been brilliantly worked out by Edward J. Mishan in the March, 1969 *Encounter* Magazine.[12] Unless a fixed payment system is adopted, all sorts of irrationalities and inequities will become a part of the system. It would, for example, be impossible under what Hansen and Weisbrod denominate a "contingent" system for the individual to calculate the value to him of a particular educational program. It is, of course, possible to argue that the purchase of a life insurance policy is not irrational simply because some individuals will pay more and some individuals will pay less. The difference, I believe, lies in the fact that all men, of necessity, die, and not all men, of necessity, may wish to borrow up to $15,000 to increase their abilities. Educational success, moreover, is a somewhat more chancy affair than death. Indeed, most major universities do not possess accurate retention figures. One of the major advantages of such a program is the tonic effect it would have on business practices within the institution. Colleges and universities would be compelled to arrive at some defensible figures for the full costs of tuition. The practice of subsidizing programs of graduate instruction out of undergraduate tuitions and fees would have to be abandoned, and colleges and universities would have to face up to the problem of honesty in the assessment of costs.

The problem of the education of women is the single most important stumbling block to such a system. As Kingman Brewster has remarked, "no one wants to marry a negative dowry." This, of course, assumes that the education of women is not really economically rewarding and in the context of current American practice that is all too clearly the case. Women do not aspire to or enjoy careers. The impact of such a program, however, might be wholly different from that anticipated. Women might, just possibly, come to assess more realistically their roles and their opportunities. The emphasis might shift in female education from preparation for matrimony to preparation for a career. Clearly such a system would find it difficult to increase the waste of female talent which is at present characteristic of our society.

Such a system would not be self-liquidating. That should be recognized at the outset. There will be costs of administration and accreditation. There will be major losses with individuals who fail to complete their training or fail after completion of training to achieve a taxable income status. These costs will simply be borne by the federal government. They will not be inconsiderable but will constitute a fraction of the current federal subsidies to higher education.

Even were such a program initiated, equality of opportunity would still evade many of the poor. The young adult, whether through his earnings or through his assistance to the family in the form of labor, is still an asset. If he is the eldest child (even among the poor the most likely to continue his education beyond the secondary level) his assistance will be most acutely needed for the care of the family. If the prospective student is older and the head of a household, he will be unable to seek further training or education unless some sort of hardship stipend is available to his family.

Forgone income is a factor in limiting adult education, moreover, not only with the poor and those with established families and continuing needs.[13] These costs, however, are more easily borne by the middle and upper-middle income groups and do not ordinarily operate as the factor which excludes the potential student from further education. I propose, therefore, that present endowment and loan funds ordinarily used for scholarship and fellowship purposes plus supplementary payments from the state be used to provide payments in lieu of forgone income in such cases where its absence will create hardship. The only equitable way to establish "hardship" is a simple means test.

Such a provision is essential if we are to make any serious attempt to provide educational equality of opportunity. As the result of such a program, the young adult with aspirations for education beyond secondary school would become an asset rather than a liability to his family, for payments would be made to the family rather than directly to the student. Obviously such payments should not be so large as to cover the whole of the hypothetically forgone income. As in every choice where venture and risk are involved, the student must be encouraged to put something of himself into the enterprise.

Finally, educational opportunity is limited by the access the student has, even at the elementary school level, to guidance and counseling, to activities and programs which have as their purpose the early establishment of realistic vocational objectives. Such a program on a national scale should be established and funded by the federal government. Perhaps such a program is, at the present moment, one of the most important steps we could as a nation take for the upgrading of abilities in the United States. At present the poorest school districts and the smallest schools have, almost universally, the least adequate programs in counseling. Students make unrealistic assessments not only of their own abilities and aspirations but of the vocations on which they have set their hearts. There are, in our society, very inexact notions on the part of the young adult about the adult world of work in all of its fulfilling and creative variety. There must be a much more creative and emphatic program for the early identification of vocational objectives than currently exists. The disadvantaged suffer most from our lack of such a program, but much of the restiveness among college and university students is due to their inability to see the AB degree as anything meaningful to their adult lives. Too often their vocational choices are initially made by their parents or are the consequence of totally extraneous considerations. As an optimum we wish to create an educational system in which the student knows what he wants to do with his life and has the opportunities to achieve his objectives. The only way to make a rational choice possible is to provide a realistic assessment of the costs and rewards of every kind of vocational endeavor. I am convinced that when adequate programs of guidance become available and the hidden costs of higher education for the individual are widely known, the link between status and the AB degree will at last be broken.

It has been argued that the poor are, because of their poverty, such determined "risk avoiders" that a program which through loans loads the individual with sizeable debts would be so unattractive as to lead to its failure. I believe this assumption to be fallacious. The fact is that loans now constitute the most distinctive way in which the poor finance their educations. "The marked distinguisher," Gurin and Epps write, "between the income groups is the greater importance of loans for the *Severe Poverty Group.* Three times as many of the students in the *Severe Poverty Group* as in the *Comfortable Group* report having *all* their college costs covered by some kind of loan."[14] As an added incentive, however, repayment of the loan might be pegged to the achievement by the individual of the average income in his particular occupational category or the achievement of a set income figure ($8,000 per year) whichever is higher. Under such conditions the debt would not be collectable until such time as the student or trainee was capable of paying.

The politics of such a program are complicated but they are, at least, hopeful. Costs are the chief factor and no one, at the present moment, can anticipate with any accuracy what they would be. If $5,000 per year were made available to every eligible student and all of those 3.5 million people who annually become 18 years old took advantage of it, the cost would total $17.5 billion for loans alone.[15] Not all 18-year-olds would take advantage of the program but to those 18-year-olds who decide to study must be added those who are beyond 18 and wish to change vocations or add to their skills. It seems unlikely to me that the figure would go much beyond $20 billion and the aggregate before repayments balanced withdrawals would be less than $100 billion. To be sure, these are large and even frightening sums. Their impact, however, will bring a reduction of political pressure. For the first time education beyond the secondary level will be taken very largely out of the political sphere. It will, in fact, become private and individual. High and middle income families might still prefer to finance the education of their children. That option will be open to them. Their ability to finance their own education will reduce the pressure on the resources of the National Youth Endowment. Nor can it be argued that the Endowment will compete with other programs for tax funds, for as an independent corporation the Endowment would borrow funds directly from private lenders and in turn make its resources available to students and trainees registered in accredited programs. If the initial impact of the program is felt to be too great, it could be instituted selectively on a geographic basis or on the basis of national income distribution figures granting priority to those areas where average family incomes are lowest.

From a political standpoint the flaws of the present system of federal support for higher education are serious. The state institutions are placed in direct competition with private educational initiatives. Support is spotty and uneven with a major emphasis on the sciences and areas such as medicine and dentistry. Those studies are most heavily subsidized which will eventually yield the highest incomes to the recipients of the subsidies. Choice is limited by granting the subsidies to the institution rather than to the individual, and the large university rather than the smaller school is the chief beneficiary of federal largess. Any program which opens opportunities for larger numbers of potential students and trainees than the present programs is bound in the long run to be politically the more attractive. Programs such as the GI Bill long ago established this point.

In summary, I have been arguing for the establishment of an independent corporation, The National Youth Endowment, which would possess the authority to issue bonds and borrow money and in turn lend money to students and trainees studying in accredited institutions. Students might pursue any course of studies or training at any time during their adult lives with the approval of the Endowment and meeting certain standards.

I have no intention of making adult education free. I do wish to make it responsible. I have no intention of providing a forced and unnatural equality. I do hope to open up opportunity. I have no intention of forcing the affluent to pay for the education of the poor, but I am determined that the poor do not continue to pay for the education of the affluent.

I do not expect any one system to solve all our problems, educationally or otherwise. If the system I propose provides a greater measure of diversity, a greater measure of opportunity, a greater measure of equity and a greater measure of individual and institutional responsibility than the present system, that is enough.

[1]Angus Campbell and William C. Eckerman, *Public Concepts of the Values and Costs of Higher Education*, Monograph No. 37. (Survey Research Center Institute for Social Research, The University of Michigan, Ann Arber, 1964), pp. 8-38.

[2]Bennett M. Berger, "The New Stage of American Man—Almost Endless Adolescence" in *The New York Times Magazine*, November 2, 1969, p. 32.

[3]See Gideon Sjoberg, M. Donald Hancock, and Orion White, Jr., *Politics in the Post-Welfare State: A Comparison of the United States and Sweden*, The Carnegie Seminar on Political and Administrative Development, Department of Government, Indiana University, (Bloomington, 1967).

[4]H. S. Ferns, *Towards an Independent University*, The Institute of Economic Affairs, Occasional Paper 25 (London, 1969), p. 5.

[5]*Ibid.*

[6]Patricia Gurin and Edgar Epps, "Some Characteristics of Students from Poverty Backgrounds Attending Predominantly Negro Colleges in the Deep South" in *Social Forces*, Vol. 45, No. 1, Sept. 1966, p. 39.

[7]Campbell and Eckerman, p. 92.

[8]W. Lee Hansen and Burton A. Weisbrod, *Benefits, Costs and Finance of Public Higher Education*, (Markham Publishing Company, Chicago 1969).

[9]James Tobin and Leonard Ross, "Paying the High Costs of Education, A National Youth Endowment" in *The New Republic*, Vol. 160, May 3, 1969, pp. 18-23.

[10]A. R. Prest, *Financing University Education, A Study of University Fees and Loans to Students in Great Britain*, Occasional Paper No. 12, Institute of Economic Affairs, (London, 1966), cites the relevant literature.

[11]W. Lee Hansen and Burton A. Weisbrod, "The Equality Fiction," *The New Republic*, Sept. 13, 1969, pp. 23-24.

[12]Edward J. Mishan, "Some Heretical Thoughts on University Reform, The Economics of Changing the System" in *Encounter*, Vol. 32, No. 3, March, 1969, pp. 3-15.

[13]Hansen and Weisbrod, p. 46.

[14]Gurin and Epps, p. 31.

[15]Tobin and Ross, p. 21.

Faculty Responsibility
in Higher Education

When the time comes for assessing responsibility and establishing guilt, overkill is the style in our American society. We have never been content with half-way judgments and uncertain pronouncements. As a consequence our political and social life and particularly our public debate have been characterized by a series of devil theories which have periodically identified a class or group or even a single individual and have made it or him, as the case may be, into the principle of evil incarnate and responsible for all the ills troubling society at any given time.

We abandon this mythology of guilt very grudgingly even when there is overwhelming evidence to the contrary. A few years ago, for example, it was argued that everything dangerous in American life was the result of the workings of a gigantic right-wing conspiracy. This notion was so pervasive that when the late President Kennedy was assassinated in Dallas the public, and particularly the press and the news media, generally assumed, and in the course of the first few days, repeatedly asserted, that the assassin was a "right-wing fanatic." How disappointing it was to discover in the course of time that both President John Kennedy and his brother,

Robert, were assassinated by avowed Marxists whose involvement in the Left was attested to, not by hearsay, but by their own self-incriminating activities and writings. Still, it would have been so comforting to believe that the sage of Belmont, Robert Welsh, was, like some monstrous ideological Dr. Fu Manchu, trying to bring the country to its knees through a series of political assassinations and other covert right-wing activities.

I allude to this unhappy penchant of ours because I believe that there is danger in our following the same course of fixing responsibility through the creation of mythologies of guilt to account for the problems of higher education in America. No one and no group is, or can be, responsible for everything. Certainly administration, faculty, and students are not responsible for the population explosion which has so burdened and transformed our educational system at all levels. In this instance, one does not have to be an Hegelian philosopher to realize that at some point in the past twenty years changes in quantity produced changes in quality. Certainly there is a worldwide restiveness which has gripped all people and all nations, though perhaps the young have felt this restiveness most sharply. The problem, however, of rebellion against institutional forms is not distinctively a problem of youth or even an American problem, and to see it wholly in terms of the American institutional situation and American youth is to fall into a dangerous error. Finally, the Vietnam war, the civil rights crusade, the discovery and exploitation of poverty for political purposes, all have relatively little to do with the crisis in higher education. Were these particular problems to vanish tomorrow there would still be a serious crisis on our campuses.

Now while it is true that no one factor is responsible for the crisis we educators ought to examine our consciences and ask ourselves what our responsibility is in these matters. No group in American life is more ready to pass out blame and denounce inequity than the faculties of our colleges and universities. Perhaps that is because so many of us are "spoiled priests and stikkit ministers." Nonetheless, we ought to apply our moral sensitivities to our own condition and ask ourselves where we have erred and to explore what our role on the campus should be and what our powers actually are.

I believe that we have lost sight of what the objectives of college and university education ought to be. Permit me to call an interesting fact to your attention. In the late 1930s, through the 40s and into the 50s there was a very widespread and profitable debate on American campuses concerning the nature, role, techniques, and purposes of education. Genuine educational experimentation was at an all time high and curricular reform was one of the most hotly contested issues in public discussion. Today those educational concerns have all but disappeared. The debate has dried up. The issues and experiments have been institutionalized.

This, of course, is not to say that there are no experiments. There are experiments in superfluity but they are political rather than educational in their inspiration. I hesitate to call the raucous voices I hear on campus debate. The discussions are much too one-sided to deserve that name. Certainly they are not discussions concerning education. Clearly they have a great deal to do with politics. In short, the focus of campus concern has shifted in the past twenty years from educational to political concern. The career of Robert M. Hutchins, erstwhile President of the University of Chicago and now President of the Center for the Study of Democratic Institutions at Santa Barbara, is illustrative and symbolic of this shift. Even at Chicago Dr. Hutchins had certain large thoughts of an activist political nature which he felt impelled to bring to the attention of the world. For example, he was a most important and articulate member of America First and on the eve of World War II did his best to secure a victory for National Socialism by preventing the prudent rearming of the United States in the years between 1939 and our entry into the war. Be that as it may, there were many who made the same mistake and in those years Dr. Hutchins devoted most of his time to education and to participating in and fostering a genuine educational debate. Those of us over 40 recall those crusades and campaigns which gave rise to such an earnest examination of higher education in America.

But alas! the lodestone of politics soon drew the nails out of most of President Hutchins' arguments and he betook himself to a sunnier climate where he could gather a group of dedicated intellectual politicans about himself and discuss endlessly in a kind of California cloud-cuckoo land how many points a politican gets for wearing a doctor's hood. And, strange to say, after debating the twenty-third draft of Rexford G. Tugwell's Model Constitution it really did not seem to make much difference.

Hutchins' career, it seems to me, illustrates a process which has been at work throughout higher education in America. That process has been the general movement from education and educational questions to politics and the use of the university as a base for political activity.

And we delude ourselves if we think that students alone are responsible for the politicization of the university. Indeed, they are late arrivals on the scene. How many times in the past several years has the discussion of genuine educational issues by your college faculty meeting been postponed for months while your would-be faculty Senator Fulbrights discussed the situation in Vietnam, or the size of the welfare payments, or defense spending, or the desirability of telling the state legislature how to behave? If your faculty meetings resemble those at the University of Michigan, faculty meetings during the past several years have been increasingly given to political rather than educational concerns.

It seems to me self-evident that the university is not, in the first instance, a political forum. The role of the professor does not involve providing political leadership. It does not include his becoming a revolutionary propagandist. The office of the professor does not make him the moral and political arbiter of his society. To believe any of these things is to entertain a delusion so dangerous as to lead to the destruction of the university.

What then is the legitimate role of the university professor? In the first instance his role is essentially conservative. He is the keeper and transmitter of a cultural tradition. Far from being a cultural revolutionary, he is expected to transmit the heritage of the past unimpaired to the next generation. Society does not ask him to be a politician, it does not ask him to have any political views at all, but it does expect him to know Latin or German, Chemistry or Zoology, History or Accounting.

In the second instance, the university professor is dedicated to the methods and procedures of rational enquiry. He enlarges the sum total of knowledge, not by an act of faith or through a religious or political commitment but through an application of his mind to a particular problem. He believes that in the world of reasoned enquiry truth is not determined by votes or the liveliness of one's sentiments but by existential reality and he believes, moreover, that there is a method for exploring that reality which can be taught as a discipline. He is quite unwilling to see teaching degraded to an exchange of fuzzy opinions.

Moreover, he believes that the quest for truth requires the open exploration and debate of all the aspects of the question. He does not believe that a genuine social science is possible which excludes from exploration certain assumptions concerning human society. He does not believe that a genuine economics is possible which permits only certain economic views to be heard. He does not believe that a valid American history is possible which excludes, misinterprets, or misappropriates important portions of the American past.

Usually, the professor at his best is a critic. His criticism, however, rests upon his ability to present and weigh alternatives rationally. He should be able to tell us better than most men what the costs of a particular line of action or program within his field of competence will be. It is not his role to choose ends for us but rather to enable us to assess what the consequences will be. He will do this humbly and without arrogance realizing that the unanticipated consequences of rational action must also be reckoned a part of any rational plan. He will not and cannot be a utopian hawking political patent medicines from the privileged and protected podium from which he speaks.

Now, of course you give your assent to this for you realize that what I have said is a part of the polite parlance of academic life, but in fact many professors reject the idea of the university as an open forum in which truth is ascertained. Elisabeth Mann Borgese recently voiced a widely held view when she denounced the work of Professor Arthur Jensen in the field of educational psychology at the University of California at Berkeley. His investigations were, according to Elisabeth Mann Borgese, racist and ought to be prohibited. What she was saying is that only "socially approved" ideas ought to be explored at the university. Of course, in the Union of South Africa one can find parallel attitudes expressed on the same subject though ideological content is different.

If this were an isolated instance it would not be a question of serious moment. However, it is not. The possibility of seriously exploring alternatives on the college or university campus has been increasingly vitiated.

Some issues are simply ignored. Although religion plays a major role in the life of our society most state universities refuse to acknowledge its existence and refuse to treat theology as a science.

Some groups are prohibited from taking part in the discussion. Until recently it was difficult for a Roman Catholic to be appointed to a post at a major university. The *bon mot* that "anti-Catholicism is the anti-Semitism of the Liberals" was not without its basis in academia. The University of Michigan, for example, did not appoint a Roman Catholic in the history department until 1954, more than one hundred years after the university came into existence. Now it is possible, of course, that Roman Catholics don't make good historians, though there is good deal of evidence to the contrary.

Some views are subtly, or not so subtly, excluded. How does it happen that in the history department to which I belong out of over fifty faculty members only one is an identifiable Republican? Is it that Republicans are as the English say simply not "clubable" or as the Germans put it, "*Gesellschaftsfähig*"? I think that unlikely. I believe it is far more likely that a process of selection and exclusion has been at work for nearly sixty years which has now produced a marvelous homogeneity of viewpoint. No wonder students don't really want to debate; want simply to have their prejudices confirmed. They have picked up their bad intellectual habits from their elders.

And finally through the operation of what I call "misplaced expertise" some professors, men, indeed, who possess acknowledged stature in the world of intellect, believe that their achievements in one field of intellectual endeavor qualifies them to speak in every instance and on all subjects with unquestioned authority. Not only do they believe they have the right to speak in such a fashion but that the authority of their voice ought to silence any opposing views; indeed that these views ought to be silenced by force if necessary.

Let's take a second example, chosen, one might say, almost at random from the *New York Times* of October 10, 1969. The quotation which is both long and amusing is from an interview with Dean Acheson, former secretary of state in the administration of President Truman. Dean Acheson said on that occasion:

> "Immediately after the war I had a great deal to do with nuclear scientists. There were people like Robert Oppenheimer, whom I admired very much. Oppie was one of the most naive people I knew. How he reached his age and knew as little about the outside world as he did, I don't know—though he was extremely cultivated and read widely in many languages.
>
> "I accompanied Oppie into Truman's office one day. Oppie was wringing his hands, and said 'I have blood on my hands.'
>
> "'Don't ever bring the damn fool in here again,' Truman told me afterward. 'He didn't set that bomb off. I did. This kind of sniveling makes me sick.' It made me slightly sick as well.
>
> "What also made me sick was the scientist's feeling that by making a bomb they knew everything there was to know about foreign relations and could bring peace to the world. The *Bulletin of Atomic Scientists* is the greatest bit of nonsense since the *New Republic*.
>
> "The intellectual, strictly channeled into one discipline, wants to run them all," Mr. Acheson went on. "This is why Dr. Spock gives me a pain, why Bill Coffin—a hell of a nice fellow—by being a Protestant clergyman knows everything about international affairs. He doesn't. When I was a trustee at Yale I wanted to give him a hemlock cocktail to relieve him of some of his responsibilities."

Permit me to drive home the point and its implications by a third quotation. This time my quotation is from an article, "Barbarism, Virtue, and the University" by Professor Sidney Hook in the Spring number of *The Public Interest*. In that article Hook quotes Professor Carl Schorske who says that the individual scholar can be protected in the pursuit of truth only if the scholarly community recognizes "a responsibility for the implications of its findings for society and mankind." What Professor Schorske is saying is that academic freedom is a value and ought to be protected only when the professor is in agreement with his colleagues. Or to put it in a blunter and more forthright fashion, "Professors ought to be permitted to teach only so long as they find themselves in agreement with the current orthodoxy."

Professor Schorske is not, as one might legitimately suspect, a discredited fanatic. He is not the representative of a minority position. He is the finest sort of representative of the liberal establishment, an establishment which defends its own right to speak with the rhetoric of academic freedom but demands censorship and silence from every other view, group or position in society. Little wonder our youth is totalitarian when they drink daily from such poisoned springs.

The only place where the professor has a right to play a determinative role in decision-making is in the classroom and it is precisely in the classroom that he has made such egregious errors. In the final analysis there are few policies in the college or the university other than academic policies which are not legitimately the province of administration and trustees. It is only within the classroom and those areas of education which are contingent upon the classroom that the professor has a right to speak and be heard.

Why is that right not exercised more carefully, more effectively and more decisively? I have suggested that a most important reason for the failure of the professor really to determine what should happen in his classroom is that he really does not believe in academic freedom, that he is more interested in what happens in the classroom of his colleague than he is in inculcating the virtues of reasoned enquiry in his own.

However, there is another and perhaps equally important reason for the failure of academic freedom in America. To put that reason in its bluntest terms, it is timidity and cowardice on the part of the professor. Tenure is a mask for mediocrity and timidity. Why, if a university violates the consciences and the rights of professors do they not protest with their feet? There is plenty of academic protest in America today but few professors are fighting to get out rather than to stay in. Nearly two years ago a regent of the University of California remarked to me: "They said that if we fired Clark Kerr that every 'name' professor at the University of California would resign. Well, we fired him and not even Clark Kerr left."

Little wonder students feel they should be able to behave irresponsibly and without accountability to the institution or the parent society when their intellectual mentors cloak themselves in the medieval robes of tenure and insist on their right to do as they damn well please. If there is one pervasive movement in American life at the present moment it is a movement in the direction of the abolition of all special privilege. Those who believe that the future belongs to groups seeking to enlarge the privileges of either students or faculty misread completely the signs of the times.

As tenure now operates within the academy it only serves to strengthen the forces that help to keep in place the liberal establishment; it only serves to hasten the completed homogenization of thought within the academy. It operates to exclude those who entertain views which diverge from those of the orthodox position, for these neophyte rebels never receive tenure. And once the conformist has received tenure he is absolved from all further institutional and social responsibility. The purposes of academic freedom are not well served by academic liberal court jesters who know quite well the limits of permissible criticism of the prevailing orthodoxy and are careful to keep within those limits. There are even on our otherwise liberal faculties the equivalent of the German 18th century *"Hoff Jude"* the "Court Jew"; a conservative who is here and there tolerated in order to keep up the generally "enlightened" tone of the faculty.

The academy is not an asylum or a refuge. It is a place of daily, hourly contention. The engagements are intellectual, and mastery within the framework of a clearly defined set of rules should be dependent upon superior knowledge and more adequate experience. As faculty we transmit the past, we are critics of the present, and we anticipate and prepare for the future. We are able to perform these functions not because our intuitions are sounder, or morals are better, or our enthusiasms are healthier (though all of these may assist us), but because we have subjected ourselves to the discipline of a science which arms us against the inadequacies of the person and the illiberalities of the passions and their momentary enthusiasms. Ultimately, those rules of enquiry which govern our discipline are the only methods by which the life of reason can be maintained. The only determinative rights which we as faculty

Alienation and Relevance

There is a striking parallel between the crisis in government at the national level in America and the crisis in the universities. In both cases the institutional structure has recently increased gigantically in size and in the scale of operation. Along with this increase in size has gone a tremendous augmentation of power both real and potential. However, it is a characteristic of this power that it is diffuse and focused only with difficulty: that it is all but impossible to bring this power to bear effectively on the problems of the state and the university. The problems which bedevil both the state and the university are frequently not problems which can be solved by the application of power. Along with the augmentation of size and power has gone a singular inability to match commitments with resources so that the state and the universities in spite of mega-dollar budgets find themselves perennially impoverished. Finally, and most importantly, each finds itself alienated from its constituency. Each has discovered that it is increasingly difficult for it to project an objective which will move men to its single-minded pursuit. It is not that men no longer believe in government and education. Indeed, they believe passionately in both. It is rather that they no longer understand either the purpose or the designs of big government or big education. While the power of both institutions has steadily increased, their authority has declined. Ultimately authority is far more important to education than power, and power without authority in the state soon gives way to tyranny. This parallel between the state and the university is instructive.

What is necessary in order to restore the institutional authority of higher education? How can higher education regain the confidence of those over thirty and command the respect of those under thirty who listen with reluctance and dissent without debate?

It would be false to assume that all our difficulties are institutional in origin, that they arise from the fact that the university has either done too much or done too little. It must be said at the outset, and the fact faced with candor and resolution, that the most important problem which higher education faces today is the growing wave of irrationality and anti-intellectualism which has caught up large numbers of both students and professors. Student and professor activists inside the university and certain ideological groups outside the university no longer believe that truth must be the essential consideration in the academy.

Both the extreme Right and the extreme Left hold the same destructive view. Both Mark Rudd of Columbia and Governor Wallace of Alabama stand in the schoolroom door and, seen from the vantage point of the academy, they both hold the same low view of reasoned discourse. They believe that force ought to be substituted for sweet reason, that power ought to replace persuasion and that only "socially approved" voices and views should be heard. They believe that toleration is a weakness rather than a strength in intellectual enquiry and they are in the deepest sense of the word anti-intellectual. They aim at nothing less than the destruction of the life of reason. The university and the parent society have no alternative to repression. These groups cannot be permitted to disrupt and destroy the institutions they so obviously do not understand. They constitute a small minority and it is possible that had university administrations not been long accustomed by their faculties to bearing fools gladly, these groups would already have disappeared from the campus scene. Their disappearance, however, will not restore the authority of the university.

If the institutional aspirations of education are once more to become credible, universities must regain a sense of modesty and a selectivity in the formulation of their objectives. They cannot be all things to all men. The notion of the multiversity is rejected with justice by students and by perceptive faculty. They reject it not simply because it is impossible to administer but because it is an institution without goals. It does not know its own mind. The able administrator in the setting of the multiversity is not a man characterized by unusual educational vision but someone whose social acoustical equipment is highly refined and who acutely senses all the many needs of his society. He is committed to servicing those needs and adjusting and compromising among these many conflicting interests. Little wonder that in such circumstances the teacher feels he is an unwanted encumbrance and the student senses that he is a forgotten man. To compound the problem now by expecting the university to become a court of last resort for the solution of the major social problems of our time will only deepen the crisis which the university faces.

Until there is a restoration of genuine educational purpose there will be no restoration of confidence by society in its institutions of higher education. Higher education has as its chief goals the education of young men and women in such a way as to make them capable participants in our complicated technological civilization, sophisticated and creative members of our common culture, and active and concerned citizens.

In order to ensure circumstances in which teaching rather than research or community service is the primary objective of the university, government at all levels must forgo the temptation of easy recourse to the enormous resources of the university. Recently there has been a great deal of debate concerning the use of the talent and facilities available in the university for defense research. It is not inconsistent to argue that under very exceptional circumstances the university ought freely to use its talent in the defense of society, and still maintain that both the government and the university would be better served under most circumstances were both basic and applied research in the national defense area done in autonomous research institutes. The same case can be made against the use of the facilities of the university for the solution of social problems.

Much of the debate concerning university research at the present time misses the point. War research is no more illicit or licit than peace research. The only sound test is whether or not research enhances or diminishes the primary teaching function of the university. And it must be confessed that in spite of the brave talk to the contrary and considerable administrative legerdemain, research has become the tail that in many instances wags the dog. Faculty members on fractional appointments who spend the greater part of their time in other than teaching activities distort and confuse the educational purpose of the university. Foundation grants for centers and programs which are often inconsistent with the needs and basic educational directions of the institution are as dangerous to the university as government, civic and business research for which there is no clear-cut teaching mandate.

"Where there is no vision the people perish," is an observation which is as true of institutions as it is of nations. In education, however, our pressing need is not for a single and unitary vision but rather for visions as different as possible. Education cannot be genuinely relevant to our society and to its needs unless it is diverse both in objective and technique. The possibility for educational diversity in America is immense; but in reality American education is homogeneous and uniform. The privately endowed colleges do poorly what the state universities do only a little better, and a handful of determinative major universities, as alike as peas in a pod, set the tone and direction for the whole educational enterprise. American education has become a single mechanism; its professors and students interchangeable parts. Under these circumstances, even student riots are monotonously, repellently alike.

Among the most important functions of education are those of widening the options available to men in the solution of their problems and in the improvement of the quality of their lives, yet our universities steadily diminish and dilute the differences between themselves. Students are still able to choose the quality of their educations; they are unable, however, to do much through their own choice about the kind of education they receive. It is important that we re-establish a free market in education. It is important that the church-related school survive, not as a secularized ghost of its former self but as a school with a genuinely religious vision of the world, a school in which men learn to serve God and their fellow men rather than themselves. It is important that private humanistic colleges with their commitment to civilization and decorum and their quiet emphasis on freedom remain an important constituent of our educational system. It is essential that we have genuine experimentation in curriculum and method and not the pseudo-experiments hatched by administrators and departmental chairmen who need an excuse for hitting the foundations or the legislators once again for funds.

We cannot have this diversity, however, until the federal and the state governments drastically alter the role they play in financing higher education. American education will become diverse and relevant to the needs of both the student and the nation when, and only when, the student is forced to pay a very substantial portion of the total cost of his education. Privilege without responsibility is a very dangerous condition; privilege without either responsibility or choice generates unbearable tensions in the society, which makes such privilege possible. State schools which compete unfairly with private schools through discriminatory tuition rates have been the chief force in leveling and homogenizing American education. If we genuinely desire diversity we will do all in our power to encourage students to pay for their education through a tax on future earnings. If we genuinely wish diversity, we will insist that such educational grants as are made by the federal government will be made directly to the student rather than to institutions of higher education.

Only when there is a free market in education, with the student and his parents able to choose from among schools diverse in kind and quality, will we be able to say honestly to students: "We do not pretend to supply the sort of education you wish or need. If you really want a totally unstructured, ungraded course of study, segregated, revolutionary and socially relevant, you can get it at, let us say, Columbia or Brandeis or Rutgers, but you can't get it here.'' The growing sense of alienation among students arises in substantial measure from their inability to choose the quality and kind of education they believe relevant to their lives.

Not only should there be a diversification in the kind of college and university training available, but diversification should bring into existence a wide range of educational alternatives. Apprenticeship programs, proprietary schools, technical institutes operated by industry for the training of specifically needed talents, a strengthening and broadening of the junior and community college programs are all of considerable importance in the problem of making education relevant to the needs of the student and the needs of society. The American public must be disabused of the notion that the AB degree holds some sort of magic. For some time it has not been a mark of status and certainly it is not a guaranteed pass to higher income.

The right of entry into a craft union is often more difficult to achieve than entry into the most exclusive college. It strikes me as odd that the New Left, which has been so concerned with the indiscriminate admission of all minority-group students into our colleges irrespective of their qualifications, has had little or nothing to say of the restrictive practices which deny the right of entry, of many of these same minority groups, into those favored unions which possess monopoly advantages in our economy and society. Someone should say clearly that the way to status and achievement in our society is not through learning Swahili but through learning English. Someone needs to say clearly that the way to affluence does not lie through an AB degree, granted by yesterday's second-rate normal college, but a marketable skill which will secure for its holder and his family the dignity of achievement.

Nearly every professor has in the past several years encountered, in what he thought a rather sober discussion of an academic question, a sudden denunciation by a student member of his audience.

The student does not challenge the professor's method or even question his data but simply rejects his position as immoral, as fascist or racist, or as simply irrelevant. There is no debate or discussion, no attempt to identify the question or purposefully expose the issue. It is assumed that absolute right prevails on one side and that moral obtuseness, Marxian false consciousness or plain wrongdoing characterizes the other side. The issue is not joined; it is not even discussed. Question periods at lectures are not occasions for refining the position of the lecturer but are seen as opportunities to present long, rambling denuciations and counter-lectures. The student usually ends his harangue with a plea for relevance and the lecturer, if he is smart enough, gathers that the young man or young lady (it is sometimes difficult to tell just which it is), is alienated.

Recently the *London Times* reported an international meeting of philosophers in Vienna in the following words: "While their elders and betters solemnly discuss the epistemological significance of the phrases 'Johnny has lost his pen. I have found a pen. I know Johnny lost it,' the students are racing through the corridors, shouting 'What about the Soviet invasion [of Czechoslovakia],' burning Russian and American flags, and wrestling with their professors for microphones during debates.

"It is disgusting, say the students, that three thousand of the wisest men from every country of the world should have gathered together in the largest philosophical talk-in in history and have nothing forceful to say about the Russian tanks on the Czech border less than fifty miles away. If philosophy has any real function is should be performing it now."

Clearly, what the student seeks is a relevant orthodoxy rather than an agonizing enquiry. Faced with some of the toughest choices in history, and living in a period when traditional certainties and traditional values have been challenged and opposed by alternatives, the student is really calling upon his professor for a clear and definitive answer and one preferably couched in a currently fashionable vocabulary and bearing the marks of current social concerns. To the student, education is irrelevant if it cannot provide a solution; preferably, of course, a solution which costs the

147

student nothing and whose weight is borne by the non-student sectors of society. The student wants to know what to think rather than how to think.

And the student has far too many professors who are willing to tell him what to think rather than attempt to teach him how to think for himself. The student has learned his lessons only too well. His professors, especially in the humanities and the social sciences, have all too often been exponents of an established orthodoxy rather than masters in the art of reasoned enquiry.

The situation is not to be mended by diversifying orthodoxies. That is the student's solution. He wishes to replace the liberal orthodoxy with a New Left orthodoxy, a WASP orthodoxy with a black orthodoxy, a permissive and tolerant orthodoxy with a repressive orthodoxy. What the student wishes is a substitution of orthodoxies rather than an end to all closed systems. His efforts will only compound the problem, for the liberal ascendancy in today's colleges and universities is like the pre-1918 Austrian Empire—"an autocracy ameliorated by inefficiency"—while the student Maoist dictatorships would end altogether the life of reason.

The professor, if he is to re-establish the authority of reason must not only admit of the possibility of his being wrong but must have the openness of mind necessary to, as Lord Acton said, "make out the best possible case for error." He must actively court diversity and contradiction rather than seek a world of like-minded men. He must continuously engage in a great debate not only with his students and his colleagues but above all with himself, and as President Truman said: "If he can't stand the heat, he should get out of the kitchen."

The ideological and cultural uniformity of higher education in America is a disgrace. Why is it that our colleges and universities have conformed themselves over the past two decades to the orthodoxy of secular liberalism? Why has the atmosphere been so increasingly hostile to open debate? Why does it take the crisis of the exclusion of the Negro from the university to make us see that not only people, but ideas have been excluded by higher education?

The authority and the relevance of the university lie in its ability as an institution to explore systematically and rationally the problems men face. Its success is not dependent upon current fashions in ideas or current solutions to particular problems. Its success derives from its ability to take the long view and ask the hard questions, and the hardest of these is the question the professor asks of himself, of his colleagues and of his society, about the possibility of being wrong.

Faculty Diversity
and University Survival

I need not tell you that the university, and even the whole of higher
education in the Western world, is disturbed by a crisis un-
paralleled in our history. There is the distinct possibility that the
American university, as we have known it, will not survive and will
follow the French, Italian and German universities in what Fritz
Stern has recently characterized as "unspectacular decay." If we
are to place any faith at all in the anonymous article in the
December 1970 number of *Encounter* entitled "Campus Revolt:
California's Balance-Sheet," the process of destruction in California is already well advanced.

No one can accurately gauge the impact of this revolution on our
society but equally no one can doubt that the triumphant, naked
and undisguised anti-intellectualism and anti-rationalism which it
represents is one of the most portentous events of our times. How,
under these circumstances, do I dare address you on any subject so
trivial as the question of a balanced faculty? Why should you concern yourself with the question of "ideological diversity" when
departments, disciplines and the university itself are in danger?

I wish to discuss these subjects because I do not think them to be trivial; indeed, I believe these questions to lie at the root of the present crisis in which we are involved. I hope I am not misunderstood. I do not mean to say that the lack of faculty diversity is the sole cause of the disorders which exist within our institutions of higher education, nor do I wish to imply that by appointing a few professors who style themselves conservatives, believe in limited government, and are non-Keynesian in their economics, that the crisis will be banished and right order will be restored. The restoration of learning, of debate, of integrity and civility will be a much more involved process and will take a much longer time than it takes to make a few found appointments. But I am prepared to assert that unless those appointments are made any other attempts at university reform will either not touch the vital issues or will be in vain.

Why is faculty diversity the keystone to university reform, the *sine qua non* to university survival? Faculty diversity is such a crucial issue, in the first place, because the integrity of learning is at stake. One of the most disturbing graffiti I have ever read was one penned on the wall of a men's room at the University of Michigan. It read quite simply, "The University of Michigan is a big fake." (Fake, I remind you is also a four-letter word.) Now I don't propose to read the mind of the student who wrote that disturbing line, but reading it I agreed that the university was a fake. It was a fake because it pretended to an honest and open exploration of the truth and the human condition, an exploration which I could nowhere find.

In the humanities and the social sciences fashionable orthodoxies had almost everywhere replaced multiplicity of viewpoint and rigor of enquiry. It was not that disturbing questions were raised and then given the quietus of a resounding refutation; no, the questions were never asked at all, the issues were never joined. It was always simply assumed that there were no limits to government intervention, that the rights of the polity always took precedence over the rights of the individual, that the processes of centralization and bureaucratization were natural and inevitable processes, that big business was always rapacious in its conduct and anti-social in nature, that one could not, as one of my colleagues, now emeritus, was fond of saying, "be a good historian unless one was a big D democrat," that the future would inevitably be welfare socialist, that foreign intervention on the side of oppressed classes and races was always desirable, that the achievement of liberal social objectives abroad was always more desirable than the attainment of more limited and restricted notions of national self-interest. The list could be lengthened indefinitely and the focus shifted depending upon the discipline under discussion. But the student, whatever his discipline, was forced to conclude that a wide range of issues were simply not discussable in the university classroom, were indeed "non-questions." Neither the student nor the professor could, under those circumstances, take seriously the university's claim that it was engaged in a free-wheeling, wide-ranging exploration of the truth. And it can be no surprise that no one came to that conclusion. Instead both the student and the professor came to regard the university as a political and cultural power base, which given the dependence of our society on the skills of the mind, lent a decisive advantage to that ideology which established its control over the university. When in the course of the Free Speech Movement at the University of California at Berkeley in 1964 the New Left announced it intended to revolutionize American society by seizing control of the university it intended quite simply to replace one orthodoxy with another. The New Left intended only to replace regnant liberalism as the power brokers within the university. They did not really mean to change the rules of the game. After all, the student Left had been taught by their liberal mentors that power rather than free and open enquiry was the name of the game. Anyone who did not get the message in the 50s and the early 60s that it was a good idea to be a liberal lacked the subtlety of mind required for an AB degree. Only a few years before, Roman Catholics found it all but impossible to be appointed to positions in a leading university. I make this charge deliberately for anti-Catholicism is one of the major undiscussed scandals of our intellectual tradition. We all know the *bon mot* that anti-Catholicism is the anti-Semitism of the liberals. Most of us are blissfully unaware of the way in which this *bon mot* is reflected in the personnel policies of our major universities.

Secondly, the lack of diversity of viewpoint in the humanities and social sciences robs our intellectual and cultural life of the contribution which pluralism has made to our society as a whole. Of course I am not arguing here for a quota system. I find the idea of quotas nearly as repulsive as the homogeneity which characterizes the present system. Nor do I believe that difference or eccentricity of viewpoint ought to take precedence over intellectual excellence. Nonetheless, I think we must be very careful that we do not discover that conservatives, Catholics, and women never meet the standards we set and that as a consequence we condemn our departments of the humanities and social sciences to a comfortable conformity.

Who is to challenge received opinion when all the sources of contradiction and refutation are excluded from the debate? Out of 69 full-time members of the history department at the University of Michigan we do not have a single professor whose primary study has been the field of religion in America. Our economics department does not have a single non-Keynesian among its tenured members; our philosophy department does not have represented any tradition except Anglo-American analytic philosophy; our political science department is almost exclusively left-liberal in its orientation. In such an atmosphere is it really possible for either the student or the professor to arrive at the truth? He has every inducement to ignore the evidence.

It has always seemed odd to me that in a society in which the adversary principle is the very heart of our system of justice, in which the two-party system is an unwritten aspect of our constitutional arrangements, in which the dialectic of ideas is the basic reason for our toleration and our insistence upon the right of free speech, that we should exclude the widest and freest sort of debate by design and oversight from our universities.

What are the consequences of such a system? What have the consequences been for the study of history? Rather than assert my own view of the costs of the present state of historical study I prefer to quote an address made by Harvard's Professor Oscar Handlin to the recent meeting of the American Historical Association in Boston. Handlin's liberal political credentials are gold-plated. Handlin pointed out that the crisis in history is the work of the historians themselves. "Confused by new gadgets, internally divided and distracted by the racket outside, they have allowed their subject to slip into the hands of propagandists, politicians, dramatists, journalists, and social engineers."

But that is only a part of the problem. The charge I make against my colleagues is not that they have deliberately lied, falsified or propagandized, though these are all increasingly a problem, but rather that they have not systematically sought the truth. They have been content to live in the parochial world of contemporary liberalism. They have belonged to a kind of "flat-earth society" for intellectuals. Lord Acton laid on historians the charge to "make out a better case for the other side than they are able to make out for themselves." Acton did not suppose that such a sympathetic effort would lead to the exoneration of murder, injustice and deceit. Not at all, for Acton insisted that the historian end by being a hanging judge. His elementary sense of decency and justice demanded, however, that there be a fair trial. I state categorically that no historical personage, event or movement can get a fair trial at the present time. The contemporary atmosphere of the historical profession is the atmosphere of a Cuban people's court.

Where there are no challenges to error truth soon becomes irrelevant or is abandoned in the name of some "higher" cultural objective or some more important social goal. I do not wish to suggest that a conservative orthodoxy would be any more truthful or any conservative establishment any less self-serving. I doubt even that it would be any better mannered though the standards set by the prevailing orthodoxy these last few years are rather easily challenged. Thomas Jefferson's fear of priests and the influence of established religions was not due to any deep-seated hostility to religion itself. Rather it arose out of his disgust with closed systems and superstitious conformity. Establishments have always and everywhere exhibited the same behavior. It would be sad if after disestablishing religion in America we were to establish a new

155

clerisy with full powers to excommunicate and sanctify. Like medieval bishops they now establish the license to teach, the license to preach and in many cases they determine the right to publish by their *nihil obstat*.

Up to this point I have been speaking as a professor. What do perceptive students think of the situation which exists within the universities? Let me conclude by quoting at length from an article which appeared in the December, 1970 number of *The Yale Alumni Magazine*. The author is Douglas Hallett, editorial page editor of *The Yale Daily News*.

> Nothing would be more repulsive to the true conservative than to argue that the university should impose philosophical quotas on the various departments. He, above all others, realizes that men cannot be changed by authoritarian direction. Still it does seem wrong that there are no followers of Milton Friedman's "Chicago School" in the economics department, no traditionalists in the Yale chaplaincy, and only one aging conservative in the political science department.
>
> It does seem wrong that no history course at Yale admits that the Vietnam war may be not only a product of reactionary anti-Communism, but also a product of post-war liberalism's confidence in its ability to remake nations 11,000 miles away as well as at home.
>
> It does seem wrong that every sociology class begins with the supposition that the racism of our institutions is responsible for our domestic ills, rather than deep-seated personal prejudice which takes time to cure. And it does seem wrong that the academic community is unable to see in the impatient, angry cry of student radicals a mirror of its own arrogance and willingness to impose its solutions on others.
>
> Although America has always been a liberal nation, its liberalism has always been tempered with a rich conservative tradition. In that tradition has always been the genius of the nation's sense of moderation and self-control, its ability to change and adapt without suffering dislocation and social collapse. Today we find the nation rethinking its commitment to liberalism. The failure of Lyndon Johnson's domestic and foreign policies has cast into doubt our powers of reason, our ability to control ourselves, much less other people. . . .
>
> But just as this is happening, just as the nation is seeking new standards by which it can guide itself, American universities have shut out the conservative tradition which many contend is uniquely suited to providing these standards. History is increasingly ignored; culture is made "relevant"; religion is politely mocked. Universities cling to the illusion of their self-mastery even as those who have uncovered the myth seek to destroy them in their hatred. . . .

It is difficult for me to improve on this statement; only you can improve on the situation which it describes.

Education in the 1970s: Consolidation and Reform

The success of American education at all levels ought to be a matter of considerable pride for every American. No society, either in the past or the present, has devoted such a high percentage of its total resources to education. No society has made education so widely available, so free of class and political influences and so dedicated both to the needs of the individual and the requirements of society. Were money and effort alone the key to success the future of American education would be unclouded and its ability to fulfil the expectations of society unquestioned.

However, it is the very successes of American education which have made its failures all the more evident. These failures now not only challenge our complacency but they raise real questions as to the viability of the system. It is a matter for self-congratulation that American education has taken the children of poor immigrants and slaves and turned them into a nation possessing the knowledge and skills which enable us to maintain our position as the freest and most technologically advanced society in the contemporary world. It is a matter which is much less praiseworthy that a recent study made by Louis Harris and Associates for the National Reading

Council found that perhaps as high as 24 percent of our population are, in fact, functional illiterates lacking the "reading ability necessary for survival." A total of 34 percent of the sample studied were unable to complete a Medicaid application. Neither can we congratulate ourselves on the overall quality of education when we come to realize that the same study reports that up to 8 percent of Americans with some college training have serious literacy problems.

These are grave failures but the total record is even more dismal. In the not too distant past our public and private schools were the laboratories of democracy which inculcated and taught by example the civics of the American system. There was a general awareness that participating citizenship required not only a commitment to and knowledge of the American political system but that our system could only function because of the presence of a sustaining ethical system. The great merit of American education was that it went beyond the intellectual formation of the child and inculcated in him those virtues and decencies which are the *sine qua non* of a democratic social order. Today the education of the total child, intellectual and moral, has disappeared or is on the point of disappearing from the public schools. Civic virtues cannot be separated from virtue generally and it is imperative that the schools return to an emphasis upon moral education. Moreover, it is apparent even in the best schools that the education of the child thwarts, alienates and stereotypes when in fact it should result in increased creativity, the humanization and acculturation of the child and his induction into the world of work and socially approved activity. The rebellion so apparent in every school is not simply a manifestation of the age-old distaste of school days and school ways. It is a response to huge and impersonal school plants, poor and heartless teaching, rapid curricula, and an ossified educational bureaucracy which is not responsive either to the needs of the student or the expectations and demands of society.

Contemporary education does not even produce the skills and training needed by our society and it frequently frustrates the individual by its failure to provide him with a realistic assessment of vocational opportunities and training in marketable skills and disciplines. To a surprising degree we are not preparing our children and young adults for a creative, productive and satisfying life. This is so much the case that a recent student of American education characterized it as "the great training robbery."

What ought we to do if we wish to restore health to our educational system and our society?

In the first place, competition must be fostered and increased throughout the educational system. We can no more afford a monopoly in education than we can afford it in newspapers, or automobiles, or any other good upon which our society is dependent. The public school must be forced into competition with private schools and privately-marketed educational services. The fostering of educational competition and educational diversity rather than the reinforcement of educational monopoly must become the object of federal and state educational expenditures. To this end the federal government should allocate support to elementary and secondary education through a voucher system which will enable the parents to choose the school which their child will attend. It should, moreover, foster experimentation with and expenditures for contract education by private "knowledge companies" and it must provide incentive payments to schools and to teachers who demonstrate an above average capacity to motivate and educate the child.

There should be a uniform system of testing of every elementary and secondary school pupil which will clearly establish teacher and school performance. Teachers and school administrators must be made more fully responsible for the frightening failure to provide basic education. Were 34 percent of the finished and marketed products of any American industry radically defective, an aroused society would justly call for investigation of industrial management.

Secondly, we need pluralism in education because the requirements of our society are various and social. Religious and political groups which constitute and strengthen our society through their variety have every right to expect that their special educational conceptions and views be preserved and transmitted to

159

the next generation. Conformity and uniformity are not characteristics which our society as a whole values. They are absolutely destructive in the field of education.

In the third place, we need to make our schools smaller and more responsive to the constituency they serve. Buildings must be small and intimate rather than monumental and factory or prison-like. "School parks" which embrace on one campus children from the elementary school through junior college are educational antheaps. High schools of from 1,000-3,000 pupils are unmanageable factories in which the student is lost and in which discipline is maintained (if, indeed, it is maintained at all), only through a host of petty and stupid regulations. In such a situation teachers and counselors do not know their students and principals do not know their teachers.

The size of school districts must be reduced so that school administrators are responsive to and school boards reflect the needs and wishes of the constituency which they serve. It is odd that the very people who are entrusted with the transmission of democratic values are so little responsive to the communities which, in theory, they serve.

In the fourth place, we must develop a national program of civic and moral education. No one should underestimate the difficulties in designing such a curriculum just as no one can now underestimate the need. The tacit consensus concerning values and motives which existed up to a generation ago in our society and in our schools has collapsed. The assimilationist ideal has disappeared and while few of us would wish to see its restoration nearly every parent is aware that elementary and secondary school education ought to go beyond intellectual formation to the civic and the moral education of the child. Sex and drug education which is conducted outside an ethical context is bound to end in failure and cynicism. The skills and knowledge necessary for material success in our society must not be permitted to take precedence over the inculcation of those virtues necessary for the good life.

No doubt there are dangers implicit in any program of civic education, but the dangers rampant in a society devoid of any commonly held sentiments of virtue and decency are even greater. If the control of curriculum and teaching remains at the local level, if parents are enabled to choose from a variety of competing schools, and if school boards are able to choose among alternative text books, curricula and methods of instruction, there should be no fears of mass indoctrination and ideological manipulation. It is of the utmost importance that the aspirations of our people and the mores which are essential to the functioning of society be communicated to our children.

There must also be a recognition that all good education is vocational education. The purpose of education should be to induct the student into the world of work; it should also enable him, to be sure, to play an intelligent role in the political life of his community and it should assimilate him to the ethical adult world of responsible commitment. Any education which is not vocational in the large and extended sense of that word is bound to end in failure.

But to make such a program meaningful we must provide at the elementary school level guidance and counseling, activities and programs which have as their purpose the early establishment of realistic vocational objectives. Such a program on a national scale should be established and funded by the federal government. Such a program is, at the present moment, one of the most important steps we could take for the general improvement and upgrading of talents in the United States.

So far we have spoken only of the crisis which exists in elementary and secondary education. No one should underestimate, however, the seriousness of the problems which now beset post-secondary education. It is as a result of post-secondary education that the young adult is equipped to enter the world of work and adult commitment.

One of the major reasons that young adults find post-secondary education so unattractive is that they come to it too late. To reach man's estate physically and psychologically and yet to be confined to a world of economic dependency and child-like school work is one of the reasons for the boredom and irresponsibility of many secondary school students. The years the American child spends in elementary and secondary school are far too long, the courses redundant and tiresome and their effects stultifying. We must

161

strengthen and intensify instruction at the elementary level and reduce by two years the customary eight years of elementary school which the average child must attend. Secondary school education can, with a strengthening of content and curriculum, be reduced by one year and the normal school-leaving age be brought into some more healthy congruence with the years of middle adolescence. At fifteen or sixteen the student should be in a position to think concretely about a vocation and should be prepared to seek those kinds of training necessary to achieve his vocational objectives. Those who desire on-the-job training at age sixteen should not find their way barred by anachronistic child-labor legislation.

American education, while it has not failed, has been so unsuccessful in recent times that it is now necessary to call into question many of its basic assumptions and many of its methods of operation. Until we are willing to revamp totally the educational process from the kindergarten through the graduate, professional and technical schools we will not secure the kinds of education we all desire. This calls for a radicalism and openness which has not recently been characteristic of the educational establishment. It also calls for cooperation among all the interested parties: private and public schools, federal, state and local governments and agencies. Ours is a pluralistic society which has benefited enormously from that pluralism. There is and can be no one single solution to this immense problem, but there are ways of bringing the total resources of the community, both private and public, to bear on its solution.

Who Killed the Liberal Arts?

A popular song of several years ago reported that "on a clear day you can see forever." This juxtaposition of the transitory and the eternal, of the temporary and the permanent, is what liberal education is all about but, unfortunately, there are few "clear days" and "forever" seems to be a word which has dropped out of the vocabulary of college professors. There is a fond conceit common among this generation of intellectuals that the permanent things don't really count, a kind of *Realpolitik* of the spirit which insists that not by every word which comes from the mouth of God does man live but rather by bread alone.

One is reminded of that marvelous scene in *Ape and Essence* by Aldous Huxley in which visitors from New Zealand, members of some scientific expedition of the distant future, visit the degraded survivors of atomic warfare living in the area of Los Angeles, California. The culture they find is one which lives by grave robbing. The graveyard they work is the luxurious Forest Lawn cemetery. Their bread is baked in communal ovens whose fires are stoked by books from the Los Angeles Public Library. As an armful of books is consigned to the flames the theocratic high priest triumphantly announces, "In goes *The Phenomenology of the Spirit,* out comes the corn bread." One is tempted to say that these decadent barbarians had at last solved the problem of relevance.

The attack upon the liberal arts is, to put the matter in its bluntest, simplest terms, the attack of those who conceive of education as the analysis of means against those who regard education as the contemplation and evaluation of ends. For those who see education as the analysis of means a loaf of corn bread is always more important, more relevant, than *The Phenomenology of the Spirit.* It is, I believe, only when the end is conjoined to an appropriate means that liberal education is possible. The education of doctors who do not revere life, of engineers who have no anthropology or sociology in the large sense of those words, of professors of poetry whose only skill is their ability to analyze metaphors, of political scientists whose behavioralist preoccupations rule out the whole realm of value, of historians whose obsessive preoccupation with the present make it impossible for them to study man as he has commonly been or to discuss the future as we feel it should be—this education represents the triumph of means over ends; its practitioners are the enemies of the permanent things and they, if anyone, are responsible for the present moribund state of the Liberal Arts.

The question of responsibility, however, remains, "Who killed the liberal arts?" And, what were the reasons which produced the crime? In the March, 1966, issue of *Harper's Magazine,* the distinguished American classicist, poet and translator, William Arrowsmith, published a critique of graduate education entitled "The Shame of the Graduate Schools." Permit me to quote from that article:

> It is my belief that the humanists themselves have betrayed the humanities. Through a mistaken loyalty to a cramped and academic sense of order, the humanists have turned their backs on men and expelled the native turbulence and greatness from their studies. Thus the humanities have been distorted, and their crucial, enabling principle—the principle of personal influence and personal example—has been neglected and betrayed in a long servile imitation of the sciences . . .

That last phrase is the phrase I wish to discuss with you, "the long servile imitation of the sciences" which has been characteristic of the humanities and social sciences during all of the past century and more especially during the past three decades. It is, I believe, this mistaken conception of science and its application in the humanities which is the seat of our difficulties. The practitioners of the liberal arts have, in fact, abandoned what the Greeks called *paideia* and the Romans called *studia humanitatis* for a method of scientific analysis and the employment of their knowledge as a means to environmental control. The quest for relevance is rooted in the Baconian dictum that "knowledge is power" and in the dictum of Marx that "the purpose of philosophy is not to understand the world but to change the world." Knowledge thus becomes not an end but a means; a tool or a weapon with which one meets and conquers the world. Finally, the conception of the humanities as the analysis of means rather than the contemplation and evaluation of ends lies in the growing "professionalism" of academics, the belief that men may make their fortunes in the academy as well as in business or industry. Increasingly academicians find themselves in the position of those Protestant missionaries who were responsible for the Christianization of Hawaii described by Alexander Wolcott as "men who set out to do good and did well."

From what I have said to this point in my argument you may well believe that I am here mounting an attack on the views so well presented by C. P. Snow in his very influential essay of ten years ago, "The Two Cultures and the Scientific Revolution." You will recall that in that essay Snow blames our problems on the fact that we are not scientific enough. He argues that a mastery of the environment through technology will save us all and solve our problems, at least those worthy of consideration and capable of solution. He denies that there is any distinction between science in the Aristotelian sense of an ordered enquiry into things as they are and the conception of science as a technique for mastery and change. And, finally, in a significant chapter called "Intellectuals as Natural Luddites" he says, "If we forget the scientific culture, then the rest of Western intellectuals have never tried, wanted, or been able to understand the industrial revolution, much less accept it. Intellectuals, in particular, literary intellectuals, are natural Luddites.''

If you believe, however, that I conceive of our world as two cultures divided by method and disputing goals, you are wrong. And, in fact, I wish to assert that both Snow the scientist and Snow the novelist are one and the same man and that they are a part of one and the same culture and that culture is dead wrong. The problem confronting humanistic studies is not the problem of retooling and becoming scientific. That is Snow's solution. The solution to the problem demands a much more radical shift than that. I believe that Snow and contemporary science suffers from the same malady as the contemporary literary intellectual: he lives entirely in the world of means and does not know how to confront the world of ends. He has perfected the most sophisticated and highly rational means and these are turned again and again to the service of irrational and subhuman ends. The choice is not, therefore, between science or poetry, between the inward and the individual vision or the outward and social vision but rather it is a choice between a rational world which insists that both our ends and our means be rational and consonant with our dignity as men and a world which is essentially anarchic and meaningless and possesses only such order as we impose on it in the pursuit of some basically irrational end.

Consequently, I am not arguing that we ought to abandon either science or technology. That is both undesirable and impossible. When men have learnd to grow two blades of grass where one has grown before, they never give up the knowledge which makes that possible. We need not less but more and better science. We need not less control of our environment but more complete understanding and control. Those irrationalists of the present moment who have for one reason or another rejected science and technology and wish to return to some tribal utopia before the invention of the wheel are fantacists. They deserve the misery and the degradation to which their choice would confine them.

But having said this, it is well to point out that I am not in agreement with Snow that the only kind of intellection is scientific in

Snow's narrow sense and that the only problems needing solving are those which are responsive to technological manipulation. I believe that the poet is no less a scientist than the physicist and that neither of them is a scientist so long as his only concern is with manipulation rather than the order of being. The problem therefore, is not that of rejecting science and substituting irrational institutionalism. On the contrary, it is the problem of directing science once more to totally rational and humane ends.

Facticity, the substitution of empirical data and a false objectivity for an analysis of purpose, is by common agreement the chief problem of the humanities. Arrowsmith put the problem in the following fashion:

> Worse, modern scholarship seems to have no means of editing itself, of eliminating its own wastes. Having forsworn value judgments, it is reluctant to judge what is valuable and what is waste in its own works. And so committed had it become to the idea that every scrap of information is useful, and that every discussion of a "problem" or crux must at least be known, if not accepted, that it is literally mired in its own speculations. . . . As the waste and detritus of scholarship accumulates, the burden of ever-greater bookishness is imposed upon the latest generation of scholars.

Facts become ends in themselves far divorced from structures of value and the order of being the means serves the purpose of a surrogate or substitute end. You will, of course, have realized that this situation is as true of the so-called natural sciences as it is of the humanities. Positivism is equally pervasive in both areas.

But not only does this misplaced empiricism lead to the destruction of intellectuality, it has the most important consequences for the way in which men behave. Etienne Gilson in a very important but now little-read book, *The Unity of Philosophical Experience*, remarks that:

> So long as, and in so far as, science itself kept faith with its own nature, it remained the healthy exercise of reason, reason seeking to know, because knowing is its natural function. Even the most stupendous progress made by the physical and biological sciences entails no disruption in the continuity of Western culture. While man remained in control of nature, culture could still survive. It was lost from the very moment nature began to control man. . . . Moreover, the constant accumulation of hitherto unknown facts and of their recently formulated laws was destroying the old balance between the human and the physical sciences, to the advantage of the latter. This,

167

however, was not the main point. It lay rather in the fact that before their un-
expected success in finding conclusive explanations of the material world, men
had begun either to despise all disciplines in which such demonstrations could
not be found or to rebuild those disciplines after the pattern of the physical
sciences. As a consequence, metaphysics and ethics had to be either ignored
or, at least, replaced by new positive sciences; in either case, they would be
eliminated.

When this development eventuated, technique was finally
divorced from rational intention. It assumed an autonomous status.
Men began to do things, not because they were humanly desirable
but because they were technically possible. The ought and the
should disappeared from the vocabulary of the scientist, the sociologist and the political theorist. They are replaced by data col-
lected by men wearing the mask of objectivity and caught up in the
cult of relevance. The consequence of this, Gilson remarked,
"is the acceptance of nature such as it is. Far from making up
for the loss of philosophy, the discovery of the scientific substitutes
for it, leaves men alone with nature such as it is and obliges him to
surrender to natural necessity. Philosophy is the only rational
knowledge by which both science and nature can be judged. . . . "
Doing what comes naturally then becomes the only test of the
validity of any action.

For a while, in the course of the 18th century, it seemed that this
scientific, natural ethic might indeed replace the much older
scholastic-Aristotelian conception. That extravagant hope was
short-lived, for a science and ethic based upon empiricism soon dis-
closed that every act was in fact natural. It was the Marquis de Sade
who effectively stripped away the euphoria of natural philosophers
by demonstrating that incest, murder, rape and cannibalism were
indeed natural.

At the level of empirical observation, immediate cause; at the
level of the fact then all experience becomes meaningless and all
life feels what Czelaw Milosz called the "suction of the absurd."
The notion of a value-free science is, moreover, just as absurd as the
notion of a value-free social science, or value-free study of the
humanities. Both rationality and life involve choice, are indeed a
commitment to a belief that being is ordered in a certain way. This
conviction about the order of being cannot exist in substantial con-

tradiction to the empirical evidence but always goes beyond the particulars of the evidence. All valuing, all ordering is a great hypothesis which is tested over and over again and which the particulars of experience either confirm or refute.

It is, however, precisely this ordering and valuing process which has been rejected by contemporary intellectuality. Either the intellectual or the artist rejects all order and value and asserts that the cosmos is essentially meaningless, experience chaotic and life anarchic and accidental, or he assumes that such meaning as exists, exists not in the nature of experiential reality but is an arbitrary meaning imposed upon recalcitrant and anarchic events.

If either of these two closely related conceptions be true, then it follows that our response to existence must be an irrational one. If no meaning exists, or if such meaning as exists is an arbitrary one as various and as subjective as the egos which impose it, there can be ultimately no social agreement. All knowledge must under such circumstances become socially irrelevant or relevant only to a particular ego at a particular moment. Social decision-making then becomes a test of wills rather than a test of minds.

Under such circumstances we can understand how facticity on the one hand and irrationality on the other become the dominant traditions in our intellectual and artistic culture. It is of course true that contemporary literary intellectuals have become Luddities, as C. P. Snow asserted. They are indeed irrationalists and are singularly dangerous men. They are dangerous because as poets they are "the unacknowledged legislators of the age" binding and loosing men with more power than that of a medieval pope. The worldview of Dostoyevsky or D. H. Lawrence is not a very satisfactory world view; the world of Gide and Thomas Mann is positively sick and ugly. The world view of Norman Mailer and Allen Ginsberg is corruptly revolting. In all of this I find myself in substantial agreement with C. P. Snow. The liberal arts cannot be revived by committing ourselves to a blind and irrational faith or a despairing passion. We cannot reintroduce meaning and vitality into the academy by a leap into faith, by some blind existential commitment.

But neither is the facticity of science enough. A positivistic science of immediate causes which will not raise questions of purpose and value is not one which contains any promise of reuniting the two cultures or of restoring vitality to either. It is true of course that such a science can yield power; power over men and power over the environment. However, it is a power without purpose and is both irrational and dangerous. There surely is nothing more contradictory than the employment of rational means in the pursuit of irrational ends and yet that is the commonplace and everyday experience of our lives. The process of rational analysis becomes in this system of partial and incomplete rationality a method of manipulation and exploitation in which reality is regarded not as an order to be contemplated, not as a reality to be loved or enjoyed, but rather the object of an act of aggression. For such science the act of knowing is an act of aggression. Snow's science, indeed most contemporary science, is deeply Faustian.

Of course most of the positivism and facticity which disports itself in academe is not so grand and terrible as all that. Most of the pseudo-science which is eating into the vitals of the liberal arts is not so terrible as the demonic quest for power on the part of Faust. No indeed, the academic sorcerer's apprentices in the liberal arts are rather pathetic figures, dry-as-dusts and second-raters in the style of Faust's apprentice, Wagner; graduate student types whose chief concern is to find a safe berth in a good place and never to raise another question which is worth answering or incite a student to anything except the dull acceptance of the current liberal orthodoxies and hypocrisies. Counting is easier than thinking; bibliography is easier still and it all has the merit of being scientific and objective. These "scholars" are the academic Mr. Joy Boys, who, like one of the protagonists of Evelyn Waugh's *The Loved One,* put the smiles on the dead disciplines of the liberal arts after they have come from the merciful hands of the embalmers.

The reply then to my question, "Who Killed the Liberal Arts?," is relatively simple. They were killed by intellectuals who rejected the order implicit in experiential reality, who rejected the processes of valuing and ordering which are an essential part of our experience of reality and who have substituted partial orders or arbitrary meanings in their place. They were killed by those who refuse to raise large questions, who disdain rational debate, who substitute facts or will for meaning and purpose.

I am not altogether pessimistic about the future, however. Students are asking questions which no amount of evasion and fancy footwork can dodge. And they are not questions about fact but questions of values and purpose. Our students are insisting that we, in fact, become professors of the liberal arts. Permit me to conclude by citing Etienne Gilson's essay on *The Unity of Philosophical Experience* (1937) once more.

> . . . For what is now called philosophy is either collective mental slavery or scepticism. There are still men who hate both, and will not lament the passing of that alternative. . . . Against the crude, yet fundamentally sound craving of Marxism for positive and dogmatic truth, the scepticism of our decadent philosophy has not a chance. It deserves to be destroyed. . . . Not something less rational, or less constructive, but something more rational and more comprehensively constructive is required to meet its challenge. The time of the "as ifs" is over: what we now need is a "This is so," and we shall not find it, unless we recover both our lost confidence in the rational validity of metaphysics and our long-forgotten knowledge of its object. Therefore, let the dead bury their dead, and let us turn ourselves towards the future, for it will be what we shall make it; either an aimlessly drifting wreck, or a ship holding a steady course with a rational animal at the wheel.

Authority, Power and University

Men have always been puzzled by both power and authority. The source of either is mysterious and the uses of either unclear. They are quite commonly confused so that men and institutions which attempt to convert authority into power discover that spiritual realities cannot be defined in terms of Newtonian mechanics and those who seek to translate power into authority learn that no human undertaking is so difficult as the legitimation of coercion.

In recent times no one has said of either a university president or an educational institute as St. Matthew said of Jesus, "For he taught them as one having authority, and not as the scribes." John Searl, former vice-chancellor for student affairs of the University of California at Berkeley, has remarked that "the unreality of the New Left is its most touching quality." Only the New Left could seriously propose that the university campus was a great power center whose capture by the New Left would enable it to revolutionize the parent society. The fact is clear and unmistakable that in 1971 the university possessed neither authority nor power. It is equally clear that it can have no power in our society until it regains its authority and that the power which it will then be able to exert will have no relationship to the power which Chairman Mao asserts grows out of the barrel of a gun.

It is clear then that the authority which the university possesses is a social authority freely given by the whole of society, just as the support and financing of the university is, in the final analysis, social. The university cannot, consequently, exercise its authority or sustain itself if it loses sight of the wholeness of society and places its resources at the command of a financial or cultural elite or permits itself to be exploited and victimized by a deviant minority group bent upon aggrandizement and tyranny. As soon as it becomes apparent in any society that those things which in some sense are the property of all are in the possession and use of the few, no matter how fine their morals and how noble their characters, the society denounces its allegiance and withdraws its support. Moreover the very exercise of proctorship by the self-selected elite in such a situation is vastly corrupting and personally corrosive. Those who, above all others, should persuade through reasoned discourse are tempted to apologize, to lie and to coerce.

The university does not belong to the students; it does not belong to the faculty; it does not belong to any special pressure group in the society that happens to feel the call to revolution or a prophetic mission. The university belongs to the whole of the society or the corporate reality which brought it into existence and which sustains it. Every administrator who capitulates before a "non-negotiable demand" sacrifices the authority of his institution to the power of a minority. However, not only does he "de-authorize" the institution, making it impossible for the college or university to educate, but he cuts off his institution from the support and the goodwill of the society as a whole.

The destructive influences of minority groups of students and social activists in corrupting the educational ideals and processes of the colleges and universities is well known. Less well known, but no less destructive, is the fashion in which certain schools of thought occupy all the positions available within departments and even whole disciplines. In the fields of the humanities and social sciences there is hardly a proposition which goes beyond the restatement of primitive folk-truth which is not the subject of widespread and informed debate, which in every instance calls into question the very basis in reality of the opposed parties' vision of the truth. In the social sciences and the humanities there is no Truth but only partial truths, while in the natural sciences Sir Karl Popper has taught us to mistrust the generalization which does not suggest a maximum of experiments aimed at its destruction. How odd then that whole disciplines have fallen under the sway of unprovable hypotheses and undemonstrated theorems.

In these great matters which concern man and his society the humanist and the social scientist carry over into their science the overt and even unconscious commitments of their daily lives. The point from which one starts does make a difference. Religious commitment or a lack of it does make a difference in philosophy; a specific political commitment does make a difference in the theory of the political scientist; a particular view of man's nature does make a difference in the work of the critic and the vision of a poet.

In the fall of 1969 the Carnegie Commission on Higher Education took a survey sample of 60,447 faculty members in American universities. These faculty members were asked to characterize themselves politically "at the present time." In the discipline of sociology, for example, 80.8 percent of the professors surveyed identified themselves as liberals or leftists. One-tenth of 1 percent identified themselves as strongly conservative. How, one is compelled to ask, is debate on fundamental social issues possible when there is such overwhelming uniformity of political and theoretical social commitment? Sociology is not an anomaly. Most of the social sciences and the humanities show a distribution not remarkably different.

In many colleges and universities the field of the study of religion is totally excluded. Universities with professors whose specialty is the religion of Tibet do not have a single professor who specializes in Judaism or Christianity. It may be true that religion is one of the most pervasive and fundamental of man's activities, but this fact is simply unrecognized by many colleges and universities. The

175

fashionable agnosticism and atheism of most faculty members ought to concern college administrators. That those whose vocation is the exploration, understanding, transmission and criticism of ideas in a society should be alienated from and hostile to its formative influence should be a matter of anxiety. It is customary, of course, to argue that such questions are inconsequential to the discovery of truth and effective education and yet we would be justified in expressing concern were a scientist to assert that he was convinced that nature was chaotic and that there was no possibility, even in terms of probability, of anticipating regularity.

The community at large distrusts university faculties because they are so homogenous in terms of religion, race and sex. For the first time Negroes are finding on faculties an acknowledgment that the experience of being Negro does make a difference in the way one perceives the subject matter of the social science and the humanities. To be black, for example, ought to sensitize one in a special way to the economic costs of prejudice and the social costs of lawlessness. To be black ought to sensitize one in a special way to the promise of American institutions and ought to instill in one an intense dedication to the success of American ideals. I anticipate that in the long run the impact of Negro scholarship and Negro perceptions on the intellectual life of the university cannot constitute anything but an enrichment. That enrichment cannot, however, take place if the Negro scholar withdraws into his own course and segregates himself from the conflict of ideas and the noise of debate which should characterize every university campus.

What the Negro is on the point of achieving is still denied both to women and to Roman Catholics. To be sure, there is token representation of both groups on most faculties, especially those of state universities, but neither group has been permitted to make its full contribution to the life and scholarship of contemporary society. We are all acquainted with the role which 19th century liberalism played in dispelling the clouds of prejudice which surrounded both women and Catholics, but we need now to reassert those principles with respect to university teaching.

The university cannot and ought not to speak with one voice on any subject. Professors and students ought not to involve their institutions in the controversies of the society. Those compulsive newspaper advertisements in which intellectuals proclaim their support of the current orthodoxies and to which they are careful always to append their institutional identification remind one of nothing so much as the patent medicine recommendations which once filled working-class and farm weeklies. Medical faculties ought not to speak on the subject of harvesting grapes, micro-biologists on the subject of Soviet-American relations, sociologists on the subject of theology. It is a sobering truth that most contem-porary intellectuals cannot distinguish an opinion from a fact. They are convinced that thinking makes it so and they employ the Ph.D. in the way in which southern sheriffs of a decade age were said to have employed electrical cattle prods. How pleasant it would be to hear even one professor say when pressed by a television inter-viewer in the course of a discussion of a controversial topic, "I don't know." I cannot recall a single instance of that sort.

The public authority of the university is dependent upon its com-mitment to research and education rather than a general willingness to perform any task anyone or any group in society at large imposes on it. The university is not a general-purpose social institution. It is not suited to the solution of social problems, the amelioration of misery and misfortune, the reformation of character, or the transformation of culture. To be sure, the universi-ty produces skills and knowledge which will achieve all these ends, but it does not and cannot directly perform any of them. When a university gets into the building of low-rent housing, and that not even for students, as is the case at Stanford, the university is quite simply disloyal to its primary commitment. Some students at the University of Michigan are now demanding that the university provide "free" health care to all the children of the community in which the university is located. It could do so only by neglecting its fundamental commitment. The university is not engaged in the cure of souls; it is not engaged in organizing for political and social revolution; it is not in the business of providing necessary social or health services. Sometimes specific services are a byproduct of the teaching and research function of the university, but they are never to be thought of as a part of its mission.

In his Godkin Lectures at Harvard in 1963, one year before the advent of the Free Speech Movement at Berkeley, Clark Kerr noted that "the university is so many things to so many different people, that it must, of necessity, be partially at war with itself." But not only is it at war with itself, it is at war with important segments of its society. The demands which it seeks to meet are not reconcilable and the conflicting roles which it seeks to play are not compatible. There cannot be a restoration of the authority of the university until the university returns to its primary role as teacher. To be sure, the maintenance and criticism of the cultural tradition, the development and preservation of method and research in the pursuit of new knowledge are all important ancillary activities, but they are ancillary and must always be subordinated to the teaching function.

Research institutes and research professors whose essential commitment falls outside the realm of teaching should not be associated with the university. Both are terribly important in our society, but both bring pressures to bear on the structure of university education which will, in the not so very long run, destroy it.

It is quite possible that the state universities, due to a tradition which goes all the way back to the Northwest Ordinance and which found its most typical expression in the Morrill Act, will find it impossible to break the ties to service and research which the state thrusts upon them. If that indeed is the case we have been provided with yet another argument for taking the state out of the business of educating altogether.

Even were the university to eschew all the tasks and beguilements thrust upon it by society and decide to live in uncorrupted innocence and poverty, it is unlikely that it would regain its authority so long as it refuses to exercise such authority as it still possesses. So long as university administrations are not the masters in their own house they are ill-equipped to exert any degree of mastery in the world outside. At the present time the typical university president is the amoeba-like victim of every aggressive group on campus. Their powers of ingestion and cooperation have been enormous and such success as they have had in keeping the universities functioning, even at a minimal level, has followed from the fact that they have, to date, been able to meet virtually every demand, no matter how outrageous, with a concession. They have not been educational statesmen—not even educational bureaucrats—rather, they have been technicians of adjustment.

In many instances the current style of university administrators has succumbed to violence and power because, anti-intellectual by nature, they distrusted the play of mind, the open debate and the laborious process by which ideas are examined and tested. A number of them such as Clark Kerr and Robben Fleming derived their previous experience in the field of labor arbitration where the essential problems are dealt with by adroitly balancing power rather then by protecting the consumer. Clark Kerr described this new-style multiversity president aptly when he wrote: "The president in the multiversity is leader, educator, initiator, wielder of power; he is also office-holder, caretaker, inheritor, consensus seeker, persuader, bottleneck. But he is mostly a mediator."

Any university president who at the present moment determines to make his institution unique in mission, curriculum, instructional method, student body or educational philosophy will discover very quickly that his great enemy is not the alumni, or the board of trustees, or even the student body but his own faculty.

There are, to be sure, areas of college and university education in which the faculty is sovereign. They are not, however, those areas of sovereignty usually marked out by faculties. Very obviously, the faculty member either singly or as the member of a corporate body determines educational standards, has control over course content and conduct in the classroom, and is the final authority in matters of grades and certification. The faculty cannot and should not even attempt to legislate in matters of curriculum, conduct, budget, or institutional administration. Faculty meetings are neither political nor legislative bodies. In their present form they resemble nothing so much as a Polish parliament. At their best they should be consultative bodies in which the educational needs of the institution are discussed and in which administrative policy is implemented.

Only the administration together with the trustees can effectively set goals and determine policy. Trustees represent the whole corporate body of the institution. They constitute both its social and temporal dimension. They keep the institution true to itself and

179

responsive to the society which it serves. Ultimately all decisions in the institution are political decisions and the governing board is the only truly political body within the institution. It does in fact possess a constituency and exercises a legitimate power.

Although the governing board is the source of power, it exercises its authority through the administration, and its policies, in the final analysis, are formulated by the administration. The administration consults with the faculty and formulates and carries out the will of the governing body.

It is obvious that the relationship between the administration and the governing board must be one of trust and confidence, but while it is a truism it must also be added that the confidence and trust which governing boards exhibit is not infrequently abused. After all, trustees and regents are active, busy men badgered and harassed by a multitude of demands. They have a short attention span, an even shorter memory, and they are ill-informed and for the most part ill-prepared to govern the institutions which they guide. I believe it is necessary, given the current condition of higher education, to provide governing boards with a secretary independent of the administration. The secretary to the governing board will be charged not with policy formation or day-to-day administration but rather with an investigative role. His task would entail the examination of administrative proposals, budgets and appointments. He would provide the necessary extramural expertise which alone can insure that the decisions of the administration fall into line with the policy of the governing board.

Since 1964 it has frequently been assumed that students should have a special role in university governance. Disciplinary matters have frequently been placed in the hands of student governments and increasingly students have been given a role in the distinctive province of the faculty. Today at major universities students determine course offerings, decide on questions of accreditation and examination, pass on questions of academic discipline, and now seek to pass on appointments, salary increases and tenure. A number of the elite colleges and universities have recently appointed student members to their governing bodies. Many of these concessions to the youth culture and the cult of relevance have been made in the genuine desire to make the university responsive to student needs. Where those needs are educational, students are remarkably ill-prepared to judge or to pass on policy.

The point of effective student control over his education is the moment when he chooses a college or university. His choice, of course, is never irrevocable and he can always vote, as students have often voted, with his feet. Student governance beyond this point is unthinkable and no self-respecting faculty member who is concerned for the integrity of his discipline and his right to teach will prostrate himself and his discipline before a student tyranny. It has, of course, been observed that student activists and the contemporary administrators are natural allies. Both love committee meetings, both place power above principle and both are deeply anti-intellectual.

The whole question of student discipline in matters both of academic and personal conduct is much disputed at the present time. Most of the elite universities and colleges have gone over to the notion that any conduct short of a felony is permissible on the part of either faculty or students and if a court of law disciplines a student, further and other institutional discipline would represent double jeopardy and would be unfair, illegal and inadmissable.

But at the same time the student claims an exemption from institutional standards he claims an exemption from the laws and commonly held standards of his society. Administrators and students alike seem to envision the campus as an extraterritorial enclave where the rules of civility and the laws of the polity do not prevail. For nearly a decade members of the so-called youth culture have been advising the young not to trust anyone over thirty, though the one abiding impression left with the public is that the young believe, or at least believed until recently, that no matter how outrageous their behavior the society at large would make excuses and would temper the wind to the shorn lambs. The idea that local police forces should be excluded from the campus, that felonies involving drug abuse and other campus criminal activities should not be punished in the courts, that violence should not be tolerated as a form of legitimate protest and that once a student has been arrested the legal resources of the institution should be made available to him, all presuppose a separate and extralegal status for students which no sane society can countenance. If universities and colleges are to renew and maintain their status and authority in American life, that citizenry at large will need some assurance that there is, in fact, equal justice under the law and not preferential treatment for the college offender.

Every reform and every movement to return the colleges to their essential function will fail unless it is accompanied by a systematic reform of the funding of higher education. The call for full-cost tuition is the single most important reform which it is possible to make in the field of education generally. It is especially important in higher education because nothing has so corrupted college and university education as what Robert Nesbit has called "the higher capitalism." The "higher capitalism" means that colleges and universities have sold out to foundations, government and every group requesting research or service and capable of paying for it. The lure of money has been used for three decades to divert institutions of higher education from their instructional mission. Professors are aware that the rewards lie in areas outside the classroom and students know that professors no longer take teaching seriously.

Taxes, gifts, foundation grants, federal subsidies on a lavish scale and contract research cannot pay the educational bill and if we are to reintroduce order in the house of intellect we must pass the costs of higher education to the only person who can and should pay the bill: the student.

When the student foots the bill many of the present distortions in higher education will disappear. There will, in the first place, be some honesty in cost accounting and undergradate tuitions will not be used as they currently are at many major universities to subsidize an inordinately expensive program of graduate studies. Expensive innovations in instruction will show up immediately in increased tuition costs and the research professor whose chief function is to lend intellectual distinction to his institution through his publication record will be a thing of the past. Professors will once more teach three three-hour courses per semester and students will find that professors are responsive to their needs. It may seem odd that enabling students to pay full-cost tuitions is a more likely way to give students an effective voice in their educations than placing them on governing boards.

Curriculum and instruction will once more be both responsive and relevant, and it will provide the wide variety of training necessary both to the individual and the society. It is absurd to believe that once the source of income has shifted from government and the foundations to the student the "vice presidents for development" and the legislative coordinators will not soon find themselves seeing students and their parents. Moreover students forced to pay full-cost tuition even though repayment of the debt is spread over a lifetime of earnings, will calculate the relative advantages of alternative educational programs with some increased care. It is quite possible that there will be a shift away from the current pattern of the AB degree to increasing vocationalism and professionalism. The emphasis will once more be on marketable skills and the development of talent rather than the acquisition of status.

There are a number of programs in the planning stage and several at the level of implementation which will enable students to borrow a substantial portion or all of their college tuition and repay it through an income tax or social security payroll-type deduction system. A number of these programs go beyond the field of college and university training and open up the field of government-guaranteed loans to students who wish to pursue any field of study for which they are qualified. These programs are of intense interest for those Americans concerned with educational reform because they will increase educational diversity and because they will make both the educational institution and the student responsible.

Redefining Liberal Education

It is often assumed that liberal education should be broad, permissive and unprejudiced. I believe this assumption to be what I have described as an intellectual superstition. I suggest that liberal education ought to be integral, committed and biased.

I have used the word biased deliberately as the opposite of what I call the cult of suspended judgment. That cult argues that before acting, before taking a position, before accepting a theory we must wait patiently until all the evidence is in. It argues that religious faith must be forsworn, that love must either be denied or sentimentalized, that ethical commitment must be suspended and that the affirmation of intellectual certainty must be postponed until the weight of evidence becomes so crushing that we cannot conceive of alternative action. That is called keeping an open mind.

Of course, neither life nor education waits until all the evidence is in. Judgments must be made on the basis of partial evidence and action must be taken when knowledge is incomplete. St. Paul wrote, you will recall, "What we see now is like the dim image in a mirror; then we shall see face to face. What I know now is only partial; then it will be complete, as complete as God's knowledge of me." (1 Corinth., 12-13).

We must begin our education as we begin all other things with an act of faith. Without a reasoned faith which takes into account all the imperfect evidence we shall be thrown back on passion and sentimentality, on the senseless reflexes of unbelief and on action based upon conformity to the popular mood of the moment. We may suspend belief but we cannot suspend action.

William James, in his essay, *The Will to Believe*, asks "Are there not somewhere forced options in our speculative questions, and can we (as men who may be interested at least as much in positively gaining truth as in merely escaping dupery) always wait with impunity till the coercive evidence shall have arrived? It seems *a priori* improbable that the truth should be so nicely adjusted to our needs and powers as that. In the great boarding-house of nature, the cakes and the butter and the syrup seldom come out so even and leave the plates so clean. Indeed, we should view them with scientific suspicion if they did."

Then James goes on to argue something very important to the whole question of education. He says, "There are, then, cases where a fact cannot come at all unless a preliminary faith exists in its coming. *And where faith in a fact can help create the fact,* that would be an insane logic which would say that faith running ahead of scientific evidence is the 'lowest kind of immorality' into which a thinking being can fall. Yet such is the logic by which our scientific absolutists pretend to regulate our lives!"

Now, of course, William James did not mean that thinking or wishing will make anything so. He did mean that without an Archimedian point of faith no man is able to get a prize on the heavy lump of reality. In science and in morals there must be a primary assumption about the orderliness of things before we can go on to any more precise knowledge of reality. In politics there must be some basic belief that man is one thing and not another and that he finds fulfillment only in certain social modes before we can discuss intelligently those things which constitute a proper political order. In aesthetics there must be some essential apprehension of the beautiful in its general and non-particular sense before

186

we are capable of either the creative or the critical aesthetic experience.

These assumptions, this bias, these acts of faith are not, however, simply a human protest against the absurd, a trick that all life has learned and which has given it a temporary evolutionary advantage. The assumption we make that the basic reality of the universe is orderly, is good, is beautiful, is so inherently a part of our very existence that to deny it is to dehumanize ourselves.

Liberal education begins with the assumption of order and goodness and beauty. Indeed there can be no meaningful exploration of "the pursuits and activities proper to mankind" unless such assumptions are made. Nor is it my purpose to deny that there is disorder, sin and ugliness in the world. They are the all too common experience of mankind. The contemporary habit of dealing only with the depraved, the misshapen, the vile, the sick and the anarchic leaves off the examination of the evidence at the very point where it has the possibility of meaning.

There is some puzzle as to why this should be the case but nonetheless as Edmund Fuller has observed in *Man in Modern Fiction,* "It is our weakness that when we discover bad in good we are much more apt to generalize sweepingly about it than when we discover good in bad. It is easier to hate than to love, easier to reject than accept." Then Fuller goes on to say, "Truly to understand a man who is sick you must understand a man who is well. I believe that the loss of the understanding of the full nature of man is itself a major source of sickness."

Education is today everywhere dominated by a positivistic philosophy which refuses to raise those embarrassing questions which would result in a discussion of values. But behind this retreat from ultimate concerns and questions of value lies the refusal to make an act of faith which accords with such evidence as we now possess. Behind the flight from value lies the cult of suspended judgment.

Edmund Fuller, (I recommend his book, *Man in Modern Fiction* very highly) puts the problem very aptly when he says, "What some writers have lost is not an external framework of values, not just this or that set of value concepts. They have lost the basic vision

187

of their own kind. They not only do not know *who* they are, which is problem enough; they also do not know *what* they are—and this is the ultimate tragedy: for man not to know the nature of man. . . ."

The function of education is not only the discovery and study of the pursuits and activities proper to mankind; it is the integration of those pursuits and activities into one harmonious whole. Education must be integral if it is to be successful. Our partial truths cry out for completeness, our experiences need the conformation and affirmation which derives from the experiences of others. Truth is always catholic, error always sectarian and subjectivistic. Consequently, community is always an essential context for the discovery and the communication of truth.

Because this is the case, we must, if we take the question of liberal education seriously, see that our colleges and universities are genuine communities and not simply congeries of buildings, students and professors. They must be communities which provide an easy and comfortable atmosphere where students and professors not only are able to, but do, talk together, debate and enjoy one another. Such community will be impossible unless the students and faculty share some common value and dedicate themselves to the pursuit of some common good. Aristotle begins his *Politics* by saying that "every community is established with a view to some good; for mankind," Aristotle tells us, "always act in order to obtain that which they think good." Now, the individual goods of learning alone are never enough to sustain community and unless the institution and its members give themselves to some larger common purpose community will fail. It is never enough for colleges to point to their success in preparing students for graduate school or for a particular vocation. The purpose of community must go beyond these narrow and particular limits. One of the most important difficulties in higher education is the pervasive loss of institutional identity and goals. What exactly does the college community think good? What do students believe to be worth pursuing, now and hereafter?

Moreover, the college community can never pursue the goals of liberal education effectively unless and until there is genuine

188

debate and difference represented in the faculty and student body. We discern truth, as a general rule, and we elaborate its aspects through a dialectical process. Those who close off debate, who limit the views represented or discussed, whatever their motives, do a grave disservice to the educational process. One thing only is necessary and that is that honesty and integrity be evidenced by all the participants. If ideology, passion, self-interest, or animus of any kind displaces the honest pursuit of truth then debate will become little more than a facade for indoctrination. That is why it is so extraordinarily difficult to talk intelligently with members of either the extreme Left or extreme Right.

Community and diversity, then, are both important elements in the achievement of an integral education. There is, however, a still more important way in which integration ought to take place in the course of a liberal education. That integration goes beyond the identification of one commanding subject matter which then reigns as the queen of the sciences. That was Newman's dream when he sought to elevate theology to that commanding position as focal point of all the lesser disciplines. Before theology that position had been occupied by the classics, and in the late 19th century, Newman's dream having proved a failure, the study of history became the great integrative force in liberal education. It seems to me clear that integration at the level of subject matter always proves itself to be inadequate.

There are, however, at the deepest levels of our human experience, integrative forces at work which liberal education ought to uncover and encourage. Integration can never be achieved at the purely mechanical level but must reflect the way, in fact, things really are. What do I mean by this statement?

Plato, writing in the dialogue Charmides, lets Socrates state the problem in the following fashion:

> Here, then, I said my own dream: Whether coming through the horn or the ivory gate, I cannot tell. The dream is this: Let us suppose that wisdom is such as we are now defining, and that she has absolute sway over us; then each action will be done according to the arts and sciences, and no one professing to be a pilot when he is not, or any physician or general, or anyone else pretending to know matters of which he is ignorant, will deceive or elude us; our health will be improved; our safety at sea, and also in battle, will be assured;

189

our coats and shoes, and all other instruments and implements will be skillfully made, because the workmen will be good and true. Aye, and if you please, you may suppose that prophecy, which is the knowledge of the future, will be under the control of wisdom, and that she will deter deceivers and set up the true prophets in their place as the revealers of the future. Now I quite agree that mankind, thus provided, would live and act according to knowledge, for wisdom would watch and prevent ignorance from intruding on us. But whether by acting according to knowledge we shall act well and be happy, my dear Critias,—this is a point which we have not yet been able to determine.

Suppose Socrates is saying we have all the technical powers the cultivation of the individual disciplines can give us; will these, even if they include the science of futurology, add up to human happiness? Must they not be related to one another and harmonized to some other kinds of knowledge to provide the key to happiness, order in the human soul, and harmony, both interior and exterior?

Having stated the problem in Platonic terms let us go on to develop the problem within a context of Platonic ideas. It would be possible to explore the problem outside such a context but one of the most valuable aspects of the classics is that they have provided us with a widely understood vocabulary. To use the Platonic formulation, the science of sciences is "the science of human advantage," the "science of the good." "The good" here is not to be understood as a particular good but rather as the fulfillment of our human natures; the total realization of our human capacities. The achievement of this good, as Socrates argued, was a process of integration, of harmonization of aspects of knowledge and potencies within the personality so that the ultimate purposes of human existence are realized.

Let us be more specific. For Plato truth in a scientific sense, goodness in its ethical aspect, and beauty as aesthetic function, are all interdependent aspects of a higher and more inclusive good. Let us consider the consequences which follow from the breakup of the unity of the true, the good and the beautiful. It is of course altogether proper that science be divorced in some of its aspects from ethics. The study of all things begins with a consideration of the thing in and for itself, but it must proceed, if it is to be understood in its ultimate aspect to its relationship to the ordered cosmos. When the link between particular truth and ethical consequence is broken, for example, the result is always menacing and destructive. Reason alone, untempered by love and unsanctified by beauty, is a terrible thing. The world is filled with the partial logic of science, with the inhumanity of systems. Nor is beauty alone enough. We live in a time when beauty has been divorced from the good; when the ethical dimension of art has been abandoned and the truth which art should represent is despised. Beauty alone as a formal aesthetic is either a sterile pastime or the seedbed of monstrosity. Even the ethically good, the principle of justice when it is devoid of truth and beauty, slips over into fanaticism and sentimentality. Once the connecting links are broken which bind together the aptitudes of the soul, the possibility of harmony in the life of the individual and in the life of the society must be abandoned. We need integral educations because we need whole men and we need whole men not simply for the sake of society but because individual men can fulfill themselves only through wholeness.

Any discussion of fulfillment brings with it, as a necessary aspect of fulfillment, the role of pleasure. Perhaps liberal education ought to concern itself more with the relationship of pleasure to the good and harmonious life. Certainly there is a major problem in the way in which contemporary man has dealt with all the aspects of pleasure. Had some genius followed Bentham's argument and devised a calculus of pleasure there is no doubt that he would discover that by 1972 a fantastic inflation in pleasure had taken place, but as is the case with all inflations more and more buys less and less. Moreover he would note, (though it would be difficult for a Benthamite to make such an admission) that base pleasures have quite generally driven noble pleasures out of circulation. And he might, because there is a relationship between pleasure and happiness, inquire how it happens that increasing pleasure has not brought with it increasing happiness.

Pleasure is the compliment nature pays to right action and although the views of nature are nearly always short run and although nature is frequently deceived, nonetheless pleasure in all its aspects always points beyond the temporal to the joy of transcendent harmony. How then has it happened that we modern men and especially we Christians have permitted pleasure to fall to such low estate, have abandoned it to the voluptuary and the barbarian and have held it to be unworthy of the best and noblest? Why do we say, with contempt, that he or she is a "pleasure-seeker" when pleasure-seeking forms such an important part of all human behavior? Does, indeed, liberal education have anything to do with what I would like to call the rehabilitation or the redemption of pleasure?

Lionel Trilling, a decade ago, wrote an important and intensely interesting essay which he called "The Fate of Pleasure: Wordsworth to Dostoyevsky." In his essay Trilling comments at length on the rebellion against the pleasant which takes place in 19th century literature. By the end of the century, while pleasure had not disappeared from art and literature completely it had been largely displaced by the ugly, the sick and the monstrous. By the 70s of our own century matters have worsened and the decline of pleasure is now quite complete. Artists and intellectuals have increasingly turned from the themes of harmony, well-being, and sense-satisfaction. No doubt they were in part in honest rebellion against a dishonest and sentimental art which permitted men to take a pleasure or have an emotion for which they had not actually paid the price. For this they must be praised.

But there were other and more important sources for the rebellion. One of them was the feeling that pleasure was unworthy of that which was highest and best in man. Pleasure is a consequence of our creaturely natures. It is a part of our physiology and an aspect of that subtle mingling of chemistry and spirit, of necessity and freedom which is human nature. However, by the end of the 19th century Western intellectuals were in rebellion against creatureliness, in rebellion against the conditions imposed on humanity by their nature. There is a universal desire on the part of Western intellectuals to become as gods and they perceived the most important aspect of God to be an absolute and unconditioned freedom. The quest for absolute freedom is the key to the rejection of pleasure or the perversion of pleasure in such a way that nature is forced to pay her compliment of joy to an action which thwarts nature's purpose.

Trilling puts the position of modern men well when he writes " . . . To know and feel and live and move at the behest of the principle of pleasure—this, for [Dostoyevsky's] Underground Man, so far from constituting his native and naked dignity, constitutes his humiliation in bondage. It makes him, he believes, a mechanic thing, the puppet of whoever or whatever can offer him the means of pleasure. If pleasure is indeed the principle of his being, he is as known as the sum of 2 and 2; he is a mere object of reason, of that rationality of the Revolution which is established upon the primacy of the principle of pleasure."

In spite of the rebellion of the intellectuals the quest for pleasure is a fact of our humanity. We will have pleasure; if we do not find it in the natural fulfillment of our humanity we will seek it in the chemical and unnatural. If we are cut off from those noble joys we will seek our satisfactions in the base and the degraded. Our natures will not let us give an absolute "no" to our desires.

Note something very interesting. By the end of the 19th century, intellectuals had turned away from pleasure or had inverted pleasure in such a way as to cheat nature, to shortchange necessity. That of course did not mean that pleasure disappeared. Indeed, what happened is that the intellectuals had abandoned pleasure to the lowest and most unschooled in the society. Pleasure ceased to be ennobled and uplifted by art and grace; ceased to point unmistakably beyond itself to the transcendent harmony, and sank down to the lowest common denominator. It became a commodity and was commercialized. It was brutalized and barbarized, and beauty and harmony were expunged from its forms.

Liberal education can and must begin the rehabilitation of pleasure. It may be that the problem of pleasure is the most important in contemporary society. How can liberal education achieve this rehabilitation, this redemption of pleasure? It can go a long way toward reestablishing an adequate definition of what it means to be human. It can help us to establish the dimensions of our creatureliness and the futility of rebellion against our natures. It can warn us against the demands commonly made for an absolute and unconditioned freedom and it can help us to discover how those natures are best satisfied. It can, in short, help us to understand the preconditions of joy and pleasure and the consequences of their perversion.

The arts themselves, however inadequately and partially they are reflected in our individual disciplines, provide us with models of those noble joys that always arise in order perfected and harmony attained. We have all been, now, a season in hell. Let us join Dante where at the end of the Inferno he and Vergil, the very figure of the liberal arts, return to an earth where right order rather than hell's inverted order reigns.

> By that hidden way
> My guide and I did enter, to return
> To the fair world: and heedless of repose
> We climb'd, he first, I following his steps,
> Till on our view the beautiful lights of
>   heaven
> Dawn'd through a circular opening in
>   the cave:
> Thence issuing we again beheld the stars.

The Student Revolt—
Who Has Failed?

September is a bittersweet month. All of us can recall that mixture of melancholy and anticipation with which we walked down a dusty country road barefoot, the silky dust pushing up between our toes, thinking of the end of summer and the beginning of school. "Pleasant summer over" and now the anticipation and the excitement of another school year in prospect. There was excitement and a curious pleasure in putting aside the keen sweetness of summer and going back to school. Today that prospect is one which has been clouded and troubled from elementary through graduate school by disorders so grave that they threaten not only the structure of American education but even the continued existence of an orderly and democratic society. "Pleasant summer over" and no joy in the anticipation of the winter of our discontent.

It is apparent to everyone that the conditions which now prevail in our universities, colleges and schools have very nearly led those institutions to the point of no return and our society itself threatens to sacrifice its liberality in its need for order. It behooves us to analyze the causes of the present situation, not exclusively with the object of fixing responsibility but rather with the intention of recreating a functioning educational system and restoring decorum and liberality in our public institutions.

It was comforting to believe the Presidential Commission on Campus Disorders could present the public with a blueprint for the restoration of reason and stability. One cannot, however, escape the suspicion that the presidential commission discovered only those tired clichés of liberal rhetoric and those broad lies and patent self-deceptions which have become the commonplaces of liberal intellectuality. This exercise of the commission would be an amusing one were it not for the fact that its object was to deceive the American people and to sow division, hatred and distrust among the generations, the classes, the races and the parties. That such a body could have been constituted by a presidential mandate is one of the mysteries which defies explanation in this enlightened age. Whatever the shortcomings of the late and much lamented Johnson administration, it was at least clever enough to recognize its own enemies. That does not require a very sophisticated intelligence but even so it is an intelligence which seems to be lacking in the current administration.

Let us begin to answer our question, then, by saying who is not to blame. The Vietnam war, whatever its other impact on our society, is not to blame for the condition of the campuses. The German and the Japanese universities are in similar turmoil and Germany and Japan are at peace. The candid and thoughtful rhetoric of the Vice President is not responsible. The demonstrations and rioting which accompanied the Democratic Convention and the destruction of the University of California at Berkeley preceded the arrival of Mr. Agnew on the national scene. Nor can anyone seriously suggest that racial antagonism in our society is the cause. Universities in Western European states, states which are essentially racially homogeneous, are rent with disorder. And so one might extend the list through all the commonly propagated explanations of student violence. The candid observer is forced to the conclusion that these so-called explanations are no explanations at all but constitute, rather, rationalizations and apologies for violence. When the belief is widespread that, as President Fleming of the University of

Michigan recently stated, order in the universities can be restored only by ending the Vietnam war, ending poverty and reconciling the races, one can only assume that considerable numbers of influential people are more anxious to achieve their political and social goals than they are to restore order.

Before discussing the causes of violence in the schools, a major contributing factor in the American situation must be discussed. That factor is one which is frequently passed over in silence when an analysis of institutional disintegration is made. Recently a very well-informed university administrator said to me in conversation, "Drugs are destroying the universities." Drugs threaten now to become a national catastrophe for they are on the point of achieving a radicalization of the population that could not possibly have been achieved by the slogans which pass for ideology on the left. This radicalization bridges the gulf between the otherwise separated and warring groups within the society. It bridges the gulf between the races and the classes, the gulf between the generations and the straight and deviant worlds. It enlists all those who fall within the ambit of the drug culture in a common attack upon the structures of civilized and orderly life. What I am saying is not the paranoid dream of a right-wing fanatic but the announced and widely discussed policy of a half-dozen New Left revolutionary groups. Moreover, their techniques are increasingly successful.

What do drugs inject into the already complicated campus, high school and junior high school situation? They deepen the sense of illusion and paranoia, despair and utopianism which are already deeply entrenched on the campus. The drug world is one of subjective fantasy—that is the one element all types of dope-induced thought have in common. It is a world in which the paranoid utterances of the New Left take on the color of reality: a world in which utopia seems easily within reach. But in spite of these fantasies, drugs increase the sense of frustration and passivity which is such a marked characteristic of current campus radicalism. It is a frustration and passivity which is unable and unprepared to achieve its objectives through the expert manipulation of reality, and bursts forth blindly and outrageously in acts of spastic violence. Moreover,

197

the effect of narcotics is to induce a regression and atavism in the personality of the drug-user which increases both his childlike dependence and his uncontrolled and childish behavior.

Usually, drug-use alienates, as does all deviant behavior, the user from the world of accepted standards, norms and institutions. The drug-user is at war with his society for he stands condemned so long as normality exists in any identifiable sense. The most crucial attack upon authority today is made by the drug culture and it is no exaggeration to assert that drug-use is the most important problem America faces at the present moment.

For the drug-user the ruin and degradation of his personality, either incipient or actual, is projected outward on the world. He lives in a ruined society in which evil has become such a monstrous reality that only a social or economic devil theory will explain it and only the most insane and irrational cult will assuage the guilt his behavior has generated. The campus world is filled with flop-house messiahs vomiting out the agony of their degradation in a vain attempt to ease a guilty conscience.

However, drugs are not really a cause but, rather, a symptom of the terrible disorder which has struck our schools and our society. What is the source of the disorder and who is responsible? It is fashionable for members of the New Left and liberal media commentators to describe the student leftists as anti-establishment. In fact they are the sons and daughters of the liberal establishment, the pink-diaper generation. They have raised the implicit nihilism and incipient revolution of their liberal elders to the level of serious action. Whereas their elders have flirted with demonic power, their children openly acknowledge that power grows out of the barrel of a gun. While their elders courted revolutionary causes from afar, their children make the slogans and the bombs which are intended to transform society. While the elders were only intellectual snobs and liberal bigots, the children have grown to manhood in the consciousness of being a revolutionary elite. Their elders dabbled in philosophical uncertainty, fashionable bohemianism and a repressed anti-Americanism. The children openly boast that they are without morals, without belief, and hostile to every noble and decent sentiment which attaches itself to American institutions. The slander, the canard and the intrigue of the liberal parents murdered reputations; their children are willing to murder the body as well as the spirit of their enemies. Far from being anti-establishment, they *are* the establishment and that accounts for the treacle-like gobs of sympathy and compassion for them and their activities which oozes from administrators, media-masters and politicians. Compared to them President Nixon and Vice President Agnew represent the true anti-establishment.

As befits an establishment the student revolutionaries are the children of the wellborn, the well-educated and the wealthy. They may wear bib overalls and parade the rags and tatters which are ordinarily the badges of poverty but they are the products of affluent urban America and are the contemporary remittance men of upper class American society. Far from there being a generation gap separating these members of the New Left from their parents, there is the closest identity. Bruno Bettleheim writes, "There are reasons why it is mainly the children of leftist parents who become hippies or student revolutionaries in American society. The emotional content of student revolt may always be the same, yet its political content depends largely on the belief of the parents. In many ways it is a desperate wish to do better than the parent, especially where the parent seemed weak in his beliefs. This makes it just as desperate a wish for parental approval. But most of all it is a desperate wish that the parent should have been strong in the convictions that motivate his actions."

But if they are the heirs-apparent of disorder and destruction, they learn their slogans in our institutions of higher education. The universities are the centers in which these pathetic and violent minds are formed, the institutions in which the half-baked instruct the half-educated. At the university their education does not consist of a mastery of the methods of discerning analysis and discriminating judgment. They are not taught to reason and evaluate, but rather they are taught both to despair of reason and to place faith in the current slogans of social transformation and political revolution.

Richard E. Hyland, a Harvard student writing in the *Harvard Crimson*, last year observed: "I have learned only two things in my four years at Harvard. The first is that an equally intelligent, rational and valid argument can be made on all sides of any question from any and all premises. The second is that those arguments have no relationship to anything but themselves." Mr. Hyland then proceeded on the basis of these premises to go on to a defense of irrationality and terrorism. His perceptions are, however, correct and telling. One of the gravest failures of higher education is its abandonment of any final or ultimate accountability and the widespread assumption in academic circles that truth is only a convenient fiction which gives its inventor some temporary advantage. That there is an order in things and a truth about them, that human society is based on order and that the values of a humane existence involve moral accountability; these rather ordinary notions which are the commonplace experiences of the unsophisticated masses are nearly altogether absent from the academy. Educated in an atmosphere of metaphysical chaos and moral relativism, the student finds it difficult to think rationally and behave morally. When the ends and purposes of knowledge are no longer rational it is only a question of time until the rational methodology of education itself is abandoned.

It is this abandonment of rationality which is one of the most characteristic features of the student revolution. Persuasion through reasoned discourse has been set aside and mobs led and inspired by professors have taken its place. This coupled with a pliant, permissive and conniving administration, totally without principles, educational vision, or even the cunning which would enable survival on their part, pave the way to campus and social anarchy.

Irrationality is, of course, not the only factor which makes the campus the breeding ground of disorder. It is a fact that over a decade ago the universities became the strongholds of the left-liberal intelligentsia. The departments of the social sciences and the humanities are uniformly characterized by their monolithic conformity to left-liberal political and social views. Even liberal Republicans somewhat to the left of Nelson Rockefeller and William Scranton are as rare as the whooping crane. Far from debate being fostered and cherished, it is penalized and deviant social and economic views are ruthlessly ostracized. Having successfully excluded debate from the university the liberal intelligentsia now seeks to exclude it from the society as a whole, sometimes by preventing the open discussion of issues, sometimes by slander and calumny, and increasingly by suppression and open violence. I am not describing for you the actions of Austrian paperhangers, Bavarian chicken farmers and Rhineland champagne salesmen but rather the actions of professors who describe themselves as liberals and now avow a toleration, an openness and a dedication to reasoned debate, which they daily belie in their actions.

But even these factors cannot account wholly for the wave of student unrest and violence. The idea of the university as a power center from which intellectuals exert their influence and punish their enemies has been one long developing in American life. This conception of the role of the intellectual as the prophet politician, the technician of power and the source of the ideas which would transform the world and create a totally just and utopian society, has been one of the most characteristic features of that period of American life which reaches from the turn of the century (1900) to the present time and which I call "the age of interventionism." The characteristic feature of that age was the alliance forged between the practical politicians, the revolutionary intelligentsia and the elitist planners. The elitist intelligentsia provided the rationale for the centralization of power in Washington and to a lesser extent in the state capitals. It was a process wholly beneficial to venal and power-hungry politicians who have sought to enlarge at every turn the scope of community control exercised by government. This power was used to intervene decisively at every level in the life of the citizen. The unproclaimed slogan of the politicians and the intelligentsia throughout this period was "meddle, meddle, meddle"! And since it was insufficient for the scope of their talents that the citizenry of the United States alone be subjected to their capricious theorization, they embarked the United States on a series of interventionist wars abroad with the intention of transforming the world and ushering in a millennialist socialist utopia. The great thrust of our history and institutions, which had insisted that every man ought to be able to do his thing without let or hindrance so long as it did not impinge on the liberty of others, and that the role of government was positive only in the sense that it created opportunities for the initiative and inventiveness of individuals—this set of traditional American values was denigrated, legislated out of existence and destroyed by a program which sought to turn America into a statist planned society and to transform the world on the model established by the American intellectual.

Thank God that era is coming to an end. The terminal stage in the life of the alliance between the left-liberal intellectuals and the politicians is at hand. It is breaking down because the apologists for intervening power can no longer make a convincing case for their social engineering. Look at the record. After 75 years of interventionism we have a diseased polity, a social order threatened with disintegration, educational institutions at every level which cannot and do not teach, indeed which cannot even maintain order in the classroom, vast welfare programs which both impoverish the recipient of governmental largess and increase millions of indigent, a leviathan bureaucracy which is unresponsive and contemptuous of the needs of the constituency it serves, controls, restraints, penalties and restrictions everywhere for the innovative, inventive, creative, and even for the ordinary citizen who would like occasionally to choose the conditions under which he and his family live. But even this is not the saddest part of our story. We have been engaged in a series of wars and foreign operations which supposedly will bring the American way to the peoples of the earth, on a selective basis of course. It is intervention which has broken down at least in part because of the sheer megalomania of the planners who have proposed it and propagandized for it.

No one is more conscious of the end of the era of interventionism than the liberal intelligentsia itself. The politics of confrontation, the language of violence and obscenity, the employment of terror, are all manifestations of the frustrations which have accompanied their increasing impotence and their inability to persuade either by rational argument or by lies. Their view of American hopes is the view of the jaundiced eye. Increasingly they see themselves as excluded from the future which more realistic and capable men are bringing into existence. They are the petty losers who now wish to take their bats and go home. They have no vision of the future, and the past on which they like to dwell is a mythical and fictionalized version of American history which consists exclusively of slavery, capitalistic exploitation, depressions, McCarthyism and something called "repression." It is in this idyllic past of grinding poverty and heroic left-liberal revolutionaries that the decadent intelligentsia prefer to dwell. This accounts for their antiquated political rhetoric, the social ideas which derive from the 1840s, their contempt for science and technology, their posturing in the passé attitudes of the 1917 Russian revolution, the "poor boy" clothing they affect, the beards. Those who belong, or aspire to belong, to this alliance of power-hungry professors and power-hungry politicians would of course like to live in the past when their great and heroic deeds enjoyed the patina of success and when their power stood at its apogee.

Their sense of impotence and frustration accounts, too, for their preoccupation with death and decadence. The so-called literature of the moment ground out by establishment hacks is, as you know, a catalogue of sickness, social disorder, deviance, disease and death. The very group that once proclaimed the creation of a bright new future as its distinctive mission has now become the self-appointed undertaker of our civilization.

There are many technical aspects of current campus life which have made important contributions to the failure of higher education. Questions of size, teaching and research, the absolute autonomy of student newspapers and publications are indeed important, but secondary. What happens in these areas of campus life is symptom rather than cause.

I do not wish to conclude on a despairing note. It is evident, I believe, that the violence and disorder which we see in higher education is the outward manifestation of the collapse of an establishment. The alliance of professors and politicians has finally begun to break down. It is breaking down because the vision of American life which they projected was not congruent with the needs and hopes of ordinary Americans. The professors and politicians together simply could not make the system work.

203

I believe that we are returning to an earlier ideal of what America should be. It is an ideal of engagement and involvement, but non-interventionist both on the domestic scene and in foreign relations. We shall come increasingly to decide issues in terms of individual interest in domestic affairs and the vital interests of America in world affairs. We are turning away from an ethic of involvement based on ideological and open-ended commitments abroad and at home. We are finding variety, diversity, free choice and the individual solution of problems not only the only attractive solutions, but more importantly, the only workable solutions. America until recently prided itself on a variety of lifestyles, of options and choices, but we have also insisted that the price of experimentation and difference is often failure and that those who fail ought to be permitted to drive home the point of their failure. There can be no lessons in either society or history if the state as "lady bountiful" constantly intervenes to disguise the consequences of failure. I believe that after the present moment of testing a new America will emerge. It will be truly revolutionary for it will transform the world by its example rather than through intervention and compulsion. Let those who belong to yesterday gradually filter into the prisons and skid-rows of tomorrow. I choose to rehabilitate the American dream.

III. Christian Education

The Idea of A Catholic University

In 1852 when Cardinal Newman wrote his introduction to *The Idea of a University Defined and Illustrated* he discerned only a practical role for the Church in the matter of university education. He wrote then: "The view taken of a university in these discourses is the following:—that it is a place of *teaching* universal *knowledge*. This implies that its object is, on the one hand, intellectual, not moral; and on the other, that it is the diffusion and extension of knowledge rather than the advancement. . . .Such is a university in its *essence*, and independently of its relation to the Church. But, practically speaking, it cannot fulfill its object duly, such as I have described it, without the Church's assistance; or to use the theological term, the Church is necessary for its integrity. Not that its main characters are changed by this incorporation; it still has the office of intellectual education; but the Church steadies it in the performance of that office."

Newman's vision of the role and purpose of the university is still as profound and perceptive as it was more than a century ago. I am convinced that if the universities survive into the 21st century it will be because they turn away from the model of the multiversity and return to the vision held by Newman. The university must return teaching to the center of its concerns and it must be in the broadest sense of the word religious in its orientation even though religion or theology is the support rather than the purpose of university training. Intellectuality in the Aristotelian and Thomistic sense, the life of the mind is the purpose of university education. It is not the inculcation of piety, the formation of virtuous character, the teaching of wisdom or the inspiration of charity. Piety, virtue, wisdom and charity are indispensable to the good life, now and hereafter, but they are the affections of the spirit rather than the achievements of the mind.

Nor is the university a center for social reform and political revolution, a vehicle for the achievement of social justice, a place where the races are leveled up and the minorities recognized and rewarded for their contributions to the commonwealth. It is not a place of social adjustment or of group or personal therapy. The urban crisis will not find a solution on its campus nor will the conflict of the classes nor the hostilities and angers of warring groups in our society find healing and reconciliation in its ivied halls. No doubt the skills, the social and philosophical inventiveness, which have always accompanied intellectual excellence and are so bright an aspect of university life today will make their indirect contribution to the solution of these problems which our society confronts. Providing those solutions is not, however, the direct business of the educational endeavor and in asserting this I believe that I am at one with Newman's conception of the university.

So far I have spoken of the university in general, secular and religious, Protestant and Catholic. Does the Catholic university in the 20th century have a distinctive educational mission? Is it qualified in some special way to deal with the intellectual, the philosophical questions of our age? Does it have a mission to our own times which it uniquely is capable of carrying out, or does it simply do poorly what the secular universities and the state universities do so much better? To put it bluntly, do Catholic intellectuals and teachers have a contribution to make to the life of the mind which can not be effectively made by any other group in our society?

Christopher Jencks and David Riesman in their exhaustive study of American higher education, *The Academic Revolution,* ask the same question, and although Jencks and Riesman display no confidence in its affirmative answer by Catholic higher education the point they make is worth quoting in full. Here is what they say:

> ... The important question, however, is not whether a few Catholic universities prove capable of competing with Harvard or Berkeley on the latter's terms, but whether Catholicism can provide an ideology or personnel for developing alternatives to the Harvard-Berkeley model of excellence. Our guess is that the ablest Catholic educators will feel obliged to put most of their energies into proving that Catholics can beat non-Catholics at the latter's game. But having proved this, a few may be able to do something more. There is as yet no American Catholic university that manages to fuse academic professionalism with concern for questions of ultimate social and moral importance, but there are Catholic colleges like Immaculate Heart that suggest the possibilities. If Catholicism is to make a distinctive contribution to the over-all academic system, it will have to achieve such a synthesis at the graduate level. It was there that the Protestant colleges failed, and it was that failure that made the Protestant counterparts of Immaculate Heart useful but largely irrelevant to the over-all system. Unless a few Catholic universities can do better, they too will be engulfed by academic professionalism.

If this, indeed, is the case, what ought Catholic higher education to be doing and what are the intellectual issues it should be exploring?

The first thing Catholic higher education must do is recognize that it is Catholic, that is Catholic spelled with a capital and not a small "c". There are, of course, many advantages to Catholicism in America accruing from the fact that Catholicism is not the established religion of the American polity, but self-confidence and self-esteem are not among these advantages. The consequences of living in a culturally and religiously alien land should not be underestimated. In the case of Catholicism the pressures to conformity and the rewards for assimilation have been nearly as great and nearly as disastrous as they have been for American Judaism. Our Catholicism threatens to become more American than Catholic and we are in danger of accepting all the amiable and trivial badges of

209

WASP uprightness and uptightness that chiefly characterize American society.

Father Andrew Greeley of the University of Chicago's Center for the Study of American Pluralism put the matter facetiously but accurately recently in discussing the young Irish priests. Here is what he said:

> The young Irish clergy are trying their best to act like Methodists and in the process have finally yielded to the WASPs on those twin bugaboos of 19th-century Protestantism: the parochial school and clerical celebacy. And a mystic could hardly be ordained a Catholic priest in the United States today. He would do very poorly on his group-adjustment scores. When he ought to be in his T-group, he would very likely be in Church praying or out on the bogs dreaming. What in the world would American Catholicism do with a priest that dreams and prays? Of what relevance are saints?

If, then, there is to be such a thing as Catholic intellectuality we are going to have to discover some intellectuals who are unabashedly unself-consciously, decidedly Catholic. To echo a 19th century poet, "Let us be ourselves a little." I am not calling for a hasty retreat to the comforts and the isolation of the Catholic ghetto. Far from it, I am urging that Catholics wear their distinctive Catholicism into the everyday WASP world, into the humdrum secularity of ordinary life, not simply for their own sakes, (they cannot be good Catholics without doing so), but for the sake of that everyday world. We must remember that the Constitutions of Vatican II are not a license to assimilate ourselves to the world but rather a command to assimilate the world to the faith which we hold from the apostles.

Now assuming that we are Catholics, what are the marks of our distinctive intellectuality? What contributions to American higher education can Catholics uniquely make? I believe that there is a range of Catholic concerns which are not simply fascinating but irrelevant religious oddities and intellectual eccentricities but which go to the very root of the travail and agony of the contemporary human condition. Thomas F. O'Dea in his book, *American Catholic Dilemma*, stresses the fact that Catholic thought has emphasized ontology rather than history. There is an element of truth in the assertion if one does not carry it too far. This stress on ontology, however, is not a weakness but a source of great strength.

The basic questions of our time are not, as is so often assumed, the "relevant" questions of poverty, war, urbanization, medical care and the thousands of institutional arrangements by which men live. They are, on the contrary, those age-old intellectual and spiritual questions of meaning, order and value. Without meaning in some ultimate sense every path, every road, every highway is a lonely trail to oblivion. Without values happiness is even more senseless than grief, and beauty becomes as frightening as our encounter with pain and ugliness and evil.

It is a fact, moreover, that meaning, order and value are the perennial humanistic concerns of university education. They have only recently been displaced by "value-free science" and positivistic analysis. If the confusion and anguish of our times means anything, it means that mankind is crying out for purpose, is asking those hard questions which secularistic intellectuality has for so long neglected and despised.

Sir Isaiah Berlin in his essay on "Political Ideas in the Twentieth Century" explores this problem at length:

> The central point which I wish to make is this: during all the centuries of recorded history the course of intellectual endeavour, the purpose of education, the substance of controversies about the truth or value of ideas, presupposed the existence of certain crucial questions, the answers to which were of paramount importance. How valid, it was asked, were the various claims to provide the best methods of arriving at knowledge and truth by such great and famous disciplines as metaphysics, ethics, theology and the sciences of nature and man. . . . There were, of course, sceptics in every generation who suggested that there were, perhaps, no final answers. . . . It was left to the twentieth century to do something more drastic than this. For the first time it was now conceived that the most effective way of dealing with questions, particularly those recurrent issues which had perplexed and often tormented the original and honest minds in every generation, was not by employing the tools of reason, still less those of the more mysterious capacities of "insight" and "intuition," but by obliterating the questions themselves. . . . It consists in so treating the questioner that problems which appeared at once overwhelmingly important and utterly insoluble vanish from the questioner's consciousness like evil dreams and trouble him no more . . .

It is precisely in asking those questions anew that Catholics can surpass Harvard and Berkeley and all the state universities taken together. Let me be specific.

I believe that Catholicism has a vision of the wholeness of man which is essential to the humanities, the social sciences and the arts. No doubt great literature is, as Thomas Hardy said, written to the sound of breaking commandments. But breaking commandments alone does not make great literature. Too much of the human experience is left out. If we ought, as Lord Acton cautioned the historian, always to look for the cloven hoof we ought too to look in every man for the divine image. A comprehension of body and soul, the ideal and the real, of nature and grace, of necessity and freedom, of joy and sorrow, of creatureliness and divinity, of all the contradictory and complimentary elements which we as men find in our natures is essential not only to literature but to any meaningful experience. Literature, the representational and the performing arts cannot be restored until we have restored our vision of the wholeness of man. Where are the Catholic critics, the Catholic artists, the great Catholic performers and builders who ought to be creating and renewing the image, the habitation and the expression of the whole man? Let us leave off taking our cues from the despairing and decadent culture of our times and with the aid of the Holy Spirit proceed to make all things new. We cannot, however, achieve harmony, dignity, clarity and beauty in the realm of imaginative literature, in music or in the representational arts until we discern once more the wholeness of man.

Not only do Catholics have a special perception of the wholeness of man, they have a feeling for the integrity, indivisibility and universality of the human community. That common humanity, however, does not reflect itself in a uniform expression. It is various, unique and bound by time and culture to particular and peculiar historical expressions. Let me be more concrete. We American Catholics are an immigrant church. Ethnicity has been the richest and most vitalizing element in the American Catholic experience. If anyone knows about minorities, ethnicity and the dreams and hopes out of which the American reality was and is constructed, it should be ourselves. Franciscans and Jesuits named this landscape for the saints; the English first and then the Irish and the Germans for many years gave us our priests and bishops. All the ways of being human Europe's culture could count helped to people this land with Catholics, and yet what have we made of this vast heritage? We have neglected it; we have apologized for it; we have concealed it where possible and we have secretly despised it as representing something less than American, less than successful as defined by the dominant non-Catholic majority. Where is the American Catholic university where Catholic ethnicity is intensively explored? Have we helped the Poles of Detroit to an awareness of the proud cultural heritage of which they are a part? Have we really appreciated the gifts and the limitations which the Irish immigrants brought with them? Have our Catholic universities assisted our Spanish and Mexican-American Catholics in the realization and full expression of their ethnic and cultural heritage? It is, of course, quite right that the churches in the Southwest should so often be built in the best Spanish colonial architectural style, but how much more laudable it would be had Catholic universities developed a systematic program for the exploration and preservation of Spanish-American culture.

It is right and proper that as Catholics we should be concerned with the fate and culture of the American Negro, even though most Negroes are not Catholic. It is even more proper and pressing that we not forget or neglect all those others who have the very special merit of being of the household of the faith. Where are the Irish, the German, the Polish studies and the special programs of ethnic and cultural identification which would give the great silent majority definition and cultural integrity? Too often these days they are justified in complaining that the Church, their Church, has forgotten them and their needs and aspirations while it has sought to accomplish the popular and the politically expedient.

Let us devise university programs and centers which will discover for ourselves the full meaning to our citizenship and to our Catholicity of the ethnic experience. However, in order to set such a program of ethnic studies in motion we must turn away from propaganda and self-seeking to a dispassionate and intelligent study of our past. We as Catholics are ready for that now and it is high time that Catholic universities took up the task.

Catholics have been no less concerned with the dignity of man and a reverence for his existence than they have been with his wholeness and his ethnic and racial differences. Catholic medical science, Catholic psychiatry and clinical psychology and Catholic pedagogy and social work ought to be different simply because Catholics believe that technical solutions should always be consonant with the dignity and integrity of the human beings they serve. A course in medical ethics is not enough to preserve a dignity which is on every hand threatened by an amoral science and a humanity which is degraded by every manipulative technique conceivable. It is only through the articulation of a vision of man which does not subject mankind to the application of every technical possibility that we can rescue humanity from beastliness, brutality and degradation. The ultimate irony of our age lies in the willingness of men who think of themselves as unselfish and their motives as good to employ means which brutalize and degrade in the pursuit of the ideal. Such behavior is possible only because natural science and technology have been divorced from the realm of ultimate value and the analysis of ends. We will be able to discover and employ suitable and fitting technical means and social solutions to the problems of man and his culture only when we have achieved clarity as to man's nature and his legitimate purposes.

Implicit in the problem of the rational and ethical employment of power, as it expresses itself in the use of the environment and the manipulation of human experience, is the way in which we conceive of the act of knowing. Catholic epistemology has insisted on the integrity and independence of the object. It has said that the act of knowing must always be an act of love rather than an act of aggression, that all knowing must imitate the divine paradigm. Science, conceived in these terms, begins in respect for the object just as it assumes the reality and independence of the world of existential experience. Technical and human applications of science which follow from such an epistemic system reject the subjective, the arbitrary and the exploitative and insist that every application of scientific knowledge and the employment of every technical means be consonant with the ends and purposes on which it is employed. Anyone who reads St. Francis of Assisi's *Canticle of the Sun,* or better still steeps himself in scripture, knows immediately that Catholics have something important to say on the problem of ecology. One is forced to ask, "Why have they not said it?" "Why are they not saying it now?"

Finally, it seems to me that Catholic intellectuality is especially favorably placed to bridge the gap in the human sciences between the particularity and relativism which exist in the historicist tradition and the generalizing emphasis on essence and regularity which has been so important an element in Western humanism. As you all know, the 19th century saw the dissolution of essence philosophies and the adoption, in the study of human culture, of a thoroughgoing relativism. It was a philosophical position which stressed uniqueness, the moral autonomy and ambivalence of every act and subjectivity of all structures of meaning. Initially this philosophical position yielded increased understanding. However, when its positive elements had been exhausted the position became a solvent of all order and meaning, a source of pessimism and a weapon in the hands of nihilism. Catholicism implicitly shares both the world of essence and the world of historicism. Catholic intellectuality alone can, I believe, at the present moment bridge the gulf between particularity and generalization, essence and the individual, the moral norm and the personal situation, the cultural value and the unique creativity of genius. But, alas, one asks in vain to have the great Catholic historians, sociologists and anthropologists pointed out to him. Where are they?

Let us look at the field of the study of the law, for example. As Catholics, both individually and institutionally, we are often accused of being legalists. There is reason for the accusation and we should seek to turn it to our advantage rather than spend our time explaining that we have given up the practice of seeking indulgences and the Friday fast. It is high time that great legalists appeared on the scene. The legal tradition of the Western world has virtually ceased to exist and has been replaced by a relativistic sociology and fiat law based upon the power of the state to coerce. In many important respects current legal theory in the United States is indistinguishable from that of the Soviet Union. Is there really any doubt as to the cause for the breakdown of respect for the law in our society when our best judicial minds quote, in effect, the words of Thucydides when he said, "The strong do what they can

215

and the weak suffer what they must"? The law, especially, illustrates the sort of contribution Catholic intellectuality might make to contemporary society through a reconciliation of historically determined custom and a philosophy of order and essence.

I have deliberately refrained from speaking on the subject of theology. Too many ill-prepared and ill-equipped Catholic intellectuals are speaking on that subject already. I do wish, however, to emphasize a Catholic intellectual stance which should, I feel, be operative throughout the Catholic university and operative especially in the study of theology. Suspended judgment, adequate consideration, thoughtful debate and discussion and a sense of time and tradition which reaches back into antiquity and projects itself forward to fulfillment of prophecy; all these are essential attributes of any scholarship worthy of the name. The unseemly haste, the ill-prepared thesis, the hasty conclusion, the quest for acclaim and approval, the desire to be in style, to be daring, to be innovative, to shock; all these are unworthy objectives and are especially unbecoming in the study of theology. We have the divine assurance, let us not hurry. If we take our time we shall have something to say to the world; if we do not take our time we shall only add to the chaos and confusion which now press in on us from every side.

We American Catholics are the most advantageously placed group in our society. We have not exhausted the energies and potencies we brought to America from the peasant societies and working class backgrounds from which we came. We are upwardly mobile, energetic and we still believe in the American promise of freedom, dignity and opportunity for all men. We preserve, in however diminished a form, the great heritage of our European cultural tradition, and our Catholic community embodies certain social and intellectual ideals indispensable to the survival of contemporary society. We are a city set on a hill, a chosen people. What we do as a Catholic community will be determinative for our society. No group in American history has ever been so challenged or presented with a like opportunity.

That opportunity is not essentially political or directly practical and activist. We will not achieve our destiny by electing a Catholic president or by doing our bit to remedy the urban crisis. All men of goodwill would do as much. Our mission is something different. We are called to leaven the lump. We are called to assist in the restoration of meaning and order and value in a society which is the freest and most prodigally generous in all human history. We are called upon to make opportunity meaningful, to make freedom orderly and to turn the blessings of prosperity to truly human purposes.

If the Catholic community responds to this challenge it will be largely because Catholic universities have reconsidered their objectives and rethought their purposes. We cannot achieve these goals if the ideal Catholic university of the future thinks of itself as a Harvard with a Catholic faculty of theology or a Berkeley where the academic year opens with the Mass of the Holy Spirit. We must, in fact, be ourselves. Our goal must be intellectual excellence in the context of Catholic concerns. If we pursue that goal consistently and selflessly and if we make the tremendous sacrifices of dedication and money necessary, we shall succeed in making that combination of man's effort and God's grace that is the basis of every great culture and every enduring community.

The Church-Related College

There are many who argue that the church-related college is an anachronism; that at best it represents the pressed-flower school of education and that at worst it is constitutionally incapable of recognizing or dealing effectively with the major concerns of our society. In a megapolitan culture the church-related school usually lacks the stature which hugeness bestows and it discovers that its resources must be husbanded and its priorities constantly debated while its secular competitors outbid it, outdazzle it and outspend it on every hand. Its president learns every day anew that being different is a very expensive undertaking, and institutionally the church-related school finds it extremely difficult to resist the powerful pull of the gravitational mass of secular education. It is indeed the ancient Christian problem of being in the world but not of it, a problem made more difficult by the fact that a substantial part of education is secular in its concerns and worldly in its orientation.

Is it really very difficult to understand why, increasingly, church-related colleges are quietly de-emphasizing their church connection and reshaping their purposes to conform more completely to the secular model? Is it hard to understand why students, faculty and administration model themselves on the state universities and the handful of great private secular schools rather than going their own way and keeping to their own purposes? But to persist in this homogenization of American education will not only lead us to betray a heritage and liquidate a great and productive tradition but will eventually vitiate all those qualities which mark the civilized, educated and rational man.

There is a bias in the universe which favors unity. It is as though nature and nature's God had determined that our central experience should be the comprehension of unity. How paradoxical, then, that God's purpose, nature's processes and man's society should so often and so compellingly seek to differentiate, to distinguish and to individualize! Those who consciously or unconsciously seek to purchase unity at the price of individuality and diversity contradict one of the most pervasive tendencies in our experience. We are able to be one effectively because we have been many individually. Our differences and distinctions in this ecumenical world are not sources of weakness and anarchy but are the very basis out of which a rich and harmonious unity can develop.

This process of diversification within a larger unity has been one of the distinguishing characteristics of our civilization. No other civilization has possessed the essential unity and fascinating mul-tiplicity characteristic of Western society. Christianity has divided and subdivided, each branch emphasizing in some distinctive way an important aspect of our common belief. Our political institutions have been structured in such a way that pluralism has been given concrete expression, and our public lives are characterized by debate and the constant, even acrimonious, discussion of alternative solutions. Our experience with diversity of belief and practice has led us to recognize that alternative life-styles, alternative political solutions, alternative social institutions and, most especially, alternative educational programs are a major source of strength, stability and richness in our society.

How sad then, how close to tragedy, that because of cultural and economic pressures the private and especially the church-related schools have been driven into a corner from which only heroic exertion can free them! It is time that the power, influence and resources of the state be employed in the fostering and preservation of differences rather than for the purpose of undermining the private educational enterprises of its citizenry. There is not a private school in America that has not suffered from a national education policy which penalizes differences and rewards the collectivization and homogenization of education. If we really wish diversity, if we wish to maximize the richness which alternative solutions can produce in our society, we will find ways to widen the choices available, to intensify competition and to increase the opportunities for genuine educational experimentation.

Of course it is being said that, even were the private schools strengthened, the church-related college would contribute little to the highly sophisticated, technologically advanced, scientifically oriented and completely secularized society into which we are moving. It is argued that not only has the church failed in its educational mission but that the church-related school is an anachronism in a post-Christian world.

Harvey Cox writes in *The Secular City:*

> The anachronistic posture of the church is nowhere more obvious than in the context of the university community. The church has made three attempts to come to terms with the university problem in America, all of which have been marked by a certain recidivism. The first was the establishment of its own colleges and universities. This of course is medievalism. The whole idea of a "Christian" college or university after the breaking apart of the medieval synthesis has little meaning. The term *Christian* is not one that can be used to refer to universities any more than to observatories or laboratories. No one of the so-called Christian colleges that now dot our Midwest is able to give a very plausible theological basis for retaining the equivocal phrase *Christian* college in the catalog. Granted that there may be excellent traditional, public relations, or sentimental reasons for calling a college Christian. There are no theological reasons. The fact that it was founded by ministers, that it has a certain number of Christians on the faculty or in the student body, that chapel is required (or not required), or that it gets part of its bills paid by a denomination—none of these factors provides any grounds for labeling an institution with a word that the Bible applies only to the followers of Christ, and then very sparingly. The idea of developing "Christian universities" in America was bankrupt even before it began.

The charges are wild and hyperbolic. They belong to that school of public discussion and cocktail theology which make good press for the moment but will not bear scrutiny a second time. Still the charge must be answered even though it is made by a wild man.

I wish to assert in the first place that there is a fundamental difference between a Christian college and a secular university and that the difference lies above all in the kinds of questions it asks about the human condition and the type of response it makes to the human condition.

There is an enormous and growing hunger in our society today for the life of the Spirit. Men yearn for meaning and purpose which go beyond the material substance and the technological artifacts of our daily lives. Students want wholeness and integrity, commitment and dedication, and if the present frenzy among those under thirty means anything it means that they have the liveliest fears of what Czelaw Milosz called "the suction of the absurd." What men fear today is the loss of selfhood, not through starvation or disease or war but through a total loss of meaning. The questions they most frequently ask are those great ontological questions which are the first questions of the Catechism: "Who am I?" "What am I?" and "Where am I going?" These are the questions which lie at the base of all patterns of social order. And these are the questions with which every sound education must commence. It is, of course, precisely these questions which the secular university refuses to raise.

Education which does not pose these questions and which cannot answer them becomes a system for defrauding the individual of his humanity. It equips him with the keenest sensitivity, it gives him the widest and deepest experience of past and present, it places untold power in his hands, and then it intimates that it is all to no purpose and that the man who seeks something beyond the moment, a purpose beyond an animal will to satisfaction and power, is simply expressing an outworn superstition. Is it really difficult to understand why our campuses are in turmoil and why men are fainting with fear and trembling at the thought of those things that are to come?

I say that the reason for the existence of the Christian college is that it dares to ask those great ontological questions, "Who am I?", "What am I?", and "Where am I going?" It, and it alone, can afford to face them squarely.

Of course they are asked at the secular university but they are asked not in the classrooms but in the mental health clinics operated for students, in the so-called crisis-centers which are springing up on campuses to deal with the deeply depressed and the suicidal. They are asked in all the out-of-the-way places of campus life where students can still afford to be honest without risking a confrontation with the established intellectual nihilism which forms the climate of opinion at every major secular university.

The first and most important role, then, of the church-related college is to ask the most difficult and fundamental questions men are capable of posing, questions which the secular university cannot and will not venture. They are questions with which not only every life but every society and every education must begin.

In the second place, the so-called "post-Christian" world does not make Christianity and the Christian college anachronisms, precisely because it is a world strangely like the world into which Christianity was born. To be sure, there are important differences between the Secular City of Rome in the first centuries of the Christian era and Mayor Lindsay's New York (otherwise known as "fun city") in the first century of the post-Christian era, but I propose to you that those differences may be superficial from the standpoint of the human predicament and that the contemporary Christian would not find himself a stranger in Hellenistic society.

Christianity was born in the midst of urban problems. It became a world religion in an era when a great cultural crisis gripped the Mediterranean world. It was, at its outset, acquainted with both the extravagances of belief and the paroxysms of despair which are so much a part of our world. It came into existence at a time when the world promised more to men than was ever before available but when cruel institutions and a crueler society cheated men of their humanity and defiled and destroyed their persons. The society in which Christianity came to birth was a society in which community was either disintegrating or had disappeared, in which slavery was an overwhelming reality, in which affluence and technology served to enlarge men's vices rather than to assist their virtues and in which the sense of social and communal purpose was lost. It was, in short, a society not wholly unlike our own.

To be sure, in such a world Christianity did not restore purpose and community and recreate the social order by making two blades of grass grow where one had grown before. In fact, the world was materially poorer in the centuries following the triumph of Christianity than it had been in the period of Christianity's infancy. What Christianity did then, and what it can do now, was to restore meaning and vitality.

The Christian church and the Christian college are at home in this world—not the world of the Middle Ages, or the world of the Reformation, but the tragic and problematical world of the 20th century. They have dealt, and dealt successfully, with all these problems once before and it will deal with them once more. But the Church and the church-related college cannot do this by becoming secular, by assimilating themselves to the tide of worldliness which threatens to engulf our whole society. But neither can they achieve the transformation of society by withdrawing from the daily lives of men. They must not succumb either to secularity or to isolationism and the ghetto mentality.

The church-related college, therefore, has the mission not only of asking the right questions but of doing something about the world in which it finds itself. It intends not only to inform but to transform. It believes that the student must account in his actions for the faith he finds within himself.

The Christian college has an obligation to prepare men and women to do God's work in the world by giving them the technical mastery necessary for the performance of their tasks. However, technique is not enough, skill is never adequate, and science alone always proves insufficient.

One of the most significant events of our century is the erosion and loss of faith in the notion that human problems are ultimately solvable through technological means. There is a growing awareness of the moral neutrality of technical means. We have witnessed all too often bureaucracy and rationalization serving irrational ends. We have discovered all too often that man has mastery over every part of nature with the exception of human nature. We have discovered to our disappointment that technical solutions to a particular problem often create a greater and more dangerous problem in the process. A secular society which solves the population problem by abortion, the problem of the aged and the infirm by euthanasia, the problem of human behavior by the chemical alteration of mood and action, the problem of public information by the manipulation of the population through the media, to cite only a few self-evident examples, is not a society in which any man can find his fulfillment.

But it is not simply that technology often creates as many problems as it solves. It is far more often the case that human problems simply will not yield to technical solutions. Our world needs all the technique it can muster, but beyond that it needs the dedication and the purpose which will not yield to despair and nihilism when that technical mastery fails, as fail it often will. And above all, our world needs the love and greatness of spirit which enable men to give themselves when there is nothing else to give, and the problems they confront are beyond any ready and mechanical solution.

The Christian college is the only educational institution in our society which insists that technique be tempered by the love of God and His creation. It insists that man cannot do everything which is technically possible. It teaches men to hope when there is no technical solution, and to love even when there is such a solution. It demands that our means be consonant with the ends for which God has created man.

If ever a bridge between knowledge and humane and loving purpose was imperative, if ever it was necessary for men to question their use of power and the purposes of their actions, that time is the present. The secular university cannot and will not forge this link between the world of power and the world of the spirit.

To these areas in which the church-related college teaches content, orientation and skills, must be added those very important areas where the church-related college teaches by example. In the long run, teaching by example is always more impressive than teaching a theory. "All theory is gray," the poet Goethe said, and who is there who can deny it? Every man and every institution teaches best that which is itself. What then do the church-related colleges teach when they are most essentially themselves? I believe they teach two things in a fashion which marks their students throughout their adult lives.

In the first place, the church-related college, when it is loyal to its heritage and dedicated to the fulfillment of its mission, teachers community by being a genuine community. "Community" is at the present time one of those magic words which evoke the aspirations and the hopes of our society. We yearn so intensely for community because our society makes life in community difficult. We do not have to go to Aristotle to discover that men cannot fulfill themselves in isolation and estrangement from their fellow men. We know it instinctively and we feel, every day, the consequences of the decay and loss of community which is taking place about us.

Why do you suppose it is that the alumni of small and particularly church-related colleges remain so intensely loyal, not only to the institution but to the friendships and associations formed at college? I believe it is because, having for the moment outgrown the family and its attendant community, the young adult is enabled for the first time to form a community which is distinctively his own. The role of the college in providing the young adult with a model for community is one of the most important roles the college has traditionally performed.

It is precisely this role that the large secular university has abdicated. The major universities now mirror the ant-heap societies in which they are lodged. Every university administrator who has the least insight into the current student mood knows that a major portion of his problem lies in the fact that he is incapable of creating a genuine sense of community on his campus. Community is not simply the product of living together in units small enough to permit everyone to know everyone else, though that, of course, helps. Above all community arises from a common enterprise, a shared commitment and a set of common experiences. Increasingly the church-related college finds that teaching what a community is and how it operates is one of its most important functions, for the church-related college is one of the few remaining genuine communities.

Finally, the church-related college plays a most important role in the formation of personality and the development of an appropriate lifestyle. It is more successful in enabling its students to develop a mature personality, one which combines within itself both a radical freedom and reverent traditionalism, because it insists that there are models available that possess a sanction greater than that of momentary popularity. Has the meaning of the elaborate costuming of the present generation of students puzzled you? I believe they are in desperate search of a model, not just any model but one who is free, heroic, committed. Christians have always felt the closeness of such models in Jesus and his saints, and it is not corny or fake-pious to say that we cannot grow into maturity unless we appropriate to ourselves some of their characteristics.

C. S. Lewis remarked on a number of occasions that it is not difficult for us to understand evil. Our experience of the universe leads us to expect it. Everything runs down, wears out or falls apart. The puzzling thing in our experience is "good." There is no problem of evil but there is a very real problem of good. One of the most puzzling things about human behavior is the universal desire "to be good." Now, of course, not all of us make it, but everyone, and especially if he is young, wants to be good. But our conception of how to be good depends in great measure on the models available to us. I do not wish to contend that the only models of goodness available in the world of higher education are located in the church-related colleges. That is nonsense. It does seem to me, however, that the likelihood of discovering the right model is better in a church-related college than it is at Megalopolis University.

The qualities of personality and the kind of education I have been talking to you about are not anachronistic. They are exactly the sorts of things our whole society is discussing, the values we instinctively know that we must possess if we are to survive, or if we are even to want and seek to survive. It is mistaken to assume that the great questions of our time are scientific, institutional and technological questions. They are human questions.

227

In the measure that the church-related college seeks to answer these questions and fill these human needs it will have fulfilled its mission. If it decides to whore after false gods, if it decides to secularize itself and model itself on the insufficiencies of the state university, it will have lost its purpose and failed utterly. There is nothing quite so pathetic as an amateur secularist. "If the salt lose its savor wherewith shall it be salted? Then it is fit only to be thrown out and trampled underfoot."

What Is Christian
Education All About?

Everyone likes to believe that what he does is the most important thing in the world. Teachers are no exception and most of them take education very seriously indeed. When all the other good arguments for the importance of teaching have been made, the best argument for the Christian remains the argument that he is following the divine mandate to "go and teach."

But just as obviously, that mandate is not a command to go and teach just anything in the belief that the Father's educational mansion is modeled on the multiversity and that God is rather like a permissive and indulgent university president who can find room within the university structure for just about any activity and can accommodate just about any behavior.

In fact, Christian education is very distinctive and special. It is not, of course, wholly different from secular education in the kind of information which it imparts. This common subject matter has led many Christian educators to believe that there are no real differences and that the Christian college only does poorly and parochially what the secular college does more adequately and with greater cosmopolitanism. The most distinguished and affluent

Christian colleges today seem to take as their slogan, "Let us be like the Egyptians."

How then is Christian education distinctive if the body of knowledge it teaches is a common body of knowledge shared by the secular college and university? It is distinctive in three ways: in the first place, in asking and answering the question, "What does our knowledge mean?" Does not special knowledge, in fact, always point beyond itself to some larger, more coherent and adequate explanation or is it simply a subjective and transitory organization of anarchic events which give a man or group of men a temporary advantage in the struggle for existence?

In the second place, Christian education ought to be different from secular education in the way it teaches. If the test of Christianity is the way in which we show our love for one another then the atmosphere of the Christian campus ought to be wholly different from the atmosphere of the secular campus. The content of physics may be the same on the secular and the Christian campus; how physics is taught ought to be quite different.

In the third place, the use we make of our knowledge ought to be different from the use made of knowledge by the secular society. There is an active side to Christian knowing which goes beyond the Aristotelian ideal of the contemplative act. Christian education ought to move men to action even as it has taught men to know. Jesus said that "not everyone who says 'yes, yes' will enter the kingdom of heaven."

Christian education differs, then, in three important ways from secular education. It differs in that it asserts that knowledge should lead the mind of the knower to a larger and more adequate comprehension of order and meaning. It is different from secular education in its method and in its pedagogy. And finally, it is different from secular education in the use to which it puts knowledge. Let us examine each of these characteristics in turn and discover, if we can, their practical pedagogical significance.

A recent essay in a popular magazine discussed the disappearance of humor from the American scene. The essay remarked on the sudden and mysterious end to the great tradition of humorous writers, great comics, funny-men, clowns, burlesque, minstrel shows and vaudeville jokes, comedies and motion pictures, which even in the worst of times kept men laughing and helped them to gain some perspective on the human condition. The question which the essay raises is a fundamental one for our society. Why is it that we cannot laugh?

I believe that if we answer the question of why we cannot laugh we will at the same time be able to answer the question of why substantial numbers of men no longer want to learn. Humor disappeared from the college campus just when the love of learning began its retreat.

Both tragedy and comedy are explorations of order. Behind each there stands a cosmos, an ordered system whose lawfulness is ineluctable. The tragic hero is the man who does not know that order and discovers and affirms it through his suffering. He verifies the order of the cosmos in his own disordered and suffering existence and at the end his pleasure is not the pleasure of catharsis, as Aristotle asserted, but the pleasure of affirming that God is in his heaven, that order does prevail and man can move confidently in a world that would otherwise not make sense.

And humor, likewise, is a dramatic affirmation of order. Those who have a joke played on them are literally surprised by order, and the viewer who laughs, laughs not at another's misfortune but because he knows the prevailing order and anticipates the consequences of its violation. He sees the banana peel upon which the clown is about to slip. Whereas in tragedy both the viewer and the actor are ignorant of the order and discover it together, in comedy the viewer knows from the beginning what the order is. If I am at least partially correct about the nature of comedy and humor, is it possible that comedy has disappeared, not because we have fallen upon bad times, but rather, because our intellectuals and even ordinary men and women have ceased to believe that order exists. In an anarchic world neither comedy nor tragedy can exist because, quite literally, nothing makes sense anymore. The theater of the absurd is a drama which presents us with bits and pieces of experience which in their totality are devoid of any meaning.

And I need not point out that secularized education has become a kind of theater of the absurd. The student is presented with the most diverse and complicated vignettes of man's experience of the environment in which he lives and the human condition with no attempt to reconcile it to ultimate meaning, purpose and values. Such education is a tableau of what is, in which no one ever raises the question of what ought to be or asks why one human choice is better or worse than another.

And yet it is this very question of meaning which preoccupies every student at the college and university level. I do not believe that this generation is better or more moral, or more clever, or more beautiful, or more intelligent than past generations. Old men seek to ingratiate themselves with the young by affirming that the young are all of these things. This generation is simply less distracted than past generations by poverty, war, material affluence, and has had to face in its most acute form the question of meaning, of value, of purpose, of order. My generation could evade those questions because of the depression and the great war and the experience of material affluence. For the present generation affluence will no longer hide the spiritual poverty in which they are living nor everyday concerns conceal the metaphysical anxieties which they confront. Our students are telling us that it is not enough to know and to be and that knowledge and being always point beyond themselves.

How important order is to the life of society! It is in those marginal situations; the time between waking and sleeping, nightmare, mental disease and the confrontation with death, in which meaning seemingly goes out of life and primordial anarchy appears to reassert itself and the demand for order becomes most acute. It is then that we as men insist that existence is dependent upon the discovery and the affirmation of meaning.

Then humanism and materialism and the stylish positivism and pragmatism of the academies are not enough. An altruism which is based on sympathy alone will prove insufficient, for unless man, his experiences, and the moment in which he lives point beyond himself he will be caught in the wasteland of his subjective ego and will be subject to a shifting and amoral sentimentality.

Every class in a Christian college ought to begin with the question, "What does it mean?" The answer of the secularists and the positivists is that it means what we want it to mean; that meaning and morality are convenient fictions which we invent for our sentimental and selfish reasons.

Unless the teacher confronts the question, "What does it all mean?," he has not the faintest chance or hope of truly educating. The multiversity is a tower of Babel not simply because the human proportion has been lost but above all because men have ceased to ask those ultimate questions of value which form the basis of integration and order. That order does not have its source in ourselves, is not a projection of our subjective wills, but is the manifestation of God's loving providence. From the grammar of ethics to the track of the stars that order is present and endures. Every statement of fact, no matter how bald, raises the question of "why?" That question demands an answer. The Christian educator will not evade and equivocate but will raise the question himself boldly and freely.

The great questions of meaning and value, of order and integration are not ones which can be evaded. They are written into our very natures. We "rage for order" and if the teacher does not ask the question the student will immediately sense the emptiness and superficiality of the instruction he is given.

What I have just said does not mean that the Christian has a set of pat answers, of easy and thoughtless affirmations. He does not. What he possesses is faith and hope and an enduring confidence that the multiplicity of experience has some central unity and purpose. He, too, is often baffled and torn by indecision but this starting postulate is order rather than anarchy and this alone enables him to confront the chaos of experience boldly and with self-assurance. He can ask the question "Why?" because he is confident that there is an affirmative answer. He understands the nature of sacrifice and renunciation, for example, and can affirm their absolute validity and necessity, not as a sentimental gesture but because they are a part of God's reconciliation with his created order. How can I teach the humanities until I ask what it means to be fully human? How can I teach the sciences until I raise the question of why things are one way and not another? As a Christian I can raise these questions confident that I will not turn away baffled

233

but will glimpse, at least in part, the ultimate mystery of unity and order which lies at the heart of the cosmos.

No, we as Christians have no pat answers. Indeed all we have is difficult questions and confidence that some day we shall know. And knowing this as Christians and as teachers we ought to warn against pat answers and easy solutions. Order and integration are so difficult a work that only God can achieve them. At the moment, the halls of education are filled with strident voices hawking easy and painless moral, social, economic and political solutions. The young are angry that age-old human problems are not banished overnight by recourse to some utopian system, and the old are confident that every human problem has a technological solution. But the Christian is not convinced and the Christian educator affirms once more that the solution to human problems lies not in utopian schemes or technological breakthroughs but in discovering and doing the will of God. Order is not ours. It is not our creation and we cannot will it. Order is God's work and man can do no more than discover and affirm it. As teachers we ought to begin with a suspicion of the easy solutions which men offer. As Christians we ought to make doubly sure we do not confuse our wishes with the will of God and give His approval to our favorite schemes for human amelioration.

I have said that the second area in which Christian education is different from secular education is the way in which it teaches. I do not wish to limit teaching to the experience in the classroom. I believe that teaching takes place as much, and perhaps more, outside the classroom as inside. Let me give you a practical example by way of illustration. My son and I were recently walking about the campus of a large state university, other than the one at which I teach, and viewing it with the fresh eyes of visitors. This university has more vast and gigantic buildings per student head than any other school in the country. My son remarked that the message the campus gave him over and over was that the individual did not count, that the only important thing was the collectivity. To many students at the university that lesson may be the most important one of their lives—reinforced as it is by such masses of stone, brick and cement and emphasized by its tens of thousands of intellectual ants who go their purposeful ways across the campus.

The most important thing that a student can learn, should learn on a Christian campus, is that someone cares, and cares about most of the things which touch a student's life. It is hard to believe that God cares when no one else seems to. It is hard to believe that God is watching when no one else seems to be watching. Students everywhere seem to me to be saying, "Look at me, I am a person. I want you to recognize my humanity and regard my personality. Treat me like a human being and not a thing." A great deal of what students do at the present moment is an effort to get the attention of a world which seems to have ceased to care about people.

And so we must as Christians create the kinds of educational institutions which express God's love for the individual and our obedience to Jesus' command that we love one another, not in some great collectivity but in terms of the personal and unique needs of each different and difficult human being.

In practical terms that emphasis means that, in the first place, the Christian college is on a human scale in terms of numbers, buildings and space. The administrators and faculties of a Christian college should know the difference between a collectivity and a community. Collectivities are assemblages of human beings in which the social cement which marks a community has been lost. No hope is more widely shared in America today than the hope expressed in that poster glimpsed from a campaign train by candidate Nixon, "Bring us together again." Our society threatens to become a great collectivity in which we are forced to live side by side but in which we are all separate, alien and hostile.

Woodstock Nation has that appeal of loving togetherness and that more than anything else accounts for the mythical popularity of that rather sad and burlesque travesty of community. Many students now believe that every campus can be recreated in the image of Woodstock, but that, too, is an illusion. How sad it is that the broken image of community which Woodstock represents is the most compelling image of community available to contemporary youth! But it, too, represents an anonymous ant-heap society in which no one really cares and the normal bonds of community are replaced by drugs and sex and momentary sentiment and mood induced by music and site.

The Christian campus ought to be a genuine community. It ought to care enough about every student to be both free and demanding. How do we express our love and concern for individuals? We do it by learning what their needs are and by serving those needs. But we do it no less by making demands on the individual, calling him to perfection and the expression of his full humanity.

This latter point is very important at the present moment for there is a great temptation in contemporary culture to confuse a loss of standards with liberation and repersonalization. The encounter group craze, desacralization of the liturgy, the decay of dress and manners, the coarsening and vulgarization of speech, the ethic of confrontation are all ways in which we demean and diminish our own stature and that of our fellow men rather than methods by which we free and augment human potential. We show we care by making demands upon the object of our affection. But in making those demands we lay on no one a burden we have not assumed. The Christian teacher must begin by loving and respecting his students. This love, however, should never express itself in a meaningless permissiveness. By all means, the trivial fact, the meaningless action, the sterile rule, and outmoded code ought to be abandoned. Let us exercise care, however, and be certain that we do not alter the substance of the law when we change its expression.

One of the most important things a Christian school can do is to offer a model of community. Community, of course, is not achieved in three days. That is a part of the mythology of Woodstock. At the root of community is an overriding sense of common purpose. At the present moment many Christian colleges are in danger of losing that distinctive purpose. They are in fact becoming just like their multipurpose counterparts in the secular culture. To them I say, dare to be different, dare to be yourselves. Tell your students when they arrive on campus what your school is and what, as a community, it seeks to achieve.

One of the most surprising things about Christian monasticism is the great variety of form and purpose which Christian monastic communities have exemplified. Why has Christian education been so sterile in producing new forms and addressing itself to new purposes? Surely the conventional curriculum and the AB degree are not the only ways in which God's educational work can be done! Let us have genuine institutional and curricular uniqueness but let us make certain that the changes we make are the product of an overriding vision, a shared goal and not simply a reflection of a desire to be novel and stylish.

I have argued that a Christian education differs from a secular education in terms of the use to which that education is put. Christian education is vocation education. We are all of us called to the service of God and our fellow man. Christian education recognizes this and insists that we think about the purposes for which we prepare ourselves. The priesthood of all believers and the idea of the calling, I need not remind you, are central tenets of Lutheranism. They have become in the last five centuries an important and distinctive Lutheran contribution to all of Christendom. Let us, for a moment, examine the implication of these two teachings for education.

They are closely related doctrines and they are directly relevant to the Christian educational ideal. They insist that we both share Christ's ministry and that we achieve our beatitude, our sanctification in the ordinary world of work and service. Saint Theresa of Avila, a Spanish 16th century contemporary of Martin Luther, remarked, "God walks among the pots and pans." Indeed he does. He walks wherever men quietly put aside self and serve their fellows as carpenters, fishermen, tentmakers, physicians, and even as doctors of the law.

There is in America at the present time a growing estrangement between the intellectual elite and men who earn their livings in occupations of lower status. There is a frequent complaint voiced that college students who are apt to demand "all power to the people" really know very little about the people, that they are snobs and elitists at heart who show little understanding for the needs and aspirations of ordinary men. They do not, the charge is made, so much serve society and their fellow men as demand that society serve them. Students, it is said, constitute a privileged order exercising power and enjoying benefits without showing any responsibility. I am struck by the fact that these are precisely the charges the Reformers of the 16th century made concerning the medieval clergy. The charges are not without justification.

The remedy is Christian commitment and Christian service. Perhaps students should declare a moratorium on telling others what to do and simply do their part, "do their thing," in the parlance of the moment. To what does God call us? The gifts of the spirit, St. Paul tells, are various and diverse but "all these are the work of one and the same Spirit, who distributes different gifts to different people just as he chooses." The occupation of construction worker seems an unlikely one for Jesus but that was his profession.

We need in America and throughout the Western world a rededication to the ideal of Christian service and self-sacrifice. Where are the volunteers in nursing and education, the ghetto teachers, the small-town doctors, the impoverished ministers and priests, the nurses, and those who through tithing and self-sacrifice served with their money a society which their talent could not directly reach and influence? The great voluntary associations which were once thought to be one of America's finest achievements are dying on the vine because men and women are no longer willing to make the contributions of talent, time, service and money necessary to sustain their activity.

Surely a good education ought to awaken in us a desire to employ our talent and our skill in behalf of our fellow men, not by imposing our will or our ideas on them but by quietly ameliorating their lot and raising their hearts and minds.

Many students are determined that the world shall be made better but are convinced that its improvement is dependent upon their wish alone. The environment, the poor, the oppressed and the alienated cannot be saved, ransomed, served or reconciled without sacrifice, and when the pinch comes secular sentimentality will not make men strong enough to bear the cross which service of any kind imposes. Christian education, then, teaches us what we ought to serve, how we should serve it and the kind of costs we can expect to pay in a life devoted to service.

Of course no Christian college does all of these things well, and some colleges which call themselves Christian do none of these things even poorly. Still we all know what we should do and from time to time our conscience disturbs us. Perhaps as Christian educators we should begin the school year by imploring the Holy Ghost to move our minds to broad sympathies and to stir in us the disquiet and discontent out of which renewal is born.

Time, Eternity
and the College Campus

All of us live a very considerable portion of our lives in the eternal present. We believe, incorrectly to be sure, that tomorrow will be like today; that we will always be eighteen, or thirty or forty-five and that the mortality which is the lot of our fellowmen and their institutions will not really touch us or the fabric of society which makes our lives possible. While we are willing to concede that change exists, we hastily add that we do not change, only our world and our society change. In short, we are reluctant to admit that we are pilgrims and strangers and that earth, in spite of all its glory and its wonder, is our habitation for only a little while.

It is increasingly difficult in our society, moreover, to attune ourselves to the transcendent. There is, in the first instance, the constant temptation to turn these stones, this hard awareness of our loneliness into the soft bread of immediate sensate experience. Sometimes the temptation takes the form of an idolatrous regard of technique and science which transforms the spiritual quest for excellence and goodness into the material quest for quantity and satiety. Sometimes the temptation takes the form of urging a substitution of political for religious action, an effort to legislate the

Kingdom of God, immanentize the eschaton, to substitute revolution for revelation and the mysterious action of providence.

In the second instance there is the constant temptation to substitute the transitory transcendence of intoxication and ecstacy for the genuine experience of religious transcendence. Of course, these temptations are not new. They have been the common experience of mankind. Were we better acquainted with the Old Testament we would all realize how unoriginal our secularism is. What is new is the pervasiveness and insistence of the secularism with which the denizens of the city of this world are buffeted and the remoteness and paleness of the city of God. Heaven has lost its credibility and God who once walked with men in the cool of the evening seems remote and unreachable even, and perhaps especially, on Sunday morning.

For this reason the Christian college finds its role especially ambiguous and confused for it has as its mission the preparation of men for eternity. But the fact is that the Christian college cannot be simply otherworldly; it cannot simply turn its back on the secular, however much that might ease the painfulness of its situation and quiet the confusions which surround its role. Men are of the earth, earthy they are, not, as Jacques Maritain was fond of saying, disembodied spirits, or angels, and although they are pilgrims and strangers on earth this is the place where they must achieve their salvation and develop the full stature of their personalities, both natural and supernatural.

It is important therefore to make once more the distinction between the process of secularization and the ideology of secularism. Secularization is the process whereby Christianity has progressively brought the total content of time and creation within the sacred context of God's redeeming grace. In many respects the Reformation was a turning point in this development for it took the common offices of secular life and raised them to the level of a calling. It had, of course, been the intention of the medieval church to sacralize all human activity and the sacramental system moved a long way toward the accomplishment of this end. All in all, the Christian purpose has been to bring all creation and all human life and its activities under the sacred canopy of Christ's redemptive ac-

242

tion. The movement known as secularization is only the completion and the confirmation of this development. It insists that it is God's will that men achieve their salvation in the world and not out of the world.

Secularism, as an ideology as distinguished from secularization, insists that the transcendent and the sacred are irrelevant to human concerns in this world. Secularism either insists that religion is a meaningless delusion or a pernicious reflection of man's alienation. It envisions man as totally a product of the natural order and its so-called humanism insists that man's only fulfillment and happiness can come as a satisfaction of the natural man. It excludes the sacred totally and with this secularism Christianity and Christian education have nothing in common.

What Christian education in the present seeks to achieve, then, is an increase in secularity; an emphasis which will bring our creatureliness in all its manifestations within the reach of the saving grace of the incarnation. Consequently, Christian education must prepare the student for life in the world but at the same time it. must point beyond the world, beyond the here and now, beyond the natural man. It is a difficult, almost an impossible task.

An indispensable quality in the maintenance of a balance between the demands of heaven and the requirements of earth is the preservation of our personal and institutional innocence. Jesus said, "Unless you become like little children you cannot enter the Kingdom of Heaven." Only the innocent can remain in the world and not become cynical; only the innocent can confront our human condition directly and remain pure in heart; only the innocent can make Job's affirmative confession of trust and allegiance; only the innocent can know fully and completely and still maintain confidence and hope in the providential purposes of the Almighty.

Innocence does not mean, or even imply, ignorance. Innocence is able to face all the enormities of a totally sensate and depraved society and still maintain its simplicity and purity. Among intellectuals living in the present hour it is the most important and least common of all the virtues which distinguish the Christian. In every college and university there is tremendous pressure to force conformity to the ugly world of the secularists, to gain the world at the price of one's soul. Sophistication which is so highly prized means loss of innocence, a rejection of the values and standards which are the marks of the Christian. Every ugly, depraved and diseased sentiment is exalted and sophistically justified. Academic reputations are built upon a spurious scholarship and science which has as its objective expunging the divine likeness in the human creature. The meanings of words, the coin of the realm in things intellectual, is twisted and turned so that they convey, not the truth of things but the sick fantasies of the secularist elite. It requires the innocence of the child, however, to say, "But the emperor has no clothes" and reestablish in one moment of unconscious insight God's eternal truth.

Innocence, moreover, requires that the self be whole, integral and undivided. It requires that the individual and the institution know its purpose and possess a full sense of its selfhood. That is, to be innocent requires that we become a seamless robe. The opposite of innocence is guile. Among the impure of heart every man knows his advantage. Everyone has made his calculation. Everyone has his price and it's usually lower than ever he dares admit to himself. Fads flourish and are rewarded. Cults abound and the intellectuals now, as then, have itching ears yearning to hear some new thing while the truth is neglected.

Seeing this the saints cry out their hearts in desperation and the wise are filled with fear and trembling in the expectation of what is to come. Do we dare to be innocent? Do we dare not to conform to the secularism of our time? Where are the great dissenters of this generation? Surely they are not the grubby conformists of the so-called youth culture. Surely they are not to be found at faculty cocktail parties where the badges of intellectual conformity are paraded and the slogans of academic group-think are exchanged.

Without innocence the pursuit of truth is a meaningless charade. How can anyone discover anything if he lacks the openness which is characteristic of the innocent? Look about you at the university and college scene. Are you impressed by the abundance of open minds? I am not. On every hand I find positions which are not discussable, demands which are non-negotiable and minds which are unchangeable. I find, in fact, every attitude which seems to insure the failure of any educational effort.

Let us renew then the Christian's dedication to innocence in ourselves and in our educational institutions. Let us begin by calling things by their right names, by insisting on God's truth whether it is found in nature or revelation. Let us continue by devoting ourselves completely and without calculation of worldly advantage to the pursuit of truth and virtue, refusing to be involved in cults and fads, refusing to bow down before the secularist idols of our times. Finally, let us renew our innocence by opening up ourselves to the voice of God as it comes to us from revelation and from nature. The world constantly points beyond itself. Let us be open enough to weigh the evidence.

There is a second virtue which is essential in maintaining the practical possibility of Christian education. That virtue is the virtue of prudence. The medieval scholastics made prudence the first of the virtues and their devotion to prudence was not misplaced. How many destructive and imprudent things are said and done these days, inside and outside of the classroom? Promises are made which cannot be fulfilled and expectations are excited which it is impossible to satisfy. Shorn of any religious context it would still be wise for educators to behave with greater prudence and circumspection. As educators, are we certain that we have not oversold education? Have we not made promises so large that we can, in fact, never deliver? We have said that education will make men good, will make men happy, will make men just, will make men powerful and rich when we know in our heart of hearts that education is a very wasteful and chancy proposition which sometimes succeeds and often fails. We have held out the most extravagant hopes to our society concerning the benefits and the role of universities and colleges. We have said that they will solve the problems of the cities, reconcile the races, bring peace to the earth and usher in such an age of mellow feeling and community spirit as to make selfishness and poverty a thing of the past. Any sane man who is not guilty of the grossest self-deception knows that colleges and universities can do none of these things, are indeed, unequipped effectively play any social, economic or political role. The idea that the colleges and universities of America should undertake the reformation of society strikes me as a notion of such overweening arrogance and affrontery as to invite the hubris which punishes all over-reaching.

In these matters which touch the secular side of education we need to exercise prudence in our dealings with students, parents, trustees, regents and legislators. Prudence dictates that we restrain the educational puff, that we refuse to issue the fraudulent promissory notes which have become the medium of exchange in our culture.

We need too, however, to instill in our students a sense of prudence. We need to tell them that no wise man ever does everything of which he is capable, that every man regardless of the justice of his cause ought to calculate the effects of his actions and words on others, and that every sane man demands less than is due him. It is an injunction of prudence as well as a demand of God that we do not provoke to anger. It is time for the temporal and spiritual consequences of confrontation to be spelled out.

You will say, with some justification, that these injunctions are the commonplaces of civilized behavior. It is nonetheless true that without innocence and prudence the Christian college cannot be saved from the encroachment of secularism in its most blatant form. This is the case because the swollen claims and the politics of academic confrontation are anathema to the charity, decency and decorum which are the *sine qua non* of Christian education.

I wish to make one more point with respect to prudence. In advancing the just claims of religion we ought to exercise the same prudence as characterizes our conduct of secular education. We must recognize and deal honestly with all the uncertainties and the ambiguities of the religious position, claiming neither too little nor too much. We must not oversell religion just as we must not oversell education in general. We must meet scepticism honestly, openly and bravely.

In Catholic colleges and universities in the age before the new dispensation the school year always began with the celebration of the Mass of the Holy Ghost. By that action students and faculty acknowledged their dependence upon God's inspiration and the teaching power and authority of the Holy Spirit. Their action was one of humility which affirmed man's dependence upon God for every right thought. Man needs to be reminded anew that Promethean intellectuality which challenges and defies God and sets up man and his vanity as the final arbiter of all matters will result in disaster. "Let us build a tower which reaches heaven," they said, and they proceeded to construct Sproul Hall on the campus of the University of California at Berkeley. There can be no Christian education without the requisite humility on the part of administration, faculty and students. Unless God's inspiration and order is recognized and man's fallible creatureliness acknowledged, man's attempts to exploit knowledge always end in disaster. We are told that the Socratic injunction, "Know thyself!" which was inscribed in the temple of Apollo at Delphi, really meant, "Man know that thou art mortal and not a god and do only those things proper to a man." Let us be humble in our knowledge before God who is its source and inspiration.

Let us be humble too with one another in the quest for truth and the pursuit of knowledge. Unbalanced faculties which represent only one interpretation of discipline or one political viewpoint are not a testimony to the humility of any group of intellectuals. True intellectuality begins with the assumption that we, any of us, or all of us collectively, might be mistaken. I am not advocating an intellectual ecumenism which abolishes differences by glossing over them. On the contrary, I wish men to debate with intensity but with humility the differences which separate them. The Holy Spirit would behave strangely indeed were he to speak only to Democrats, or modern language analysts, or Keynesian economists. The Holy Spirit, I have always assumed, is less arbitrary and snobbish than the Cabots and Lodges of Boston.

I believe these three virtues, innocence, prudence and humility, must inform any Christian educational effort. Beyond this it is fair to ask, however, for a somewhat more positive educational program. What ought we to do and what ought we not to do if we are to strike a balance between the demands of heaven and the needs of earth?

In the first place we must realize that, as Alfred North Whitehead once remarked, "Religion is what men do with their solitude." If there is no solitude, there is quite simply no religion. If we are sincere about desiring a religious atmosphere on campus we will begin by reducing the amount of activity. The office wall of every college chaplain ought to be decorated with the motto, "Don't do something, just sit there." Judging from the frenetic activity which characterizes most college religious programs one could never guess that Jesus withdrew, occasionally, alone to pray and that at least once he spent 40 days in solitude. Most college chaplains would have managed a dozen protest demonstrations, a short stay in jail, and would have inaugurated a number of social welfare programs given an equal amount of time. I believe it far more likely that religion will be destroyed by well-meaning activity than that it will succumb to quietness. Let us all learn, students and faculty, to sit and wait upon the Lord.

It is important that we learn to pick and choose among our activities and that we do not spend all our time galloping from crisis to crisis; this week racism, next week police brutality, the following week ecology and the environment. Choose one activity which you believe has special merit and make certain you spend as much time thinking about it and praying about it as you spend in activity which you suppose will accomplish your purpose.

In the second place, when you act make both the inspiration and the goal of your action specific, concrete and personal. There is little merit in the world in subscribing to large, vague and usually ill-conceived plans for social amelioration and political reform. The Christian way of consecrating the world is through dedicated, specific action. Do you wish to change the world? Become a nurse or a doctor, a lawyer or a teacher, a housewife or a good, decent, loving, overworked father and bring some dedication and sacrifice into a world perishing from selfishnes. That is what Luther meant when he talked about a calling.

There is a common belief afoot in the world that men can accomplish nothing in a group of less than a hundred thousand. That is why a love marathon such as Woodstock requires such vast congeries of human beings in order to be rated a success. I dare you, teachers and students, to be a loner, or if you need company in an undertaking ask for the kind the saints have always enjoyed.

Avoid movements, crusades, fads, cults, sects and all those social forms which enable men to hide from hard work and hard questions and still enjoy the congratulations and approval of a group. If you are serious about revolution, why wait? Make your revolution now. Put on the new man; do your thing, though it would be a good idea to make certain that you have properly prepared yourself with the discipline and skills which alone can give your effort some chance of success.

Finally, those who teach and those who learn at a Christian college in this tempestuous period of social change ought to think seriously about the danger of secularizing God's transcendent purposes. We all want to believe that we are doing the will of God when, in fact, we are often trying to make God do our will or at least making our will appear as the will of God. We must remember always that man's secular order, man's laws, his culture, his social and economic arrangements are the products of his creaturely condition. They stand under the judgment of God. They are not and never can be His will. The close identification of a particular economic, political, social or cultural order with the will of God is blasphemy and idolatry. In such an arrangement what man does is worship himself and his judgments. Eventually all of man's arrangements are found wanting and go down to destruction.

At the end of the Middle Ages the reformers attacked just such a close identification of human institutions with the divine will. They quite rightly pointed out that sinful man is never justified in arrogating to himself and his society the purpose of the Almighty. Today a new medieval synthesis is on the point of creation. It seeks to identify the institutions, purposes and ideals of liberal humanism and the welfare state with the divine purpose. It too, however, stands under the judgment of God, is being judged now and found wanting.

Be certain, then, that when you teach you do not too closely identify the things of heaven and earth, time and eternity. It is one thing to say that it is God's will that the poor be fed. It is quite a different thing to say that it is God's will that a specific program

DATE DUE

GAYLORD			PRINTED IN U.S.A.